1

Arise: Becoming the Better You

Hidden in God Publishing
South Bend, Indiana
www.hiddeningod.com

Unless otherwise stated, Scripture is taken from the King James Version which is public domain.

ISBN-13 978-0-578–79602-4   Paperback
LCCN: 2020923318
Printed in the United States of America

TABLE OF CONTENTS

"ARISE"

BECOMING THE BETTER YOU

SECTION ONE

The Dark Beginnings of Living in The Past

CHAPTER ONE

The Wonder Years of Weariness

1. WHERE, WHEN AND HOW IT ALL STARTED

2. THE TRAUMA OF FEAR AND TORMENT

3. THE EMOTIONAL AND PHYSICAL SEPARATION

4. GROWING UP A CHURCH GIRL

5. THE DISAPPOINTMENT

6. THE COUNTERFEIT ESCAPE

CHAPTER TWO

The Weight of Brokenness

1. MASQUERADING THE HEAVY BAGGAGE

2. HOW TRAUMA CREATED MENTAL DEPRESSION

3. HOW A BROKEN SOUL MAKES YOU A SLAVE OF THE PAST

4. WHY MUST I FEEL OR BEHAVE THIS WAY

5. BROKEN, BUSTED AND DISGUSTED

CHAPTER THREE

Your Past Affects Your Present

1. THE FALSE CONCEPT OF LOVE

2. ARE YOU PRESENTLY LIVING IN YOUR PAST?

3. THE HEARTS OF FATHERLESS DAUGHTERS

4. HOW OUR PAST AFFECTS LOVE AND OUR RELATIONSHIPS

5. WE ATTRACT WHO WE ARE IN TOXIC RELATIONSHIPS

6. THE REPERCUSSIONS OF BROKEN FATHERS

7. BROKEN SONS BECOMING BROKEN MEN, HUSBANDS,AND DADS

8. THE INFLUENCE OF SINGLE MOTHERS RAISING SONS

SECTION TWO

BETTER DAYS ARE COMING

CHAPTER FOUR

THE INTENSIVE CARE UNIT OF GOD

1. LETTING GO AND LETTING GOD

2. MY SOUL, MIND AND SPIRIT UNDER CONSTRUCTION

3. OUR HEALING IS OUR RESPONSIBILITY

4. LOVE IS HEALING

CHAPTER FIVE

THE ROAD OF RECOVERY

1. WHEN GOD SPEAKS

2. SEEKING GOD IN THE LOW VALLEYS

3. WHEN YOU KNOW BETTER YOU DO BETTER

4. REPENTANCE AND RADICAL FAITH

5. A RENEWED COMMITMENT

6. THE TRANSFORMATION OF FORGIVENESS

7. THE NEW REVELATION

CHAPTER SIX

FINDING AND DISCOVERING A RELATIONSHIP WITH GOD

1. WHAT IS RELATIONSHIP?

2. THE RELATIONSHIP IN MARRIAGE

3. RELATIONSHIP VERSUS RELIGION

4. ON A PERSONAL AND DEEPER LEVEL

5. THE POWER OF PRAYER

6. RESTORATION OF FATHER AND DAUGHTER RELATIONSHIPS

7. A NEW LIFE OF COMFORT, PEACE, JOY AND LOVE

8. CHOOSE TO EXPERIENCE A LOVE LIKE NO OTHER

SECTION THREE

LIVING IN THE PRESENCE OF MY BETTER DAYS

SECTION THREE

GOD ISN'T THROUGH WITH ME YET

CHAPTER SEVEN

PAIN TO PURPOSE

1. AWAKENED FROM A DREAM THAT CHANGED MY LIFE

2. ALL THINGS ARE WORKING TOGETHER FOR OUR GOOD

3. HOW MY PAIN WAS PURPOSED FOR GOD'S GLORY

4. EVERYONE IS GIVEN A GIFT FROM GOD

5. WHAT ARE YOU PASSIONATE ABOUT?

6. WHAT DOES A FULFILLED SOUL FEEL LIKE?

7. THE COST OF DELIVERANCE IS PAIN

CHAPTER EIGHT

"ARISE" I AM WHO GOD SAYS I AM

1. A SPIRITUAL AND MENTAL PERSPECTIVE OF SELF DEVELOPMENT

2. THE CONFIDENCE, COURAGE AND FREEDOM TO TELL MY STORY

3. MY STORY IS FOR THE VICTORY OF GOD'S GLORY

4. THERE IS POWER IN THE WORDS YOU SPEAK

5. PURPOSE WILL SHARPEN YOUR IDENTITY

6. A PURPOSE FULL OF CLARITY AND DIRECTION

7. THIS MIGHT BE THE FINALE BUT MY JOURNEY HAS JUST BEGUN

8. MY PRAYER TO YOU

CHAPTER NINE

YOUR SETBACK WAS YOUR PREPARATION FOR YOUR COMEBACK

1. THE JOURNEY OF MY PURPOSE WAS THE UNCERTAINTY OF MY PATHWAY

2. WHO IS THE MAN WITH THE MASTER PLAN?

3. ARISE

INTRODUCTION

Born and raised in the Midwest of Gary, Indiana, the early 80's era was fun, colorful, unique, and the collective memory of a generation known as Generation X. During this time of my life as a child, growing up in an urban middle-class home in that shadowed house on Carolina Street was full of evil, despair, and the desolation of fear, attacks from the dark side, which separated my family and left me feeling broken, empty, and hopeless. The separation of my family made me that fatherless child carrying baggage of insecurities, resentment, bitterness, rejection, distrust, lack of self-confidence, stress, depression, and the walls of offense which distorted and conditioned me to have a false perception of myself and the world around me.

I was that little girl who didn't receive the affirmation of love, security, and emotional acceptance due to the lack of paternal instruction, security, support, and presence. This lack of affirmation created bags of brokenness. A broken child who became a broken soul who fought to survive by burying the baggage and masquerading repetitive pain for countless years, which would later suppress internal negative thoughts and emotional behavior through feelings of inadequacy and unworthiness in my teenagehood, womanhood, intimate relationships, motherhood, and throughout 20 years of marriage.

The psychological and emotional impact paralyzed me and conditioned me to become desensitized from the start of those humble beginnings where the fatherless wounds rooted in and the thick and tall walls of offense were built for my false security and the comfort of my isolation to help me cope for my survival! My survival convinced me to believe that my life was just fine and that I had moved forward from my past. I

9

believed that my past was left behind. I thought my survival meant that I had healed, been delivered, and escaped the baggage successfully! Little did I know, my personal achievements and accomplishments throughout my life were the false notions and perception of being who I was and accepting that this is who I am, and that was my wholeness. I searched for love from a man as a validation to complete me! I placed more value in how the world saw me than in how God saw me. I couldn't find my value to understand my potential and purpose in life!

I accepted my character flaws and discomfort of deficiencies by the social and family norms of my generational inheritance. The same emotional, psychological, and spiritual traits that my parents and paternal grandparents struggled through were all relatable. I was a functioning dead woman but there was hope, help, and healing in the horizon!

We all are not perfect! Even as believers of Christ, we are not perfect! Christ reminds us that we have all sinned and fallen short of the glory of God, yet we are all justified freely by his grace through the redemptive work on the cross. According to KJV(Romans 3:23 & 24), He also reminds us that we perish due to the lack of knowledge. KJV(Hosea 4:6) says, "...and knowledge is our pathway to our power." God allowed me to find my power. I had to find the power to receive authentic healing, deliverance, and the victory! All things work together for the good of those who love Him. In this life, our goods outweigh our bads, but we must understand that our bad struggles and deficiencies of life were for our better good to use our mountains as our ministries, and our tests for our testimonies. God gives us beauty for our ashes. This is the crown to our victory!

One day, I had an awakening! God allowed me to be awakened to the truth! The true and the living God had to remind me how much he loved me and that He was always with me from the very beginning! He had to purge me and prepare me for the ultimate journey. Have you ever felt in your spirit that urgency to make a radical change, even if it meant taking risks? Taking risks involves being uncomfortable by taking a leap of faith. I had to submit wholeheartedly to God to heal in order to share my story. Yet, someone standing on the outside of my life looking in may have thought, "What's the problem?" This woman has it all. My story is my truth and my freedom which gives me the courage to release and share my story publicly without shame, guilt, or fear. I had to rise to my calling and to fulfill the purpose! Through the journey of healing and deliverance, we will never arrive, but yet our spirits will arise once we have allowed God's will into our lives.

Section One

The Dark Beginnings

The Dark Days of Living in the Past

CHAPTER 1 - THE WONDER YEARS OF

WEARINESS

WHEN, WHERE AND HOW IT ALL STARTED

In my tender years at the age of six, playing with dolls and enjoying life with my mother and father at home, life was innocent, yet mysterious. The curiosity of not knowing what each passing day would bring, brought a sense of insecurity and fear like no other. One afternoon, I could smell the fresh aroma of catfish and spaghetti from the kitchen. My father was great at fishing and he would bring home buckets of catfish on many weekends. He would come home and scalp the flapping fish, and as I watched with intense sadness and guilt, in my eyes every catfish went through the torture of being slaughtered--one by one. They would try to escape by jumping out the bucket, and I would run with fear because these slippery, wet amphibians would get closer to me every time. However, regardless of how horrifying it felt to watch them die, one by one, these little creatures were still our dinner that would satisfy our cravings.

This particular evening was different, but quite familiar. It was an evening that would always be remembered for the rest of my life. Arguments flared and the fear of evil would once again cause my parents to experience their own traumatic pain that festered into verbal altercations, then the abuse. I didn't understand what and why the arguments would happen so often, but I could feel the strong conflict and tension between them. As my heart would race rapidly out of fear and the

13

unknown, I suppressed all of the pain inside because there wasn't anything I could do to change the atmosphere. I felt hopeless and helpless! I felt lonely and isolated! I had no one to go to. This had an impact on my life as a child and the fear, anxiety, and insecurities would soon start to develop internally, stronger with every passing day. How would I know what I was feeling? I was only five or six years old, and this uncertainty left me with twisting and turning thoughts that made life an uncomfortable place to live in, and I was unable to sleep almost every night wondering what would the next day bring or would I even live to tell my story.

One evening, we all sat at the table, me, my mother and father. It happened so quickly! The rage in my father's eyes reminded me of the tormenting feelings I would feel almost every night as if hell had created a portal to that house. My father became angry at my mother for something simple in my eyes, and within seconds, I could hear the screams of death, the loud cries of terror and the physical and verbal abuse she endured. This left me numb inside where my heart sunk. I was paralyzed with fear! I felt hopeless seeing her eyes filled with sadness and with heavy grief and sorrow as I would help her get up from being thrown to the carpet. My mother was in deep agony and her screams left me in a state of grief, disappointment, and complete shock. Her cries broke from the reservoir or her soul, and from the brokenness of her heart, she endured the physical and verbal abuse. For she was broken. In my innocent eyes she was a broken soul. It was like I could see her inner soul and bleeding heart through her eyes, and I could feel her pain by the posture of her body, yet I was too young to understand what I was feeling inside at this time of my life. I felt both of my parents' pain. I felt my father's pain of rage, frustration, guilt, shame, and resentment. He also was broken inside. I couldn't understand all of these emotions around me but I knew that we all felt this way.

There was a demonic presence in that house where you could feel the cold breeze of terror, like swift winds passing by and the house was filled with so many spirits. I don't like to talk about evil but I know what I experienced. Evil was surely one of many spirits in the house we lived because the encounters that would appear made it a miserable paranormal experience. The presence of heaviness was so thick that it would make your heart ache and my chest tighten. I feared for the worst because I never knew what unearthly appearances would pop up at any moment. As chills of fear would gravitate my mind, body, and soul, my mind had been conditioned to think the worst and that I wouldn't make it through the nightmares. The feeling of dreadfulness was so vivid to where it became difficult to accept evenings. The evenings felt like the worst time of day. That's when it seemed where evil appearances were exposed the most. I kept these experiences a secret because I knew that no one would believe me and I didn't want people to think I was losing my mind, but I also suspected that my parents knew something in this house wasn't normal too. I knew the things I saw and I knew what I felt was weird! The isolation and loneliness became normal to me because I had no other choice but to live in this situation. I was just a child that buried so many insecurities and vulnerabilities and I had kept these feelings buried deep down inside and made my promise not to reveal this to anyone, not a soul. No one from the outside knew what my father, my mother and I, as a family were going through and it was not my position to discuss this pain I carried for many years. It was not my strength nor was it my responsibility.

Yet, this was that evening so familiar to me because for many days to come, it left my mother completely and repeatedly broken, but it was the beginning of my unknown pain and the developments of baggage I would carry throughout my life. Fear would consume me all over again and I could feel my heart race and hear my heartbeats as I was paralyzed standing there trying to console my mother's broken heart, but yet trying to understand my father's rage. I knew that my parents loved one another, but as time went on, I also knew that they wouldn't remain together for too long. I knew that my parents loved me, but because they carried spirits of brokenness, it developed brokenness in my spirit too. Their spirits had transferred to me. I suppressed their brokenness. At this age, I was very intelligent, intuitive, and creative. I knew the meaning of survival because my parents showed me what survival was about, but they were unable to show me or teach me how to heal because as I look back over my life now, they didn't have the ability to heal through their own past, filled with deficiencies of their own pain and struggles. As a child, I had hoped that my parents would see how their individual pain would intensify and affect their struggles together as a couple. My soul had begged for our family to receive help and counsel but no help was given. We suffered in silence! When you're living in an environment where the spirit of darkness is present, your natural abilities don't have the power to defeat the evil when you don't have the knowledge and the spiritual warfare to battle in the spiritual realm. So, you become vulnerable to the demonic presence around you. Vulnerability soon became my baggage. It took a toll on my soul.

This is where it had all started. The pain would become heavier and heavier and the wounds were buried deeper and deeper. The spirit of heaviness consumed me with tears of sadness, the fear of the unknown and the emotional, spiritual and mental burden I internalized became my cloud of heaviness. Many families wouldn't discuss their deepest and most intense personal pain of what they've suffered through, but you must understand that your truth is your freedom! You just have to face it in order to fix it. My story is my truth. I can only reveal my truth of authenticity from start to finish and when you are ready to do the work and face your truth and pain, then you can prepare to fix the damages of your brokenness. You must face it yourself because no one can do it for you. I accepted that my brokenness must have been the normal way of life because I learned to deal with it. So I accepted much pain and normalized it.

My mind was flooded with the hope to survive, and to survive the nightmares that were beyond my parent's ordeal. Although it was not my fault why these circumstances had to occur in my life growing up, it was still my responsibility to become healed, delivered and set free!

THE TRAUMA OF FEAR AND TORMENT

The haunted house as I call it, is the childhood home I grew up in. These were dark days of gloom in which would be the beginning of how my fears and anxieties were developed.

We lived in a beautiful ranch style home with cathedral ceilings, spacious bedrooms and a very long backyard with a private red-wood fence. During this era of the early eighties, the community and neighborhoods were well kept and the middle-class neighbors were working-class families.

From the outside of the house, life appeared to be peaceful, glorious and full of tranquil moments but as the old saying goes, "The grass is always greener on the other side of the fence." There's a reason why this old saying was spoken. Although life appeared better from the outside, it wasn't the same on the inside. At that time, the exterior of the house was beautifully painted in light brown with dark brown trimmings. The lawn was neatly manicured with trees neatly trimmed on the front and back of the house.

It reminds me of how people can look their best on the outside, freshly groomed and smelling great with the best colognes or perfumes but on the inside it's a totally different person. On the inside, your spirit carries a stench when it's full of toxins and contamination but it's covered up at its finest. This is masquerading at its best. Isn't this the way some people masquerade their lives by covering up their pain internally?

The particular house we lived in was not your ordinary experience. It was an experience beyond my recollection. As a child, I didn't understand it! The outside appearance was totally opposite from the inside. I believe this is how my life looked to others nearly my entire life. Unfortunately, these experiences our family endured will never be forgotten. As I share these traumatic experiences during my childhood, I also shared these unearthly and demonic experiences with my god-brother. We were close in age during this time and he would come over to visit me often. His mom and my mom were best friends since their teenage years and I was an only child at that time, so I didn't have any playmates. Most of the time, I played alone. I had so many toys to play with and being an only child allowed me to enjoy the benefits of owning every toy I desired. However, I shared many dark experiences with my god-brother, who was my close playmate. As we played with many of my toys, he would just sit in a very stiff posture and stare at me with fear, listening very attentively, knowing that everything I shared with him was true. We grew up as babies and he knew me really well. He could feel my fears and he could also feel the presence around us as I discussed in detail those very frightening moments. I knew that he could see that look in my eyes. I knew that he would believe me and not judge or treat me any different, so I shared these moments with him freely and in private. Over thirty-five years later, as a husband and a father at this present time, he can still recall those chilling stories. He considers me a survivor because he said those stories stuck with him his entire life.

As demonic encounters seem more present today, I would assume that there are many who have experienced dark, supernatural encounters with demonic presence and many would not be at liberty or have the courage to share their experiences, due to being afraid of rejection and the fear of embarrassment and judgment from people as being an outcast or better yet, a basket-case. Gracefully, I've grown to courageously and bravely share my truth.

I'm quite sure that in the neighborhood me and my family once lived, there could possibly be many others who may have experienced some type of supernatural encounter in their homes and I'm almost positive that the neighbors experienced something similar to what we had experienced. I often wondered what their stories were like and did their experiences affect them in any type of way. It wouldn't be long before I would be reminded how my past fears would become a familiar dark place I never thought I would revisit.

Several years ago in a newspaper article, I discovered there was a home that sat one mile from the haunted house I lived in. This particular home was televised on the Travel Channel and many news stations and all over the world featured this haunted house as being the "portal from hell" or the "exorcism house". It was also filmed on a documentary of "Ghost Adventures" and an article written in the Indy Star. A reporter quoted, "Something was inside that house that had the ability to do things that I have never seen before — things that others carrying the highest forms of credibility couldn't explain either," a reporter told IndyStar via email. "There was something there that was very dark yet highly intelligent and powerful." Indy Star

This was a home where a family once lived through the horrific torment and evil activities that forced the family to move out. That particular home was later demolished in January 2016. It broke my heart to read about the tragedy of this family's life, especially how the children are affected now.

Many neighbors, local officials and social services will never forget the dreadful day of trying to rescue the family from this home and they will never forget the emotional and mental impact that affected them personally. It was also mentioned that the police officer assigned to help the family immediately quit his job due to the spiritual torment and the mental impact he suffered.

The statement from the reporter who investigated the story of that home expressed the encounters in the most mysterious, yet mind-blowing way. It was a story very chilling and very similar to the home I once lived in, yet many decades later in the same neighborhood where the house I lived is currently abandoned, and still standing.

Several years ago, my father decided to visit the abandoned home. He stated that he was hesitant, curious, yet brave enough to take a drive and walk to the front lawn. He described the dilapidated state of the exterior structure and the chills he felt as he walked closer and closer to the front door. Right at the very moment when he felt the attempt to open the door, that familiar experience he once encountered would be the last time he would ever think about putting his hands on the door again, yet alone step his foot on the property.

As I think about my life, I believe that my humbling beginnings were for a purpose and these traumatizing experiences from my past were intentional for my transparency to something greater in the future. You're probably wondering how could living under these circumstances become anything close to becoming better? Living my life would have its way of helping me to understand the reason why I struggled with so much baggage and scars for my spiritual deliverance and revelation to know that the truth we live is our story. The truth hurts but it also heals and it reveals! Once again, it gives us freedom!

Once we start to accept the true meaning of our pain and struggles, God will begin to uncover what we've hidden for so long and to recover our souls from darkness into the marvelous light. The light is the awakening of becoming a better version of ourselves. The Enemy is Satan and his mission was to destroy my mind during my innocence. My childhood sudden attacks in that haunted house was a warfare but I wasn't spiritually, emotionally or mentally equipped for the battle. It was God's grace and protection that covered me!

Demonic presence and spiritual warfare is dangerous when you do not understand Satan's plan and the attacks against you and the plan that God has for your life. The supernatural and demonic presence is of Satan and it's real! This was not a dream! This is not a joke! This was absolutely real life horror! We must be reminded that God's plan isn't to attack us and He allows us to experience a supernatural presence of His love in different times of our lives whether we believe in God or not! If you don't believe in spirits then how can you believe in God? God is a spirit and when he cast out Lucifer(Satan) and 1/3 of angels out of heaven, he and those fallen angels are the evil and unclean spirits we battle against today.

What's most important is knowing God and knowing how He was my protector from the very beginning and how He sustained me all of my life from the battles around me. The emotional and mental trauma I experienced could have been much worse and similar to the family who once lived in the home nearby, where the home was later demolished four years ago.

There is no greater love I've ever experienced on this earth. I give all the credit to God for allowing me to share my story. If God wasn't real and if it wasn't for His grace and mercy, I wouldn't be here nor have the strength or courage to share my experiences. As a child, my   presence. One night I was lying in my bed. My bedroom was far from my parents' room and there was a long hallway that separated each of the spacious bedrooms. As I would pray before pulling the sheets from my bed, my peripheral vision would notice quick motions as if something had just swiftly entered my room in less than seconds. I would pull the covers over my face in fear of the next sighting and hoping that it wouldn't be the most frightening appearance to kill me. I tried very hard to hold in my screams. I tried to be as brave as I could to prevent screaming but some nights were impossible. There were eyes watching me from wall to wall as I laid in bed and I knew that if I were to tell someone, they wouldn't believe me or they would think that I was absolutely crazy and out of my mind but my parents knew what I had gone through. The eyes would travel across my wall and I would lay in bed, paranoid and in extreme fear. Many nights I couldn't sleep and it was difficult for me to stay awake at school. I would fall asleep in class from being drained and exhausted from so many restless nights. My heart beats were loud and as I would perspire with fear and agony. These demonic eyes that would revisit my room time after time, had me unable to move. It felt like I was held or pinned down. As my fears grew, so were the attacks that became stronger. My heart would race rapidly when I could see appearances that I've never seen before. These appearances were not even normal. Next, there would be moving shadows appearing on my wall and these shadows would appear as images that would change in different forms as I watched in fear from my bed. It was like I was watching a horror movie but instead I was a part of this nightmare. As the shadows would form, more shadows would come forth and the movement on my walls and ceilings became too much to bear where I would scream from the top of my lungs to awaken my parents. Many nights my parents had to come and grab me from my bedroom and console me as I would cry, scream and jump all through the night. Even when they would allow me to sleep with them to make me feel secure, these images came in their room and I would ask them, "Do you see what I'm seeing?" Their calm and sleepy replies would be "close your eyes and go to sleep!" I wondered how they could sleep through all of this! The heavy presence filled the house and almost every night there was a dark encounter. Other nights, I would hear heavy footsteps walking from one end of the house to the other and back and forth throughout our hallway. The doors would shut forcefully from the family room in the middle of the night and when I would have some relief for a good night sleep, something would awaken me to the frightening, dark appearance of a man standing over my bed watching me. There was one night where I was awakened from my sleep to see the walls bleed, as blood would flow heavy from the top of the ceilings to the bottom of the floor. It flowed like a water well but never quite touched the floor. It was creepy! I was tormented and the torments were painfully adding more baggage of fear, anxiety and complete exhaustion! There was another strange encounter where my full-size doll became missing. I looked all over my rooms and underneath my toys and in every room, there were no signs of my favorite doll. Strangely, my dad came home from work to find the doll standing in front of our living room near our family room door. It frightened me so terribly bad that he kicked the doll in the air where it flew high into our cathedral ceilings. He kicked it so hard where the head flew in a different direction. This was once again another unsettling experience. I always wondered how did my doll move from my back playroom all the way to the other side of the house and stand still by the door to meet my father exactly at the time he would get off from work.

For many years while my parents were together, they did their best to comfort me through these tormenting encounters. They kept their silence about the encounters they'd experienced in this house. The only person I would talk to about my experiences was my god-brother yet, years later in my adulthood, I assumed that my parents kept these things quiet to protect me the best way they could. However, as a child, I knew that I couldn't be the only one experiencing these horrible sightings until I overheard my parents discuss a strange spot on the dining room wall. This spot would remain there for days and then it would strangely disappear for days. This strange sighting repetitively happened throughout my entire stay. My mother would even try to wash away this spot. She would use all types of cleaning products but strangely, it would still remain there. We wanted to be in denial and believe that it could just be a glare from the window sunlight reflection on the wall but that denial soon ended once evening came and the same spot on the wall was still there. My father noticed the same. This went on for quite a while. This is when I would start to realize that I was not feeling these mysterious experiences alone. They knew that there was a presence of darkness and that there was an evil presence that filled that house. We all would feel this every night. This was a force to be reckoned with and an experience we will never forget.

This house was full of evil and wickedness, yet we managed to still survive through it. I know for a fact that these evil spirits caused dysfunction in the house I lived, the arguments would escalate the more I prayed and as I would peep around the corners to watch my parents argue in their disagreements, deep down in my heart I could sense that their relationship would ultimately come to a sad end. I could feel the insecurity within. There was great pain, resentment, bitterness and the spirit of evil presence filled the atmosphere no matter where I stood in this haunted house. I called it "haunted" because that's the best word I ever used to describe this house. There wasn't any communication of love, for my parent's love for each other was covered beneath the evil forces that surrounded us as a family. This had to be the plan of the enemy and I believe that I gained more baggage of insecurity as I always feared for the unknown. Most marriages split due to the spiritual demonic presence that we can become vulnerable towards opening ourselves to, meaning we allow deception, distrust, and people from the outside to destroy what God has divinely put together. If we become vulnerable and unknowingly opened to those spiritual forces, especially when we do not have the knowledge to take authority that Christ has given us, to rebuke and to cast out those entities of unclean spirits in our homes, it will and can destroy relationships and marriages and even ourselves.

Living in this house was not always a bad experience. I had some great days and moments. My mother would often take me to church every Sunday when she had the day off from work. She had been born and raised in the church. Her life and Christian faith in the Pentecostal church, with deep cultural roots, made her a faithful and dedicated believer through prayer and reverence to God. Oftentimes, when my mother was unable to attend church due to her work schedule, my uncle would take me to church often and he would always promise to take me to McDonald's as a way to influence me to come to church with him. It makes me chuckle by the fact that he would always keep his word because I was a kid who

25

loved to eat McDonald's after church on Sundays. He knew what my order would be every time too. Once again, I was an only child at the time and the only grandchild for many years, so I looked forward to those days of getting what I wanted. Furthermore, my mother's faith in God and rearing me to acknowledge God was essential for my formative years. I didn't realize then, how important this would be in the years to come. It was those days where I would hear my mom walk throughout the house and pray in every room. Sometimes she would pray in her room, read her bible and meditate on God. Watching her would give me a source of peace and a sense of security. Most of all, it gave me a sense of God's existence! Watching and hearing my mother pray allowed me to discover that there was hope to end my misery of the demonic presence that had been tormenting me. It was my early beginnings of learning about God that developed a spirituality of desiring to know more about God. I felt a sense of protection.

My mother joined a church we attended for many years and although I was receptive to learning about God and His only begotten son Jesus, who died on the cross for our sins, I didn't surrender and commit to God like I was supposed to. Well, I reverenced God but I just didn't apply the devotions to my life like everyone was talking. I didn't develop a personal relationship with God the way the people in the church were talking about in their testimonies during service but the conviction of sin was in my heart. I knew that God was real and I feared and reverenced God but after church, I was back to doing me and doing me was everything that was not godly.

During this time of my life, I relied on prayer the most. I would say my prayers at night and ask God to make those bad spirits go away and allow me to sleep peacefully at night. Some nights I could sleep peacefully, many nights were the constant demonic encounters. These encounters would even wake me up through the night and it was emotionally, mentally overbearing and physically overwhelming. I had many restless nights that would affect my days at school where I would unconsciously drift off to sleep during class. Thankfully, I knew how to pray but I didn't know how to warfare in the spirit. I lacked the spiritual knowledge and yet the demonic spirits increased and their presence grew in strength. I felt hopeless because I felt powerless and mentally worn from feeling weary and my spirit became inflicted by the brokenness of my soul.

THE EMOTIONAL & PHYSICAL SEPARATION

That day when my life would change at the age of seven years old, my parents physically separated. Their emotional separation for many years came to the point of physical separation. My family security and structure was broken. This separation left me afraid and more afraid of our future, my future! This is when the spirit of insecurity developed in me but it was buried so deeply. The separation was a major impact to my emotional and mental state of being. This affected my confidence and self-esteem which would have an impact on my self-identity. My family structure was broken and so was my spirit. Later in life, I would have to deal with the seed that was deposited into my life but this was the beginning of more to come. Not only was the emotional disconnect between me and my father realistic, now me and my father's relationship would become physically disconnected. Thoughts would come to my mind and those reminiscing moments I missed would visualize. For, I missed those very few moments when I would think about how my father would intimately touch my mom and try to hide those moments from me. You know those intimate moments that make a woman laugh, smile, giggle and say, "stop" but deep down inside those were love-touches of affection and attention that most women love from their man or significant other. These were just thoughts of what I would miss. I would even miss those dinners at the dining room table we shared. I would miss playing those Atari games with my dad and I would miss watching him play his bass guitar on the weekends. As I sat on my bed preparing to pack my clothes and a few belongings, I felt heartaches of pain as someone receiving news of losing their loved-one suddenly without any warning. The water from my eyes began to fall heavy, one drop at a time, rolling down my cheeks and onto my clothes. The background screams was the emotional distress as the noise of pain and anger filled the air. This was the epiphany, an emotional and spiritual challenge in my life. This was a breakdown that I normalized. I didn't want my parents to split but I was smart enough to know that they needed happiness and they were better off separated. This would hurt me the most although it was the truth. My broken and most painful truth was a big pill to swallow. I was young and intelligent but I felt that this season of my life had to come to an end. I felt there must be a reason this had to happen! As my mom stood by my bedroom, she walked in the room and I just sadly stared into her teary eyes filled with red strains from crying, gently speaking to me in a low tone, she said, "Angel, pack your favorite things, we're leaving but you can't take much." I had so many favorite items, from toys, clothes and playroom furniture. I didn't want to let go of all my favorite things, not even my favorite white canopy bed. I knew that I couldn't take this with me but I had to swallow this pain and find strength to pack up my belongings in the midst of sadness, stress and confusion. I didn't know where we were going but I knew that this place I called home, that I loved but also hated too, would no longer be my place of security and it surely wasn't a place of serenity. This separation was bittersweet. I didn't want my parents to separate but I didn't want to spend another tormenting night in that house as well.

The first man in my life, my father, the man who I loved so much would no longer be here to protect me when I was afraid. The man who I wanted to be a part of my life, the man that I never felt that he connected with me, emotionally or physically would no longer be in my presence. Although he's alive and well, he wouldn't be around me and I wouldn't get to see him as much. I wanted him to experience my development of life. I just wanted to have my dad by my side!

As a child, I was lonely. I normalized loneliness and pain, my comfort zone of pain became isolation. I kept myself isolated due to the fear and insecurity, which had internalized in me. I developed the nature of protecting myself by building walls around me. I became a loner and my identity made me believe that I was an introvert. I was different but yet a gentle soul to be around and although I would make friends from time to time, they didn't last for long because the spirit of offense and fear had developed, yet I thought I was doing just fine coping with my innermost demons inside. I felt like a misfit but yet, I normalized these personal deficiencies because I had buried my pain so deeply and desensitized the areas that I felt would destroy me emotionally. As a child, you learn to cope the best way you can and you learn survival by watching your parents look like survival. In my eyes, as a child it was the look of survival and existence. As a child, I felt like I had been in a dooms-day war zone. Although I was a child, I had developed into an old soul.

As I packed my belongings, I felt stressed because I didn't have the time to prepare for a sudden move or concentrate and figure out what to pack. My heart was heavy and my mind was cluttered. This early stage of my life left me broken and although I felt an unknown strength and courage, I felt empty inside. I was too numb to talk. This is where I developed the spirit of discouragement which was my way of "shutting-down". I internalized the pain so that others couldn't see my true feelings. I had mastered the seed of masquerading pain. I thought I did a very good job because no one could tell.

For several years, we lived with close family members and left my father in that house to live alone. I never got to see him or hear from him much. Oftentimes, he would visit us occasionally because he would say that he missed us. Deep down inside, I missed my dad too. I missed his presence and I missed those memories of him listening to his favorite songs from his stereo system. The stereo system was a big deal in the early 80's and his taste of music became my taste of music. I missed listening to him play his old records from the music era of the 60's, 70's and 80's. Singers such as: Marvin Gaye, Chaka Khan, Teddy Pendergrass, Earth Wind & Fire, The Isley Brothers, Sister Sledge, Michael Jackson, Prince, Rick James, and the list goes on. I became an old soul when it came to music and I could sing every lyric and not miss a beat. Soul and pop music was also a part of my growing up as well as classic gospel music. I missed seeing my father pick at his bass guitar and trying to sing tunes from his old time favorites, Luther Vandross. He was my father's favorite singer. The soothing and sensual love lyrics that Luther Vandross would sing made me believe that intimate love must be genuinely real. Music had a special way of comforting me. As a kid, I missed seeing my father maintaining the yard and he loved to wash and shine his 4x4 blue truck. What I remembered the most was his fishing trips when he would come home with buckets of fish and he would scalp and clean the fish for my mother to fry. He was a hardworking blue collar man and his work ethics were outstanding. As I can remember, we had a few great moments as a family but it had all changed until one day he convinced my mom to come back home. I was a little excited, although I was afraid to revisit those demonic encounters in that house, I figured maybe those bad spirits have left by then. This was the way I thought as a child, so I was optimistic that things were going to be much better now if we returned to that house. At first, my mom was very reluctant and remained hesitant about returning home, but eventually she decided to give him another chance. This time when she returned home, it was not only me but a new addition to the family came with us. I was no longer an only child for seven years, my little sibling was now a part of our family. My mom was pregnant during the separation and it was very stressful for her to carry a baby while enduring the heartaches and pain from the marriage. We returned to the house but unfortunately, it wasn't long before we left this house again where my parents didn't get along. My sibling doesn't have any memories of this house and that's probably a good thing, considering those evil spirits were still lurking around and the demonic presence hadn't changed a bit. In fact, it felt like things were worse than before. Once again, my mother, me and my baby sibling left home for good this time, leaving my father behind was our final move.

In that house he had lived alone for many years and to this day, he has countless stories and experiences he endured living there alone. His stories were much more frightening than I had encountered. Due to the extreme demonic presence that had taken total control of that house and a toll on him, my father soon moved out! That house where I once knew as home, still remains empty and abandoned to this current day.

Growing up without my father and being separated from him physically developed fear and insecurities like no other. I didn't feel the emotional connection or the protection that I needed or that special "daddy's girl" bond I always desired.

At this time of my life, I was too young to discover or understand what I was going through. I was around the age of eight or nine years old and I could remember feelings of being afraid, the fear of the unknown, the fear of not feeling protected and the fear of being homeless and not knowing where we would live. As I recall these memories, I still felt the need to have my father present in my life, just to be around him because I loved my dad, even through his shortcomings, his faults and his failures. He wasn't perfect but neither of us are. I always wished for those special moments where I could reminisce and see how other dads would spend time with their children and I often imagined what it would have felt like to have my dad take me to the playground, parks, carnivals, or even take family pictures. Those special moments that would mean so much to me growing up are those priceless moments that you can't take back ever in life. It was even important to me just for my dad to ask me, "How was your day at school?" or seeing me perform at a school event. My mother would always show her support and she gave me the attention I needed but I also desired the attention and affection from my father. I lacked it! This lack of attention from the first man in my life that I'd loved so much, had developed a loss of self-worth in me. My father was a very busy man. He was a hard-worker, a great provider and he took care of our family, the house, the financial responsibilities and he was a protector, unfortunately, his time and other interests were outside of home. On special holidays such as Christmas, there were those great moments that I could recall where he and my mom bought me a kid motorcycle. I loved this little blue rider and I can remember riding it up and down the sidewalks. Another great moment I could remember was him showing me how to fly a kite in the open lot next to the house we lived in. On a sunny day in May, I stared into the beautiful sky and watched how high the kite would travel. There was a slight warm breeze and the higher the kite went up into the sky, the tighter I had to grip the string. This reminds me about life in general, it seems like the higher you go in life, the tighter the grip seems when it comes to maintaining balance, strength and the determination to hold on, to never let go!

Those fun moments of playing games, like Pac Man on the Atari Game System were the most anticipated. This was a very hot commodity back in the 80's and anyone that had the Atari Game System, definitely played Pac Man. These were a few moments that I could recall those times I missed so much and would never experience again. There were more distant days with him than there were days I needed to bond with him. I would consider myself fortunate for those limited memories with him, simply because I don't recall any of my siblings sharing similar experiences with him as I was fortunate to experience. As I grew older in age, all I had were faded memories. I no longer got to see my dad as much and when I would see him, he would either drop me off to my grandmother's house, where he would leave the house and I wouldn't see him until it was time to take me home on the weekends. There were those other times where me and my sibling would be excited with anticipation to pack our bags for the weekend and wait by the door or stare out the window and hoping that one of the passing vehicles would be him pulling up in our driveway for him to pick us up, only to find ourselves still looking out the window wishing he would come but he would never show up. When we would try to call him, he wouldn't answer the phone. There were many weekends where we waited and waited and waited, where hours would pass, leaving us having to unpack our belongings and silently hide our grief and disappointments. Those moments of feeling emotionally abandoned, rejected and neglected, is where I had convinced myself that he really never loved us at all. These were the moments where I became angry, bitter and I resented him for lying to me by breaking promises. My heart would ache during these times where I just needed to talk with him but he could not be found. The more I became optimistic about having hope that my father would change, the more it felt like buckets of disappointment pouring over my body because it didn't change at all. I had always dreamed and had high expectations of that perfect relationship with my father. It meant so much to me. It was unfortunate that those days of hope never came and the years kept passing by. These days brought us farther apart. I grew up into a young girl, developing and blossoming into my preteens and now by this time, I'm carrying bags of self-condemnation, resentment, bitterness, fear, distrust, insecurities, while yet losing myself in the process of my development, in fear of what was ahead of me in a cold world and in a society to fend for myself and to protect myself, my courage, my heart, and building walls of isolation. This was where I started to bury the seed of grief, the seed of pain, the seed of anger, and other seeds of deficiencies.

These were those baggages! The biggest seed of all was the seed of unforgiveness. I was angry with what I had endured and I had to blame somebody for the pain that left me this way. For many years, my mother, a single-parent, worked several jobs to provide ends-meet. She worked tirelessly as a single mom to make sure me and my siblings were well taken care of. We didn't have much but we were thankful for what we did have..

GROWING UP A CHURCH GIRL

During this time, my mother kept us in church. We attended church faithfully. Many times I didn't want to attend but my mom made us go anyway. I didn't like going to church that much and I had always promised myself that by the time I became an adult, there would be no more church for me. That would soon change.

What I enjoyed the most about attending the church services was the opportunity to work with children of different ages, in various projects and activities. I learned so much about God by being active with the children and it brought joy and excitement to look forward to on Sunday mornings. It had created a sense of purpose in me to work with children and since I enjoyed working with the children so much, I looked forward to learning about God on my own just to ensure that I was teaching them about God according to the basic principles of the Word of God. I was young and just entering into my early teens and at this time of my life, I discovered how much I'd really enjoyed working with children. This opportunity to work in the children's ministry continued for a few years. I enjoyed playing bible trivia and giving out prizes to the kids during early morning Sunday school. These were the best experiences of attending church and during this time of my life, I had developed and grew in God's word from adolescence to teenage years. Many years had flown by and as my mother would continue to take us to church, I became active in singing in the church choir. I enjoyed singing a lot. I always enjoyed music and singing was one of my gifts. Singing had a way of bringing peace and deliverance to my spirit and soul.

One of the greatest moments at the age of 13, was celebrating my mother's blessing to move in her first home. We lived in a medium-sized single family home and for the first time after 5 years of living with different family members, we were excited to be in a place we called home. I was thankful as a child to have family in our lives, who loved us and opened their homes to us to allow my mom to get on her feet and make a better life for us. With her faith in God, her faithfulness to the church we attended at that time, it was a long time coming and we endured patience for the wait. It was a monumental moment in our lives to finally receive our blessing of what she had desired for a long time. We were excited and so thankful to God to make this house our home with pleasant neighbors around us and in a new season in our lives to regroup and to refresh. Although our home was not the family structure of having both parents, I had adapted to a new chapter in my life. It was a new chapter in all our lives and we created a bond with just the three of us, my mom, my sibling and me. Long, were the days where I would feel those demonic attacks that would wake me up through the night and shake my bed. I may have had a few nightmares but it wasn't the same experience I had before. This house was different and by this time, my mother's faith in God grew and she would pray all throughout the house. I always observed my mother's reaction to life, as I considered her to be the "strong woman" in my life for enduring so many challenges and so much from our past. She was yet determined in doing everything she had to do as a single parent to set an example for us. That also meant, keeping us in church all day and even all night for night services to return to church twice a week. These were the moments where I was tired of being in church almost everyday and I didn't realize that these were the most pivotal days of my life! My mother was a God-fearing woman and regardless of the pain and struggles she endured, she kept her business private and stayed positive throughout the process. She never showed us her feelings. She was very private with her feelings. Although she was often disappointed and angered by my father's emotional abandonment and physical neglect towards us throughout the years, she would never talk bad about him to us. She would always say, "You will have to learn about your father for yourself." My mother's side of the family was deeply rooted in The Pentecostal belief. She was a "Preacher's Kid". From her side of the family, my great-grandfather and grandfather were pastors and my great grandmother worked in many church district meetings and my great-grandmothers worked tirelessly as a missionary and first lady of their church. My maternal grandmother worked in the church as a head usher and she was very faithful in helping out in any way she could by organizing and developing many functions within the body of Christ. Many other family members from the next generations later became ministers and pastors and both sides of my mother's family preached the word of God and their messages for all was to repent of your sins and surrender our lives to God. Being born again through Christ Jesus was the main message in the sermons and altar-calls were the most important times of the service. These were the moments where they would open the floor to anyone who desired to give their life to God.

It was a strict upbringing on my mother's side of the family and as an adult today, I've learned the importance of morals, values and standards. The ultimate message was to get your life right before God and to turn from sin to escape a burning hell. This had always placed fear in my heart and although my spirit was willing, my innermost struggles made me feel like I wasn't good enough to live up to these standards. The standards of living for God seemed boring and undeniably challenging due to the strict lifestyle. I didn't like the thought of never wearing pants and wearing long dresses. I couldn't wear fingernail polish. This was too ancient for me. I didn't like the thought of not being able to do anything and it just didn't seem like fun to me. On the other side, I absolutely didn't want to go to a burning hell after experiencing the life in that haunted house that was so traumatic. The hell sermons and messages I would hear filled my heart with so much fear and anxiety that I would get saved every Sunday but only for the sake of not going to that terrible place. Although my belief

37

in God was real and I couldn't relate to the religious part of serving God, I believed in my heart that God died on the cross for my sins. I honestly felt that there was no fun living for God due to the strict lifestyle that seemed to be the requirement. I didn't fully commit to God in the way of His word like I should have. For a very long time, I strayed in and out the church. I was considered a backslider all through the week and a saint on Sundays. I had no spiritual stability but I knew that God had a calling on my life. Growing up in a single-parent home with my sibling, we had no other choice but to attend church, no matter if we had tons of homework, we brought our homework to church. Even if we complained about a headache, my mother would say, "Well, you definitely need to go to church for healing." There were no excuses for her to accept. She believed in the word, as the KJV states, "Train up a child in the way he should go: and when he is old, he will not depart from it." This is what I would hear as a child and then it made sense once I started having children of my own because the word of God never left my soul no matter how far I had strayed away.

Even when I had countless studying and homework assignments, we did our homework in the back of the church. Even going to church during the week, I managed to still maintain good to average grades in school. My mom believed that it was important to be in a Godly environment and that God will continue to bless us and that the anointing from God was our covering. Her diligence and faithfulness in the church gave me a foundation of hope in the midst of my innermost voids and pain in life. I believed my mom kept me in church to help me through the trauma I lived through in that house.

By this time of my life, I needed God because I had completely accepted the fact that since my father didn't want to have anything to do with me and never made the effort to see us, I was determined to do well without him. Even in the midst of my weakness and baggage that created a root of resentment in my spirit, I somehow managed to gain a sense of strength. Yet, the spirit of resentment was strong in my heart and anger and bitterness had settled within me, the feelings of fear, anxiety and depression at an early age became my identity. It was the only way I could feel the emotion.

In addition, I was also angered by my father's lack of presence. It had become evident to me that he didn't care if I was dead or alive. I was worthless to him in my eyes. So, I buried these secret struggles and held them in my soul for many years and I found ways to forget that he never existed and that my past would fade away as I buried it so deeply in my heart. I began to learn more about God's love and the impact it had on my life but again, I never took it seriously enough. I took it as a form of religion. I felt that if I attend church every Sunday and throughout the week, say my grace when it was time to eat and kneel down at night to say my prayers that it was enough to make it in to the pearly gates. Every night my prayers were memorized like, "Father lay me down to sleep..." This was enough to get me into heaven. I felt that this would be my escape to heaven and I was at peace with that.

It wasn't the importance of building a relationship with God but more of building a stairway to heaven. I had developed a form of religiously trying to live my life by the law of religion, instead of developing a spiritual relationship with God. This was a form of religion that I developed and understood but yet my mom kept making us go to church regardless of how we felt about going, so it was difficult for me to understand that I had developed a legalistic approach instead of a genuine and personal relationship of intimately loving and knowing God.

THE DISAPPOINTMENT

As the years went by, my mother never complained about how tired she was from working two to three jobs and attended church on a regular basis. It felt like church was all I knew and I felt sheltered and stuck to an extinct. It felt like a routine. She raised us to keep the house clean and neat with the little we had. We were grateful with the little we had and we made the best of it. My mother taught us to be grateful at all times for what we had, even if it didn't seem like much and yet work hard for the things in life we had desired. She was that "strong woman" and she taught us to do what we had to do to survive but from a positive and respectful standpoint. Hard work paid off in due time and by the time I had left middle school, our family structure changed. Soon, my mother remarried and later so did my father. During this time, entering high school brought changes within me. Not only had I developed into a blossomed flower, I had also developed thorns as well. Many thorns had developed inside of me. The thorns of my life became the scars of my soul. These were those tender years which were more crucial to me because I was a functioning depressed young woman and I didn't know it. I had normalized these feelings from my past and never healed from them. I had attended church for so many years but never healed from my past. I still carried baggage!

During my early preteen years, I was starting to like boys and by the time I had entered high school, I was more sensitive towards my appearance. It was important to me to feel pretty and it was hard for me to accept my appearance. I didn't feel pretty on the inside nor on the outside. My level of confidence and self-esteem was at an all-time low and I wanted to feel and know my worth but I didn't and I couldn't. My insecurities grew stronger than me and the rejection was my rehearsed pain. It was cycles of pain that would haunt me. I struggled with rejection in the same manner I'd struggled with emotional and physical abandonment. The baggage of life damaged me. I would often take my time to observe people before I would even start a conversation. I had developed these feelings of distance and isolation. This is how I believe I was an introvert. I had a hard time allowing people close to me. I was skeptical of people in general! It was difficult for me to socialize. This would explain why my friendships were temporary! The numbness had started to take hold of my heart and soul. I didn't want to be around people because I always felt misunderstood. I always thought the worst and I believed that I felt this way because I carried the baggage of offense. I would always feel offended by someone, whether they looked at me wrong or made a remark that just didn't sit well with me, I had a difficult time feeling comfortable around people. Although I had very few friends that I considered friends, I couldn't explain to them what I had been suffering from. I felt that they wouldn't and couldn't understand my feelings and that if I told them, I would lose them. Those feelings of sadness grew into deep depression, yet I continued to smile, laugh, engage in conversations and socialize with people I grew up with the best way I knew how, I was also becoming an expert at covering up and masquerading the pain. The trauma from my past scarred me with experiencing anxieties and although I didn't know what was troubling me took a toll on me, I didn't want anyone to know that I was afraid and suffered anxieties. My wounds on the inside were bleeding and I didn't want my open wounds to bleed on anyone else, especially those who were nice and showed kindness towards me. I was broken but I was also not a fool.

I felt ostracized by many and I wanted friends that I could open up to, but I also had trust issues that led into seeing others as my enemy and creating walls of defense. I grew up believing that I had to protect myself because I had no one to protect me, so I was always hesitant to become close to anyone. I feared not trusting my friends. I felt that they would eventually betray me. It was painful that I couldn't trust anyone. I was afraid that they would disappoint me as I've always felt others would. I would often have late and long night talks with my mother but I didn't want to burden her with my depression. She had gone through enough, so I kept many things private and hidden from her. I psychologically feared for my life. The shame from being rejected by my peers had brought on more disappointment and more disappointment increased my level of depression. I was also in deep fear of the unknown. The "What If's" were a part of my anxieties. My unknown future of how I am going to continue to live this way? To live with deep pain and sadness throughout my life and how would I ever become successful from the emotional and mental trauma I've endured? These were the questions I often thought about. Many nights, my eyes were consumed with tears, my prayers were, "God, if you love me enough, then why are you allowing me to suffer this way?" "Why am I constantly being rejected by people?" "Why did my father reject me?" "Why am I not good enough?" "Why is loneliness so normal for me but yet so safe, yet others see it as being abnormal?" My prayers went unanswered. I never felt that I fit in. I felt like a misfit everywhere I went. I felt betrayed, talked about and looked down upon and I couldn't seem to embrace trying to fit in with others for their acceptance.

So, eventually I came to the reality of not caring about fitting in with anyone and the more I became rejected by others, the more I started to bury the pain deep inside. I learned to bury pain well enough to remain lonely and isolated because this was the way I had to cope in order to survive. This was my coping mechanism.

Attending church every Sunday was still not an option, I learned more about God and how Jesus heals but I didn't feel that I could be healed. I had too many layers of deep pain to become healed and I had seen too much for a child my age. I thought maybe physical healing was possible. I prayed and enjoyed singing songs and listening to the preacher and ministers speak and I felt encouragement and hope but by the time a new week started, I was back to feeling my old way again. I was hurting inside. I couldn't understand how to heal from open wounds that would feel like salt being thrown on it when I was faced with the agony and the triggers of my baggage. Yet, I knew that I had a few family members who loved me dearly, I felt like I was in a bottomless pit filled with thick darkness. I questioned why these feelings were so deep. Maybe, it was because my father wasn't in my life. Thinking about my father brought on more resentment, bitterness and anger. When I would think about my father during my high school years, I questioned why he didn't love me. He never reached out to me or to check on me to see if I even existed or to have a bond, that "father and daughter" relationship. He didn't care to know my personality or to be a part of my life's achievements and accomplishments in school. He didn't even know my gifts and talents or goals and desires for my future. He wasn't there for me when I needed him the most. So who am I to be loved if my own father couldn't love me? He rejected me and never seemed to care about me. So, I decided to bury him right along with the other pain, struggles and brokenness I held for so long. My soul was full and filled with heavy bags. My heart was heavy and the walls around me became thicker and taller. I thought, well maybe I'm going through changes with being a teenager, you know, that teenage crisis of transitioning from childhood to teenage-hood that can be challenging.

So I became a survivor! I never desired to date any guys at the school I attended because I didn't trust that the relationships would work out because relationships didn't seem serious in school. It seemed like almost everyone was dating a new person every month. I also wanted genuine love and I wasn't a fool. I was smarter than people thought I was. I knew that these guys couldn't give me that love that I really needed. I didn't want counterfeit affections. You love me today and you're a ghost by tomorrow. I couldn't trust the male peers. I was too prideful, angered and isolated and all they wanted was sex and thankfully I had enough self-worth and sense to not open myself to trusting guys into giving them what they wanted as a temporary satisfaction for their lustful desires. So, I didn't give them my body. I felt that since I couldn't see myself beautiful on the outside, these guys couldn't see me this way either. So, I couldn't trust a soul and I didn't trust any of the guys at my school to think about dating them.

I became angry when they would ask me out. I felt like it was a set-up to make fun of me. I had already formed in my mind that they didn't desire me. They just wanted what was between my legs. I had so many walls up that no one could get between my legs and surely not my heart!. I was even more rejected for not giving up sex and not doing what many were doing, so I accepted the pain of rejection even more and developed the spirit of offense even more. I felt offended, yet stubborn to know that since I wasn't cared for, I couldn't care less about others. I desired love but I had also built walls to avoid the feeling of not repeating cycles. I had to protect myself because I had to survive. My heart became hardened from bitterness. Even though I had a few crushes on a few guys I liked and secretly admired, I knew that they would never have a place in my heart and they wouldn't like me the same. These insecurities were frightening and I was too frightened to follow my heart. My heart was hardened!

As I got older, I declined many offers to be in relationships, even from the popular guys. Even though I assumed that I may have been attracted to them, I knew they were not the committed type. I was well matured beyond my years and loyalty and commitment was important to my old soul. So, my focus was to study and earn decent grades until graduation. These were my teenage years where the idea of being in love was the reality I desired but the fairytale I had dreamed of. Being a wounded and fatherless daughter, I didn't have a father to talk to and to give me the love, advice and attention that I had always desired. I lacked love, self-esteem and it felt so severe. I didn't think that I was attractive enough in a world where appearance is everything. I didn't believe that I had purpose or destiny. How could I have a future in this emotional and mental state of mind? I was just my parent's daughter, using space for existence. I didn't have an identity because I was a fatherless daughter and a daughter of a mother who seemed so beaten by the labor of survival, she didn't have sufficient time to discover how torn apart I was. Trying to survive had robbed her precious time and the struggle was really stressful. Depression consumed my heart and mind as if my eyes could take you on a tour to my heart, you would be convinced.

This was the point of my life that felt severe. I knew what I was feeling but I didn't have an identity, my worth or my value, although I had high morals from the fear of God and from the fear of my God-fearing maternal grandmother who was a tough lover, strict and kind and had high expectations in me, I respected her so much that I was too frightened to disappoint her. She definitely would be the last to know what I was really feeling.

In many communities, most commonly, in the African American culture, the words "depression" and "suicide" are never discussed. These are topics which were kept in silence. If you struggled with these issues, you'd better cope the best way you can and figure it out. It would be considered a shame to the family's name. These emotional hidden feelings are most times left unmanaged.

Many nights, I still had the opportunities to have talks with my mother but I never shared with her how the spirit of suicide had came across my mind, for she didn't know the level of pain that I had buried far during my childhood years. The pain was so intense and although I was a teenager who loved God and listened to God's word, prayed and read my bible, I didn't have the faith to believe that my heart and mind could be healed. As much as I desired to become healed, I was buried under too much pain and I just didn't desire to live. Since I felt my father wasn't there to talk with me and to tell me that I meant everything to him and that he loved me and that I was worth being loved, something inside of me was dying. A slow death. It felt like I was suffocating, no oxygen to breathe and there was no way to declutter the heaviness I felt. What I had become had a name. It was called depression! Depression grew from the scars of my pain. This is what I had normalized. This was all I could see. The isolation and the walls I had built made it extremely hard to develop or hold on to, no consistent friendships and relationships. I couldn't understand how the late and legendary music artist, Luther Vandross could paint the picture of love so well when I couldn't relate to love in that manner. I knew that I had the capacity to love like those lyrics he used to sing with soothing melodies, but I couldn't relate to receiving that type of love. I was broken! I didn't know how to heal and I was too ashamed to tell anyone about this pain to accept healing. I didn't know if I had too much pride or too much fear of embarrassment.

This pain of brokenness kept me bound and chained!. People, family and friends wouldn't understand it because they couldn't feel what was on the inside of me. Just like no one would have understood those dreadful nights I suffered as a little girl in fear and torment I endured and the silent cries many nights. My main priority was to just deal with it and accept the things I couldn't and wouldn't understand. I just had to get through life the best way I could. My heart painted the picture of what depression looks like. I figured maybe this is just who I was? But the more I tried to cope with it, the more desensitized I had become.

MY COUNTERFEIT ESCAPE

Even through my darkness, I knew God was with me because if it had not been for God's hand on my life, this deceptive spirit of suicide would have consumed me very quickly. So, I took a chance with death by swallowing a large consumption of prescription drugs. I went into the medicine cabinet and I took as many pills as I could possibly take to convince myself that it would be over and enough not to wake up the next day. I knew that the prescription drugs were prescribed for physical pain, but not emotional pain. As I laid down slowly in bed, I felt a little guilty for what I was about to do. I could remember thinking, "God can't forgive those who murder themselves," but I also believed that God won't allow you to suffer pain all your life that you have no strength to bear either. I said a prayer and asked God to take this pain away for good, even if it meant that I die with it. I asked God to take me into his arms and allow me to sleep this old life away. I would miss my family so dearly but I knew that they would be fine without me. I believed that I wouldn't be able to suffer again because I would escape this feeling. I felt the guilt of this being a selfish act. It was too hard to see this as being selfish to hurting others but others didn't know how I was feeling. I was tired of masquerading my feelings of being something I was not. Why did I deserve to feel this way? Why was I even born to experience this pain anyway? I just wanted this all to end and I just wanted to lightly float away like a feather in the wind and I would be at peace with knowing that this too shall pass. Drinking alcohol and smoking marijuana is only a quick fix and it's certainly a counterfeit escape to alleviate the pain. After the high has faded away, you're right back to that crash of depression. I needed a permanent fix, not a quick fix!

As I was getting very sleepy and as my eyes felt very heavy, I became extremely physically tired and exhausted. With a blink of an eye, I would just vanish into thin air. It would seem peaceful and it would no longer be a day of suffering!

As my head sunk into the wet pillow, which became soaked from my eyes, I prayed that God would protect and take great care of my mother and siblings. I didn't want to think about how awful this would be for my grandmother who had high hopes in me. I could see their faces and I could also create a visual of other loved-ones who'd I would miss but this was for my own good. My body became physically numb and my eyes closed as I unconsciously drifted away into a deep sleep that would have gone into never-ending eternity.

The next morning, I woke up! I woke up extremely drowsy and physically sick, I was in denial that I had awakened. It was a moment of disappointment. I realized those pills didn't work or maybe I just didn't consume enough but it had been enough to my knowledge. I had nearly emptied that prescription bottle of drugs to ingest for my fate to end my misery but it just wasn't God's plan. This was an attempt that no one knew about and I kept this a secret until this very day.

CHAPTER 2 - THE WEIGHT OF BROKENNESS -

MASQUERADING THE HEAVY BAGGAGE

The weight of brokenness is the captivity of our soul that is in
bondage by internal pain. Our soul is made of our emotions,
our will to make decisions and our mindset. When our souls
are not connected to the Spirit of God, we find ourselves lost,
misplaced, confused and disoriented. It brings a lifestyle of
bondage. To say the least, it started early for me. When you
have seeds of toxicity weighing you down, it makes you
broken on the inside and you find yourself trying to silently
find a resolution to the problem. It makes you embarrassed to
even accept that you are miserably unhappy with life and even
by doing things or accomplishing things you love, it still
doesn't lift the weight. It's like having a migraine headache
and taking aspirin to alleviate or to block the pain. That would
be considered a temporary fix because the root of the problem
isn't cured by blocking or alleviating the pain. The cure is a
permanent fix because it treats the condition by pulling up the
root of internal pain by releasing or detoxing your soul for the
sake of purification and cleansing. Heavy baggage is like
toxins that pollute, ferment and poison that which is within
the soul. This is known as deliverance from God. The internal
baggage is years of brokenness of unhealed wounds that
continue to bleed and creates hemorrhaging of the soul. The
weight is heavy but how would you know how heavy it feels
when you've carried it for so many years? You become
accustomed to the weight, although you have become
suppressed by the pain. The suppressed pain is what can
negatively trigger our behaviors, our perception, our
perspectives, our response, our choices and our beliefs. Years
of brokenness just doesn't fade away with time, if not healed
it becomes worse and the pain either becomes numb or it

becomes critically sensitive. No matter how intelligent we are, how many degrees we have earned, or how accomplished we've become, brokenness in our souls affects millions of people. When we have pride in our hearts it blocks our true reality and forces us to overshadow those feelings because we tend to be in denial of these feelings; it's unfortunate because we make ourselves more like the victim where it's always the other person's fault for the way they make us feel.

For many years we hide the pain by professionally masquerading the wounds. This affects our abilities to become free, forgiving of ourselves and others, embracing our identity, and finding courage, confidence to believe that we are beautifully and wonderfully made through Christ! We have to take that risk by really believing that, and also accepting the fact that it is okay to be broken, as long as we are broken in the arms of God. It took most of my life to understand that.

Your humbling beginnings may not be similar to mine. In fact, the pain you may have endured from the very beginning will always be your truth and your story for a purpose. We are all sufferers of something different that may have burdened our spirits to the ultimate degree and whether we have shared those experiences or have hidden our pain as our secrets, we can all agree that pain hurts. Pain that is never healed turns into rooted-baggage. Some of us handle pain differently from others and that is okay because God made each and everyone of us different anyway. Ultimately, our pain from our past doesn't dictate our future. God has an assignment and a mandate on each and every last one of our lives. So don't take your pain for granted. It is for a divine purpose! There's a purpose attached to your pain with a great deal of passion! It is your awakening to a manifestation of an ultimate gain for your future.

Being a fatherless daughter was the open wound that never had a chance to heal. Your open wounds may have not been your father nor your mother but something else that you may never want to face; burying it deep in your soul only makes it worse. The open wounds would soon end up suppressing into another form; physically it affects your natural body; emotionally it destroys our souls and our relationships and mentally it destroys how we see the world around us and ourselves in it.

One thing is for sure, what doesn't kill you makes you stronger. I'm sure you have hear many people say this. Well, my humbling beginnings didn't kill me, somehow it made me stronger to gain the courage and bravery to tell my story!

As I reflect back to those days of being a high school student, these years were supposed to be the best years of my life as they were for many people I personally knew. High school years are supposed to be the fun years, filled with unforgettable memories and moments with friends; the experiences learned and shared, the friendships developed, activities of school pride, weekend parties, and attending those crazy after-sets; these are those moments that later become reminiscences of conversations later in life. Although I had a few friends and grew to befriend a few associates and was cordial with most of my peers, I was still very lonely during my high school experience. This was a time of my life where rejection was at an all-time high. During these years, violence, fights, homicides and suicides were a part of this era and as the years passed and the social environment grew wicked, those unfortunate experiences became worse and more common. At this time of my life, I became resilient to my environment and my emotional walls of isolation were the walls I had created to guard my heart for protection and the brokenness that I never faced or fixed. I felt ridiculed and being made fun of by people for being myself, this grew into excessive pain that I had internalized. It was unfortunate that I had entered high school as this insecure and introverted child with insecurities of feeling inferior and a loss of self-worth and low self-esteem. I felt unattractive, hopeless, fearful and still remained isolated from friends. My future was filled with uncertainties. However, I never stopped praying even without having faith that God would restore my identity, my mind and my soul for a joy that I desired on the inside. I didn't feel that I could be happy. There were classmates that made fun of the clothes I wore because my clothes were not the latest trend or fashion but I always kept myself clean and made sure my appearance was neat and modest. My mother, raising two children as a single parent did the best she could to provide for us on a limited income; so she wasn't able to purchase the latest sneakers or for me to have a pair of shoes that matched every outfit I wore. As this was considered the most popular and most appealing way to become accepted or to become popular and accepted, I did my very best to not allow these feelings inside to affect me but deep down inside it burned like fire. I was angry, bitter and felt like I didn't belong in this uncomfortable environment where learning was the main purpose for being there in the first place. In my opinion, it felt like my school days was about whose the coolest and the most popular to become accepted. I continued to feel the pain of rejection and the spirit of offense. I was talked about behind my back by others and mistreated by some but I always remained calm on the outside. This pain of rejection was the way of life that I normalized. I never wore my feelings on my shoulder.

This, however, created walls, thick and tall walls, guarded my heart and kept me in a world of isolation. My introverted personality made me feel like a misfit. I just couldn't fit in any cliques at my school and there were many cliques from the bougie personalities to the "hard-core" or "roughneck", the nerds, who were the smartest in the class, the popular girls, in which everyone knew and the others, who were considered the average girls. I'm not sure what I was classified as but I'm sure I was in a class of my own, and that was "the loner". The one no one sees. I wasn't an attention-seeker, so I moved to the beat of my own drum. I never tried to fit in any clique because I felt that if I'm not accepted, then that's what it is and I had to accept it that as reality. I didn't want to attend school because I felt that there were too many distractions and that it wasn't the place that made me feel accepted. My isolation and distrust in people was the struggles that kept me isolated. I socially kept to myself, never having the desire to socialize with anyone, I kept my life private to protect myself from the fear of not being accepted and from not fitting in. Those four years, from ninth grade until senior year, I didn't feel comfortable in my own environment. I had one close friend I could confide in but that friendship soon ended not long after high-school graduation. After high-school graduation, I felt a sense of relief because I didn't feel that I had to be forced into an environment of feeling uncomfortable and miserable. The years of my high-school experience went by fast for many but it was in slow motion for me and every day felt like a full week. No matter what I was feeling, no one could probably tell what I was feeling, I kept a smile on my face and my smile was liked by many. I would often receive compliments from people on how I had a beautiful smile. Accepting compliments weren't always easy for me, I wasn't sure if the person was being serious or sarcastic but my replies were always "thank you" regardless of what I felt. My smiles masqueraded the happiness I really wanted to feel but don't misunderstand when I say this, my family made me happy and I was grateful to have a family, especially those family members who were active in my life and played a major role in loving me by

showing love towards me, it's just that I wasn't loving myself.
I wasn't happy on the inside.

Many years later after my mother had remarried, life seemed
to be okay but what my family and loved-ones didn't know
was that I was suffering from years of deep depression. I was
battling a mental-illness that kept me emotionally depressed. I
wasn't clinically diagnosed because I hid these feelings but I
was intelligent enough to know that I was a functional
depressant; yet I had the ability to function as a normal
teenager. I had a way of always encouraging others very well.
It was quite strange for me because I enjoyed encouraging and
inspiring others and I made it look like I had it all together
from the outside but on the inside, I couldn't hide the pain I
was feeling. I often wondered how I could encourage others
so well and yet have them feeling better and able to live life,
but yet I was left isolated inside the cage of depression that
kept me bound. I couldn't see a way out! Many nights were
worse than others. The tears were heavier and heavier each
passing night. I had no peace. I had no desire to do anything,
not even the things I enjoyed. I would just stay in my room,
isolated in my spacious and comfortable bedroom for
weekends and I would stay in my bed and curl up in my
blankets in a fetal position to cope with the pain. Sometimes, I
would sit on my bed and just write poems about what was on
my mind. This was an outlet for me to release what had built
up but it didn't heal me. Other times I would write song lyrics
to express myself as a way to escape those feelings and
thoughts. Writing was therapeutic for me. It helped me to a
certain degree. At one point, I stopped writing because I felt
there was no purpose to write; no one would read my writings
but me. My sadness and tears of stress and worry would have
me sleeping for hours. Sleeping was my escape zone. It was
the safest way for me to escape but only temporary! I knew

my mother and sibling loved me during this time of my life; yet I also felt that they could still do well without me.

So, for many years, the emotional baggage was more weight than I could carry and all through classes during my college years, those thoughts of hopelessness and despair were back again. Those feelings as to 'why I exist 'came back to haunt me again. There were many thoughts to execute that exit plan, I once made an attempt to do, once again it came back stronger. That escape plan would have allowed me to no longer bear the pain of deep sadness that I had carried from my past. I actually didn't understand why I had carried this pain for so long. My past of not having my father is what planted these seeds of deficiencies. I didn't know how to let go of these feelings. I had fallen into that trap, which was a hole of deep depression. This hole was my pit! I unconsciously buried all my childhood pain and grief, never to feel it again but I had held on to it for so long, that it would soon suppress. It suppressed many dark feelings of not feeling loved by my father, not feeling I was worth the reason to live, not desiring to live another day of rehearsing my past of pain of rejection, insecurity, emotional abandonment, fatherless hurt, lack of self-esteem, lack of confidence, lack of self-identity, lack of not be accepted in a world I desired to fit in so desperately. I couldn't understand what it was about with me that was not accepting to others. I felt in my heart that I was a pure, loving and genuine person with a great heart who could be a great friend to many. I was that lonely flower that stood alone just needing to know my worth, my value and my purpose. My heart lacked the love that I needed.

The years of my early twenties were wrecked by the burdensome of toxic relationships. I wanted to move forward in life. Although I was in college at this time, I needed change but I didn't have a plan. I didn't have a clear purpose or a vision for my life. I knew that I was gifted in computer operations, graphic arts design and writing but I felt that there was more for me beyond that. I doubted myself and I became very critical of not believing in myself. I had many dreams and I even envisioned myself of becoming a lyricist but I compared myself to so many others where it only remained a dream and that's where it remained. Through it all, I kept a smile on my face and my smiles were the outer appearance of my strength. My smiles were my cover-up, my masquerade. Sometimes, I would think about how my life could be different had my father been around to talk with me, give me advice and the paternal guidance and instruction that I needed to become that beautiful women, to lead me and to protect me from the unknown, to know what to look for from the predators who would say anything to get me to lower my standards for them, and for me to be far advanced on what to look for in a man and to know what isn't good for me; protect me from the false concept of love, and allow me to find genuine love that I solely desired.

HOW TRAUMA CREATED MENTAL DEPRESSION

That love that I desired was the love that became void, yet I repeatedly felt the discouragement and disappointment from reliving these feelings from male figures. The pain from my brokenness were cycles of life. I kept finding myself going through the same cycles of being hurt by men who were players and cheaters, playing with the hearts of women. It seemed like every passing day started looking and feeling the same. The unhealthy relationships, where I desired that fairy tale love experience were only in the fictional romantic love stories. I didn't believe that those happily ever after moments could ever exist, well at least not for me. I only read them from my Disney books I collected as a child where the prince and princess fell in love and lived happily ever after. I wanted that happily ever after experience, a love of my own. A love from a male figure, was that little girl still living inside of me as a woman. What I lacked would soon lead me into a dark path that caused poor judgment to believe false notions that I wasn't good enough to deserve the love I so deeply desired.

I knew God was able to mend my broken heart because I knew God existed but how? How could God heal what I was going through at this time? My heart was full of hurt and my mind was full of poisonous belief. It was that rooted-baggage of poisons of doubt, failure, guilt, shame, unforgiveness and hopelessness. Those thoughts came back to haunt me. What I had struggled with, reminded me of that haunted house I once lived in. Thoughts of emptiness consumed my mind, I wanted to give it one more try at love even when it felt risky. I couldn't take it anymore. I just wanted this pain to end again but at this time in my life, I had enough knowledge in God to know that if I made the poor choice to end my life, it would be no coming back. That feeling of depression would find its way back in my mind. I believe the first time God had secretly spared my life, I knew the amount of prescription drugs I had consumed and I knew that I took enough to not wake up from that deep sleep. God still woke me up from the touch of death. He wanted me to live when I couldn't see any worth in myself. He saw the best in me but I could only feel and see the worst in me.

As these thoughts became critical, I would remain in my room, lay in bed and console myself from this depression. I wrapped my body in the blankets and drained my heart from the inside out. My cries were so deep until I felt chest pains. The fire of anger was so heavy and all I ever wanted was to feel normal, to feel complete, to feel a wholeness from the inside. I wanted my internal being to feel the way I appeared to many on the outside. I thought about how God healed and delivered many from their demons and their issues, I had to encourage myself to know God is for me and my life is in his hands. I don't have the authority over my life to just take it away. So, I cried and cried until I couldn't cry anymore. As the blankets wrapped around my body, I consoled myself from the mental and emotional anguish and I said a quick prayer. I couldn't remember exactly what I had prayed about at that moment but I knew that this moment would be the moment of life or death. I knew that God's love was with me, so I figured since God loved me so much, why won't he just let me die, right now, at this very hour. Why won't He just save me from this crisis and take me with him in my sleep.

Over a course of time, I continued to have suicidal thoughts. I stayed distant from everyone and felt no desire to wear a mask to cover my naked truths. The truth was, I was deeply miserable inside. During that time, my stepfather at that time would often ask, "Why do you sleep so much?" "Why are you always in your room?" Even, my aunt would come over to visit and she would jokingly ask, "Angel, why do you stay isolated in your room?" I had never really thought what my close family members were thinking. It was all about me trying to uncover the pain but my behavior of isolation had suppressed it to become noticeable around those who were around me the most. My aunt would often say, "You know they consider people like you a hermit". A hermit is someone who lives in seclusion from society. I had never realized that while I was trying to hide my pain, that there would be family members who would suspect something was wrong with me. I thought that I was great with covering up my emotions. I was delusional for thinking this way and I realized that there was a problem with me and it had to be serious. My mother and stepfather at that time, thought I needed to be seen by a doctor, to have my brain scanned due to the extreme amounts of sleep and my dull behavior. I would sleep for hours after school, on weekends and anytime I wasn't doing anything or had to be anywhere. All medical tests results came back fine, so my mother and stepfather were relieved that I was well. I was physically in great health but what they didn't know was I wasn't fine emotionally, mentally and spiritually. My stepfather would nickname me 'Sleepy'. My mother would often think that I was literally tired all the time. She would often come upstairs in my room to check on me. Sometimes, she would even pop up in my room and just pray over me. I believe that she had sensed something was wrong, so she believed that I was just extremely tired and exhausted from school and homework. She would often say, "You better sleep and rest now because when you become an adult, there's no rest." You better rest now while you can. She considered that this was just being the typical "Angel" and that this was my normal "me". I remained quiet and thankful for her prayers. It would only be her prayers that I could rely on. I didn't think twice about sharing this burdensome pain with her. She had enough stress and worries of her own to deal with: Although I candidly and openly expressed my darkest moments of being in and out of moods from depression and never received the healing for it, I relied on prayer to cope through it. I needed more than my prayers because I didn't have enough power to fight against the attacks that were wearing down my mind, soul and spirit. You could have a conversation with me and you would never be able to discern my sadness. No one could ever discern my deep depression. No one ever did! Love was not even enough for me to remove this spirit that troubled me all the time, yet I knew that I was a very kindhearted person, very compassionate and I had a way with people when it came to those who were nice, friendly, loving and kind towards me; my love for others was reciprocal and I showed my appreciation and admiration to them the best I could. I just couldn't love myself the way I needed to. Many nights as I would be alone, I relied on a few moments of smoking "weed" or marijuana as a coping mechanism and taking a few shots of alcohol or a little sip of wine to soothe my pain. I needed that high to help me for the moment. It seemed to make my guilty conscience worse after being consumed with what I desired would comfort me at the moment because I would feel a huge feeling of condemnation in my spirit. I knew that the temporary relief of counterfeit pleasures would push me deeper and deeper into sadness. Sometimes I would smoke weed or marijuana just to clear my mind from everything that was around me and troubling me, and it would have me feeling high where I would think on anything and analyze it to the degree of why am I focusing on something that is so irrelevant to my present reality. It would make my thoughts drift far away into another atmosphere and not want to face the problems that were in front of me. Sometimes, it would make me laugh at things that weren't meant to be funny, yet it was a form of mental drunkenness that allowed me to look at my life from a strange perspective. It gave me more of a sense to perceive my problems and issues from a humorous perspective. Yet, other times, getting high and feeling high would have me paranoid, yet reliving my thoughts of my past as to why I was so broken in my soul. This feeling of mental highness had me floating and mind drifting. The things I was thinking about was beyond my control. I didn't like the fact that I had lost control of my senses. I felt I could speak without a filter. I bluntly commented on things that were on my mind without even thinking about it, so I had my moments of confessing my faults and becoming very talkative and rambling as if the other person around me even bothered to listen. I never did my vices of sin around my family, especially not my children. It was not what I wanted them to see in me and I respected them too much.

The counterfeit affections of feeling high made me feel that I was in control of the conversation but it allowed me to keep my mind off the things that triggered my tainted emotions. In private, it became repetitive that it allowed me to confess the honest truth of my heart posture. I would confess my brokenness but could never figure out how to heal from my brokenness. After feeling my high subsiding, I was back again feeling the sadness, anxiety and the depression which was an everyday struggle. Marijuana or "weed" was not my cure.

The weight of brokenness kept me inferior to others around me. It had me comparing my life with others. The comparison made me feel like I hadn't achieved a thing in life. It caused me to fester on my problems and issues and it heightened my insecurities of feeling unworthy, feeling like a failure, feeling a lack of confidence and the loss of courage. I couldn't believe in myself because I had given up on myself. I was ashamed of myself for feeling the way I was and I was mad at myself for becoming addicted to the immoral vices that were against my standards with God. I knew better and although I believed and feared God, I was yet living in unbelief due to my troubles. I knew that it was not right for me to indulge in the things that were against my standards because I personally felt the conviction in my spirit, even when I was tempted to repeat the cycle. I knew enough to know that it wasn't me and it wasn't right for me. I was not able to become a better version of myself because in secret I wasn't being truthful to myself and how I felt about myself, although I didn't commit my life to God in salvation, there was a guilty conscience that one day I had to get it together, yet I had no peace within. At this point, I didn't have the capacity to love myself. Love wasn't enough to heal me or to provide me hope. So, my emotions, vulnerabilities and insecurities remained my sufferings that I would have to deal with. I knew my parents couldn't help me. I knew that my husband and children couldn't help me and I knew that I couldn't help myself at this point. The only hope that I believed was that God would have to be the only one to help me and to save me from my demons inside or else life would be a sea full of hopelessness and deep depression!

HOW A BROKEN SOUL MAKES YOU A SLAVE OF THE PAST

Your broken soul will continue to make you a slave of your past unless you expose and admit to the things you worked a lifetime to cover up. Deeply-rooted baggage is carrying too much heaviness, the stuff from my past and the heavyweights that I couldn't let go kept me bound in cycles. Not releasing these things and not letting go will sabotage your purpose and abort your destiny! I was desensitized to my pain and being desensitized is pretending to be something that you are not. You paint a picture well on the outside to cover up the bad feelings on the inside; however dressed up on the outside, you continue to ignore the inside. I didn't believe that I needed help because I believed that I needed the pain to fuel my motivation and to pump up my energy. That was my motivation to keep me at achieving goals and it worked. I was a hard-worker with strong work ethics, easy to pick up on things when it came to landing jobs opportunities and being promoted to higher positions. Looking at me from the outer appearance, I was stable in life and very disciplined in whatever I worked hard to achieve. The silent depression that affected my life forced me to believe that the pain I would feel was all I knew right along with disappointment, discouragement, bitterness, offensiveness, and feeling victimized by become sensitive to how someone looked at me or made a comment that was offensive towards me. Those moments of feeling offended made me dare someone to say something that was critical because I was ready for that clap-back moment. I was ready to get someone told and they were going to feel my pain. The problem I've learned with the spirit of offense is the seed that can become planted in a person. Not everyone is out to hurt you and that someone who is trying to constructively provide criticism doesn't always have the intention to break your spirit or to hurt you or harm you. This evil seed makes the person paint a picture of themselves as being the victim all the time or innocent in all aspects. The weight of brokenness will have you feeling offended by the truth and blinded by the fact that you really need help. The truth is, what is done in the dark will soon come to light. Time has a way of exposing the suppressed behavior and in due season; God has a way to heal the broken-hearted.

My promise in life was to never forgive a soul, this was my validation that if someone does anything to hurt me or have wronged me in anyway shape of form or fashion, they would have to pay and it came with a price, they would enjoy my absence and never see me again. I was great at revenge and unforgiveness where holding grudges was a part of my character. I needed to be healed delivered from this. I would hold grudges and unforgiveness in my heart for years. I didn't have the heart to forgive my father for over 25 years. I tried to come to grips with it but I felt that I didn't do anything wrong to him. Why should I forgive someone who never apologized for what they did to me? Or, why should I forgive someone who didn't acknowledge my pain? I felt at this point in my life, I didn't need my father's love. I was a grown woman now and at this time in my life, yet I was still angry by the fact that I was still hurt by the little girl inside me that never got a chance to know what it was like to have a loving father. To lack the love from a father as a little girl placed open wounds that never healed throughout my developmental stages and into my adult life of being a wife and a mother. I felt like I was winning when I held grudges against people who had hurt me. I felt that they needed to feel my anger and to be reminded how wrong and evil they had been. Little did I realize that holding the grudge was really causing me to lose my power and relinquish control to them to overpower me. Holding the grudge against my father was holding him captive in my heart to never heal. It was the grudge that kept my heart in chains. I put myself on lock-down for many years and these internal wounds placed scars that produced other deficiencies. It was like fire spreading across a field and no water to extinguish the flames or to prevent the fire from spreading and endangering everything around it. I was holding in anger for years until it would cause me to boil; once I reached that boiling point, it reminded me of the old movie called, "Incredible Hulk." Although I was not a hot-headed person, the problem was, I allowed anger to grow and by not addressing and releasing the problems at hand, I had allowed anger to pile up and fester as high as a mountaintop where the "Hulk" in me would be more than incredible, it would turn into bitterness! Several people who have made me that angry or who have seen me become incredibly angry, got a chance to see that awful side of me that I didn't like. I was a mild-mannered and a nice person and I didn't bother anyone. My goal was to get along with everyone. It was just my nature but I wouldn't allow anyone to disrespect me or cross me. It just wasn't going to happen! Unfortunately, fear of being around people, especially people that I really didn't know was not easy for me. Sometimes there would be ladies that I would meet for the first time, they would either misjudge me for being bourgeoisie (bougie) or "too good" because of the way I carried myself. I guess I wasn't "*hood*" enough for them. So, they would misjudge me before they really got to know me. On the other side, there would be ladies that I would meet for the first time who would be bougie where I didn't fit their high-end standards; I guess to them, I wasn't good enough to be around. I guess they considered me to be rough around the

65

edges fir them but it really didn't matter what people thought. In the end, it really mattered what I thought about myself and it ultimately matters what God thinks of me period!

Anyhow, I seemed to always feel this need to protect my feelings. I believe that is why I wasn't quick to make new friends or attend social gatherings to meet people.. I guess it was due to the feelings of being abandoned and rejected. Being isolated was comfortable for me. Fortunately, there were better days where my social interactions were pleasant, yet I stayed my distance and stayed observant and always had my guards up. This would probably explain why I never attended any of my high school reunions or any special occasions with my alumni reunions because I avoided being uncomfortable. I was comfortable only being around close family and friends. I would always feel awkward being around a crowd of strangers or people I barely knew in a social or public setting. I didn't know why I wasn't sociable but ironically, I've been a friendly person all my life and great with interacting with people and communicating on a one-on-one basis or small group level. I believed that I was so distrusting of people because I was protective of my emotions, guarding my feelings and refused to allow anyone to nudge at those triggers points that would make me go into default of my insecurities. Although my insecurities were my motivation and so I thought, it made me an enemy within myself because it kept me in bondage of never being healed and set free in my soul. I stayed on guard at all times, I could never keep friends that would last a lifetime and when I did become close to someone, I soon became a "ghost" to them as well, they wouldn't hear from me again and I wouldn't hear from them. There would not be any conflict or any reason for the separation, I just remained distant and enjoyed the comfort of living a private life. I enjoyed minding my own business. I knew that I was an introvert of being shy and reserved, so I felt that being an introvert was just this part of me that I had accepted but was in fear of rejection and not being accepted by others because "who would want to be my friend and really care about what I was feeling inside anyway?" Especially, when I didn't make the effort to continue the friendship. I could remember having the experience of enjoying the bond and a close friendship with two ladies that were very special to me. They didn't know each other and they were considered my friends in two different eras of my life. One of them was a close friend during high school and the other was a friend during my single while transitioning in marriage. These were friends that I truly felt comfortable with. They were kind, intelligent and had some of my characteristics of being laid back, humorous and down-to-earth but soon those friendships would fizzle out and somehow we lost touch with one another. I never gained that type of friendship again with anyone else. I guess it was very disappointing to believe that maybe it was my own issues of why these friendships never really lasted. Although, I can not recall ever being in a conflict or just being a mean person because I always remained a calm and easy to get along type of person, I believed that those same feelings of abandonment, betrayal, and rejection would come back to haunt me again and make me reflect on my insecurities of not being worthy or valuable as a friend. I started to believe that it just wasn't meant for me to have close friends. When it came to dating; it was difficult. Trusting men was difficult. I didn't want to experience the nightmares, the horror of being humiliated and haunted by my past and that my past was the excuse for my failures in my present life. I felt that I had to blame these issues on something. I had enough of bad experiences during my childhood years of living in that house of spiritual demonic torment as it was detailed in the first chapter of this book. Even so, I had been disappointed in so many different complicated, yet serious relationships of dating guys who weren't committed.

In general, church associates and friends who were like family towards me and my family were not excluded from my experience of friendships. Whether by these friendships were like having a sisterhood of friends or whether it was a romantic relationship with a guy I really liked, it had been a very disappointing experience, to say the least.

WHY MUST I FEEL OR BEHAVE THIS WAY?

Letting go of the seeds of baggage is letting go of the weights that we've carried all of our lives. We become immune to the weights. We normalized the weights we carried where we've made it easy to carry the heavy loads because we have added an abnormal strength to the burdens that we weren't supposed to carry in the first place. We didn't know that we were supposed to have this baggage because we didn't know that it was actual baggage. We considered it the way of "Life". We told one another that our baggage was the way we live and the way our families lived. "It is, what it is!" is pretty much how we learned to mentally normalize what was toxic or what we should not have accepted or tolerated. That's where it starts and that's where we leave it. This is generational baggage. Baggage that was carried from one generation to another, from one era to another, from one seed to another. When we are reared under certain cultural conditions, we consider it normal because it's how we were raised. For me, it was the seeds of baggage that I carried throughout my life. I considered it normal. It becomes a mindset. When I carried seeds of brokenness which was repeated cycles of disappointments and a heartache of silent sufferings and hidden pain filled with: distrust, depression, daily stress, rejection, shame, insecurities, unforgiveness, pride, stubbornness, fear, anxieties, anger, hate, resentment, bitterness, being doubtful or negative, double-mindedness of unwavering faith and that was specifically, believing the truth but would doubt it when life would hit me the hardest; the procrastination was the arrested development that became my excuse to finish things later depending on what type of mood I was in: the list went on. We accept the way we feel as if it's a part of who we are. This is what I believe makes us normalize our rooted-baggage.

When we carry these seeds within us, we repeat the behavior of what's not repaired. These downfalls become our cycles of life. The repeated baggage becomes our character and our character is demonstrated and suppressed through our actions and emotions. Most times, our behavior is influenced by how we respond to things and how we respond to things exposes our hearts. Our children and/or grandchildren learn from us and they are taught by what they see, hear and feel from us. If they see and feel our anger, they will become angry. If they see and feel our fears, they will become afraid. If they see and feel our hatred, they will develop hate in their hearts. If this is all they see or hear, this becomes behavior seen as normal. Having generational baggage develops complacency and stagnancy in our own lives. It keeps us from growing and improving our lives. It's an impoverished mentality that keeps us from uncovering our purpose and it stunts our personal development and our spiritual growth. This is what creates the domino effect of dysfunction and it transfers from family to family and generations to generations in many families. It's the influence and mentality of social conditioning.

The weight of brokenness comes with a steep price to pay! The weight of our baggage comes from what was poured into our spirits or what we opened ourselves to; the choices we've made that have produced additional pain, misery and injury deepens the roots in our spirits and souls. It hinders us from living our best life. What others have done to us, the things we couldn't control, we tend to carry these things in our hearts and minds for many years. The worst baggage to carry is baggage that has become normal to carry. It's baggage that we are unaware we're carrying. We don't see it as baggage. This type of baggage of social conditioning puts limits on our lives when we believe the negativity of what people tell us, when we are conditioned by the limitations of our social circle, what we hear and see starts to condition us. We can be socially conditioned to slavery even after freedom, simply because we can limit ourselves to what we have been conditioned to. It's like being socially programmed by being conditioned to see and hear the world from what we've been raised and taught. It's the fear and self-doubt that will compromise and hijack our future. Revelation and knowledge changes social conditioning. When we become exposed to awareness, knowledge and revelation from God, it's what changes our social conditioning.

BROKEN, BUSTED AND DISGUSTED

Later in life, I learned that mental health of depression and anxieties were kept silent but it was a struggle for certain family members to cope with it. I believe this mental illness is kept silent because the African American culture don't talk about or discuss these types of problems due to fear, shame, guilt, embarrassment, feeling ostracized or looked down upon as being considered weak, and the cultural belief that if I've survived this long and functioning at my best, then I don't need any help now. The problem is..........you do need the help! Professional help is needed and by all means it is best to seek help from a licensed therapist or a counselor to help you

70

in any way at best but spiritual help and God's deliverance is surely necessary for wholeness and completeness to remove voids, break the demonic chains that hold us bound and the restoration we need to restore our souls once we've been spiritually purified. You must understand, it's spiritual because we are spiritual beings experiencing who we are naturally.

As it saddens my heart to hear about countless cases and news reports of how suicide is on the rampage and has taken many lives, I often think about those moments I had where deep depression seeped into my soul, leaving me feeling hopeless and powerless. It was deep depression that led me to those dark days. Those dark days had overcome my heart where I felt that I couldn't handle the agonizing stress and pain that wouldn't leave me alone. I believe I suffered from a mental illness that I wrestled with in silence. I believe it grew from the deep grief of suffering in silence as a child and not having the help to release or to relieve the pain. Trauma and grief was where I shut down at such an early age. I believe this is how it forms in many lives in our children today. It didn't take away my intelligence nor did it affect my credibility and modest character and it surely didn't make me a bad person. For me, it wasn't a genetic issue, it was a developed issue. It took away my purpose to survive. Mental illness is real and it attacks many people in silence. Thousands of men and women across the globe have committed suicide. It was very shocking to understand that over and beyond 55 pastors, men and women of faith had committed suicide since 2013. I didn't know the pastor personally but when I heard about the story of a particular pastor, whom committed suicide, it was very disheartening. He was Pastor Jim Howard who fatally shot himself. I don't know why this particular pastor I've never met stood out in my mind the most. The first thing that came to my mind was the hope that he'd lost. It was a deferred hope. Did he lose his faith or had he become discouraged, saddened or oppressed by the concerns and the cares of this life? How heavy was his heart where his belief and faith became stretched from the word of God and with the troubles of his life? Why did he feel that he had to give it all up? What was he facing on the inside at that very moment? We would never know why. We just know that many face this dark place in their lives in silence. Yes, it's a silent-killer. No one goes around telling others that they wish to kill themselves and if they do, it's best to take it very seriously. According to an online article from GodUpdates.com, Jim Howard who was the mega-church pastor of 6,000 members at Real Life Church, committed suicide in his home on Wednesday, January 23, 2019. He died from a self-inflicted gunshot wound." godupdates.com/megachurch-pastors-suicide-jim-howard/

When I think about mental illness, I think about how it can affect anyone and it affects even the most prominent and well-respected leaders who serve others with a heart of goodness, compassion and love. As my heart and deepest condolences goes out to the family and to the members of the church, it grieves my heart when souls become so broken where it becomes busted and disgusted. It's a feeling of being busted because it's being crushed by the disappointments and the confusion of life. The spirit slowly dies as the soul becomes low and impoverished. It's also a feeling of being disgusted because it's an emotion of disgraceful, sickened by offense, an emotion of deep sadness, fear and anxiety. This reminds me on how suicide is the ultimate fate of lost hope, complete doubt and unbelief. The question that ponders my heart is what was the rough journey like that got him to the place of completely giving up totally and leaving it all behind, especial when you are a shepherd to many?

One of the first signs of depression and anxiety is isolation. When you are tempted to withdraw from those around you, it is that time where you must fight even harder for genuine friendships. Good friends bring laughter, support, listening ears and open arms. Any type of emotional, mental and spiritual support can help with the battle for mental and emotional stability of our health. Isolating ourselves is a set up for destruction when our spirit is not seeking God, it can lead our soul in demise. When we position ourselves around people who care about us and love us for who we are, it is critically important to our mental and emotional stability. It can be tough to combat against facing depression. I was once there for many years and isolating myself from everyone around me, made it difficult for me to push through. Asking God for help and asking God to send you someone or Godly friendships to push onward and to build a community is an ever present need. Even when I ended my membership at a local church I once attended, I knew that there were a few members whom I became close to, they needed my moral support through words of encouragement, but it became repetitively draining for me during the time I needed help for myself. I will make this clear, that was not the reason I ended my membership at that particular church but I did feel a sense of obligation to specific people who needed moral support. I knew that they needed that unbiased friend to motivate them and to encourage them from their life of personal trials and circumstances. Although helping others in return can be helpful to us, there are those cases where some people can drain your energy or lean heavy on your spirit, when they have not made the effort to use your advice or encouragement as a supportive tool towards making small improvements or any improvements at all. You feel as though they are hoarders of information and don't become doers for motivation. It can feel like a puppy that chases his tail only to make himself and others around him dizzy! If you don't have the strength, power and virtue within, you'll find yourself completely burned-out by people.

God is an ever present help in time of need. He is able to provide you and I, with what we need and He will place people into our lives to help us for our specific needs. God can also give us wisdom to not allow people to drain us but we must ask God for wisdom and instruction. We cannot become someone else's savior. We are only servants of God. God is our savings grace! Jesus can only be their savior!

Mental illness is a trick from the enemy in which creates depression, oppression and suicide. Suicide kills many people at all ages and all races. According to one study, 90% of suicidal teenagers believed that their families did not understand them. I didn't think that my family would understand me and I was too embarrassed to even talk about it. Besides, it isn't common for African Americans to even think about talking about a topic of suicide. It was not the common cultural thing to do and it was also not popular to see a psychiatrist for help. It was just something that you didn't talk about. So, depression would continue to linger and remain along with all the other insecurities and these problems had to be dealt with alone because once again, no one talked about this subject! I can remember experiencing these dark days alone and too embarrassed to openly talk to anyone about it. I couldn't talk to anyone and I kept these dark emotions inside. This is what the enemy wants you to do. He wants you to bottle up your emotions and not tell anyone. He wants you to believe that you could have a better life on the other side, meaning a better life after death by committing suicide, by ending it all. I felt that since I was living broken inside, I was living in hell alone. I was tormented and saddened and couldn't find peace. I felt trapped and I also felt like I was in sinking sand. Every passing day felt like lifting heavier weights and every passing day made me feel convinced that I would have to make a choice to relieve the insanity. The insanity of depression, in which felt like the weights were just too heavy to carry on each day. Depression had me so isolated and depression is the gateway to committing suicide when there's no hope. I was tired of putting on a mask everyday to disguise the world and those around me with my beautiful smile and my most hilarious sense of humor, as some would compliment me for the smiles that would brighten their day. If only they knew what was feeling behind those smiles and laughter. I was just a jolly, creative, and humorous person that didn't have a care or concern in this life. Little did they know! First of all, I didn't believe that I was ever beautiful. I was often teased for having a flat-face with a long chin and I wasn't the fair-skin color complexion that most guys during my time saw as being beautiful in a society of what beautiful looks like, but yet I continued to smile, laugh and communicate without anyone who would talk to me, never ever breaking my silence of knowing how horrible I felt inside.

It breaks my heart to see how the enemy tricks so many souls into believing that they will never be anything in life or that they have no self worth, value or purpose and they believe those voices in their head and not realize that it is the enemy's voice that speaks to them. It is the enemy's voice that tells you to die. It is the enemy's voice that tries to influence you to believe that taking your life is more rewarding than living in this evil world. It is the enemy's voice that makes you believe that it's your voice. It is the enemy that hates life! The enemy is a spirit and this war we fight is spiritual but you don't have it fight alone. God leads us to a straight and narrow path but the devil leads us to a crooked path filled with mazes and puzzles of confusion.

It was a dark place in my life and the weights of darkness compelled my soul to the deepest depths of heaviness. The weights were too much to carry and many times the pain is so deeply buried where you begin to feel like you're a dead person walking. When you're feeling heaviness, unable to sleep, unable to function normally and you're not feeling your best, it is the spirit of peace that is needed to soothe and comfort your soul. When those moments in our lives start to overwhelm us and break us down, this is when we must get on our knees and pray to our Lord and Savior. Pray directly to God from your heart. Say, "Father give me the strength to fight my battles. Ask God for whatever you need and cast your cares to the Lord. He makes our yoke easy and our burdens light. In addition, find a Bible-based church to learn of God's goodness, the fruits of the spirit, salvation, receiving true healing, deliverance and learn more about God's love, grace, mercy and growing in faith with God. Most importantly, find spiritual leadership that teaches on spiritual warfare. Finding wise counsel and seeking help from someone who is seasoned in the faith can help you grow in your faith. The word states, "As one piece of iron sharpens another, so friends keep each other sharp. Proverbs 27:17.

CHAPTER 3- YOUR PAST AFFECTS YOUR PRESENT

THE FALSE CONCEPT OF LOVE

Love is so powerful! It's a state of being that expresses action. Loving someone is expressed the most through our emotions which creates our actions and through our behavioral affections in our mind. We can say, "I love you" a million times a day and it can even soften the heart, but as we all know action speaks a lot louder than words. Showing love by physical touch or by the act of service speaks a lot louder than words that are heard. I never heard my father tell me he loved me as a little girl. If he did, I really can't recall it but I loved him because he was my father; yet I hated him because he didn't love me like a daughter was supposed to be loved. The void I felt from his absence in my life would bring so much pain and confusion and interestingly, the pain grew silently and soon became my heavy weight throughout the years like heavy-loads of that rooted-baggage.

Living life in my womanhood, that child in me never healed because that little girl in me lacked the love from my father. The heartbreaks from men I've dated were repeated reminders of the little girl whose soul was broken and never healed, yet I was still trying to bring someone into my life to fill many voids that could never be filled.

I received love, compassion and nurture from my mother growing up but I didn't understand why I still needed my father's love, compassion and nurture. However, you know, that love from the very first man in a girl's life, a girl's father. The man you will always love, who makes his little girl believe in herself and love her beyond infinity because her dad shows her why he loves her so much and that it's a comfort and reassurance that is developed inside of her. She is esteemed by his affirmation! It's an affirmation of love that confirms her identity, her value and her self-worth. She has built a confidence and a standard based upon her father's love for her and what he's thinks of her, that she's more than precious, and even the most beautiful girl in the world, even when no one else thinks she is, even when she is not what society sees as beauty because her father esteems her as being the most important, beautiful and precious girl in his eyes. It's in his eyes what his daughter sees! When a girl has the esteem and the love from her father's eyes, she grows to develop an essence of beauty on the inside and on the outside in an environment that portrays the fallacy of what beauty is supposed to look like to become accepted. I longed for that affirmative love and I felt like the prey in the wilderness of my environment. I felt lonely, afraid, misused, abused, uncomfortable and insecure. This deficiency left me internally scorned with emotional baggage. I felt like that beautiful rose in an environment full of weeds that buried me and made me feel unwanted, unnoticed, isolated, unworthy and scarred. I became that rose with many thorns! The thorns were my defense mechanism that built up from the bruises of pain, unwatered, unnurtured and in an emotional malnutrition environment that created a shield to guard me from the repetitive scars. I became desensitized to not having sunlight to grow and the courage and confidence to know that although I was lonely, neglected, abandoned, deceived and rejected, I was still created for a purpose. I just didn't know what that was for me. I just didn't know what that was supposed to look like for me.

She attracts what she lacks in her life. A women with insecurities becomes attracted to a man with great confidence! It's a false sense of hope when she feels that this measure of attraction will heal and fill what she has lived without. She might use her outside appearance to attract what she defines will meet her inner soul but her inner soul and spirit attracts brokenness. Her physical appearance may be appealing to men but she may feel that her outer appearance is only what defines her strength because the outer appearance covers up the genuine character on the inside. She's lost in who she is because her inner soul is broken, yet others can't see what her inner soul feels because they can only see her disguise of contentment, and masqueraded beauty of having it all together. Her disguise is what conceals her identity. She's fearful, yet prideful and she doesn't want to face what she hasn't fixed. She doesn't want anyone to know what she's really feeling and facing. This woman can hold the highest degree of education, highest paid career, well-respected community leader in her neighborhood or the "strong-woman" that most people lean on for advice or support because she appears to have it all together, but yet she can't accept that she's hurting and full of so much pain; Pain that she doesn't know how to heal from or pain that she has ignored and accepted into her psychological state of "this is who I really am"! The reality is, she doesn't know who she really is, and therefore, she doesn't know what she needs in her life. Her perception of herself is disturbed and her perspective of life in her world is distorted. If she really knew who she was and if she really knew how much God loves her, she wouldn't carry the brokenness in her heart. Until she accepts the truth that she needs healing within her soul, body and mind, she will continue to hide it and use her outside appearance as her masqueraded beauty and strength. This is where she has invested all her money and time to perfect it, to make her feel better as a healing mechanism but the real truth is that her inside posture has been damaged and needs to be repaired. Is this person you? Was this person me? Does this person remind you of someone you know? That woman who continue to fix up the outside appearance by wearing makeup only to cover up the wounds on the inside, and/or repetitively buying clothing or jewels to improve the outer appearance, to make her feel better on the inside or using her body to attract attention for satisfaction due to a lack of attention, to gain self-assurance and gratification from others. This doesn't indicate that all women who flaunt their bodies only desire the attention of men but many women do, simply because they're deprived of love or being wanted!

ARE YOU PRESENTLY LIVING IN YOUR PAST?

Living in our past doesn't give us the divine fulfillment of our purpose in life. When we live in our past we become outdated mentally, empty emotionally and unaware of our spirituality with God. There is no room for growth. We create blockages and hindrances in areas that need to grow in order for us to evolve and mobilize in life. This would probably explain why sometimes we feel stuck and stagnant in the process of accomplishing our dreams or maximizing our full potential and goals. We become the product of our own misery! Spiritually, we become like a plant that is slowly withering away, branch by branch, leaf by leaf, when we don't trim off the dead sections of our past. Trimming and getting rid of those dead places in our lives that keeps us in bondage will allow us to live a newer and fuller life to grow and elevate. Sometimes, you have to get rid of some things in yourself and with the toxic and negative people you're around, even those you love; in order to see improvement in your life!

Even as parents, we can unconsciously find ourselves struggling to let go of the past. Are you a parent who has a deferred dream where you live your life through your children? You make decisions about your child's life because of unfulfilled dreams and the disappointments of not fulfilling your own dreams from your past. Maybe you once wanted to become a cheerleader, or a nurse or maybe you didn't get a chance to have that big wedding you always dreamed of. You will find yourself, living your dreams through your daughter and that may not be her desires or her purpose, yet you can't seem to see that this is for the sake of gaining achievement that is not yours because you have a need to gain and acclaim the fulfillment or attention for yourself through someone else's life..

Those of you who are parents and can relate to this must understand that our children's lives are defined by their own purpose and because we may regret we did not accomplish our own goals and dreams, we tend to relive our past through our children.

Although I have not struggled with this type of living in the past, I have struggled in other areas of not letting go of the past where I can remember my mother not being able to afford the clothes I had desired to wear to school. She did the best she could to provide for me and my sibling, so I wasn't fortunate to wear the designer clothes and shoes like other peers wore. It was not having the things that made me popular and not feeling accepted that created the pain of rejection, simply because I didn't look like the part for acceptance. For many years, this affected me and once I became an adult and had the opportunity to afford the nicer clothes, shoes and accessories, it was like I had become a fanatic of clothing and how it made me feel to have the best designer clothes and styles. I didn't think much about my past as I would purchase clothes that were appealing to my body type and it would make me feel good about myself to see myself as a woman to be desired but it just wasn't enough. I needed that approval to feel just as accepted and beautiful as I had ever thought I could feel. I wanted to feel beautiful on the outside although on the inside I was still hurting from the wounds of rejection. The clothes, accessories, shoes, jewelry and the most epic hair dos could not replace the pain that had been buried from my past. Although I love how feeling beautiful made me feel, it could never heal the root of my problems. Even high-end makeup and fixing up my face could not fix what I was struggling with all of my life. In my past, I didn't feel pretty enough and I didn't feel attractive as a petite, short and brown-skinned girl who seemed to be overlooked and not accepted. It had always seemed as though the lighter complexion girls got all the attention and were most appealing and attracted the handsome guys. Growing up in society, it was unfortunate and very sad that in the African American community, lighter skin girls were considered most attractive than brown or dark skin complexion girls. In my opinion, it reflects the color-ism of being closed-minded and enslaved by how skin colors are perceived in the minds of those who view what beauty really means. As much as I worked hard to look and feel my best in my brown skin and in the most adoring and expensive outfits, well-groomed hair-do,s and dresses to fit and cling to my curvy and petite shape, it still didn't heal those wounds of my past, those wounds of my school years. Even in my later years of blossoming into a young woman, the compliments from men who would stare or flirt with me, didn't heal those wounds. I viewed those stares and compliments as lusts. It was being wanted in a lustful way that didn't feel genuine of liking me but only the lusts of sexual attraction. This was not a feeling of being desired but more of feeling like being used and abused. These were feelings of being scorned. Those sexual remarks only became a temporary feeling and knowing that I'm surely not the only girl hearing these words, although I most certainly wished. Due to feelings of untrusted, I never seemed to get over what I felt I couldn't get back in those days when I was overlooked, ridiculed and talked about for not looking "the part". In my adulthood, I felt freedom to have the opportunity and that validation to know what made me feel good, especially when

I could purchase the things I desired. When I became older, it was like I had to prove to myself that I was just as beautiful, glamorous and just as important as any of those who would make fun of me when I lacked the things that I solely desired to have that I lacked in my younger days.

Another area of my past that I struggled with was fear, worry and anxiety. I had my days when I felt courageous to take on new responsibilities and I felt undefeated, then there were other days when fear would consume me. I believe that I became a habitual worrier. I would worry about my family, my finances, my future and the worry of uncertainty. Some days I even hated grabbing mail from my mailbox. It was like the fear of the unexpected, the unknown. Years later, I would discover how the struggle with anxieties of social settings and being in large crowds became more and more uncomfortable for me, if not unbearable. I just didn't understand what I was struggling with. I often wondered, was I still holding on to the fear of my childhood trauma? Was it a spirit of fear that caused me to feel paranoid? I knew fear was not a spirit of God, so how could I let go of these struggles from my past when it feels like a demonic-tie that wouldn't allow me to be great or better?

THE HEARTS OF FATHERLESS DAUGHTERS

Growing up without a father present in my life really had an impact on me. It was an impact that affected me in so many negative ways and I didn't know that from the age of ten years old, it would affect me in my womanhood, motherhood and being a wife for over 20 years. Being a fatherless daughter is like being this single beautiful rose with sharp thorns, limped over, surrounded and overshadowed by weeds and tall grass in an unmanicured lawn. The beauty of the rose is overlooked, hidden and unnoticed due to the weeds, untamed shrubs and heavy debris that surrounds it; a lack of sun can shine on this beautiful rose once it has been hidden beneath all of the weeds and its surrounding. Isn't this how life feels when God sees the beauty in us but the wild environment keeps us hidden, isolated and becoming comfortable with being in our environment and that feeling of being overshadowed and overlooked?

The scars of life and the layers of baggage, affected my ability to believe in myself, to know if there was purpose in my life to have a vision to dream bigger and a sense of identity to have confidence in myself and the security of not walking through life in fear and feeling insecure, as the fearful child I always was.

Many women around the world, living lives impacted as fatherless daughters, I'm sure can relate to the pain. We may not all have experienced the same problems growing up and developed the same wounds. We may not all have endured the same brokenness of being scarred by the conditions to the extent of our sufferings, but one thing is for sure, we all know what deep pain in our minds, hearts and souls feels like. It feels like salt poured over an opened wound over and over again. Some fatherless daughters never got to know who their biological fathers were. Some fatherless daughters grew up with a father who may have transitioned from their lives. Other fatherless daughters carry the deep desire to pursue their fathers love and gain a sense of emotional closure by seeking and hoping to reconcile with their biological father. Then, there are fatherless daughters whose dads are incarcerated and they have not had the experience to enjoy life with them. There are even fatherless daughters whose dads live near them and they have been rejected by their father due to either conflict between both parents or the father just refuses to be in his daughter's life for no apparent explanation. Nevertheless, whatever the situation is, I know what not having your father in your life feels like. It's a feeling of an abandoned little girl who needs approval as a woman. Just know that you were never alone in the past and you are still not alone at this present time.

Overall, the young girl needs the sufficient affirmations of her father and that was me. Many don't understand that this is a need for a young girl. I also needed the attention from my father, the innocent affections was what I was searching for. I needed that affirmation from my father. I can express what I was feeling and what I carried into my womanhood because it all makes proper sense as I reflect on how much I searched for the affirmation and for the affection from a man when I should have gotten it from my father. As a young woman, those false concepts of love became detrimental in my relationships. It's worse when you date someone who has narcissistic behavior which abuses the love of a gullible young girl, whose heart is very tender and delicate. It's painful when you are in fear of what you need and you shouldn't be in fear of what you are supposed to have. So, I can relate to the young girl who is searching for the love in the arms and in the eyes and in the grasp of men and most of these men would be those to pervert her, so she becomes trained that love is sex and love is abuse. This is how she begins to develop those false concepts and notions. Sex and abuse is what many young girls see as love in an unhealthy mindset. You can't point the finger at them nor can you cast stones on their behavior and the mindset, the best thing you can do or say to them is that they are beautifully broken and tell them that it's not true love. It's not genuine love because they never got to see what true love looked like or felt like.

When young girls lack their father's presence, they lack sound advice, proper guidance, a sense of protection, a sense of identity, a sense of affirmation and their input on approvals and disapproval from their fathers, relevant to who they are dating or who they meet in a masculine society. When a father hasn't been attentive and intentional about his daughter's development, it places a void in her life. She has to cope through the pain consciously and subconsciously and someone will have to affirm that she is still a queen even through her brokenness and low self-esteem. Even through my own personal brokenness of not having my father, I had to gain the strength and observe my mother and grandmothers character of how they managed life in the midst of lack and heartaches; how they behaved with love, grace, strength, living by standards of morals, values and most importantly, Godly principles, in which encouraged me through the traumatic journey of my father's absence. During these days of my life, I observed them closely to allow my innermost being to be fed the wisdom and knowledge of what I needed and how to cope in life during the lack of my own personal desires. My heart and spirit was always willing to be of good character and to do what was right even when life hadn't been fair to me growing up. It wasn't an easy journey for me and it took most of my life to heal. Unfortunately, not every young lady and woman has or had that outlet to gain the strength and courage that I gained but somewhere down the road, I had to allow my obstacles to become my strength. When I learned about what my grandparents had to go through in their lives, it gave me the mental ability to feel a sense of hope and power to know that I can overcome the many obstacles and trials I'd faced. I just wasn't sure if they had faced the same lack I had but if they did, how did they manage to cope through it? Never once did I ask them. Many women today are still silently struggling and suffering from the pain of being fatherless, whether their father left them at a young age due to a family separation, or whether the father became imprisoned behind bars, whether the daughter never got to meet her dad due to her father's transition of life or whether the father couldn't find the compassion, love, courage or responsibility to feel deserving to be in his children's presence due to his own guilt or shame. Many fathers aren't aware what their children's struggles are without being in their presence and what many fathers don't understand is, you don't have to be perfect to be a father. You just have to be there for them emotionally, mentally and physically. It's a great deal to help out financially too! The father is needed to give important advice to his young daughter and to instill into her value and worth by advising that if she has become interested in a young man, she shouldn't lay her body down for a man who won't lay his life down for her. She may always keep her dad's words of advice as a safeguard for her womanhood and well-being, for instance, "Stop seeking love from a man who doesn't love you" or stop trying to be a man-pleaser just to keep his mind on you or to keep him from leaving you" A loving father should tell his daughter that he loves her and he should show her what genuine love truly means, and that pure love isn't always receiving tangible things. Love is shown to many daughters by just having their dad's presence! Just having a dad to hug and hold on to and to know that this man will be the first man to ever love her! It starts off with a love that is innocent and as she becomes a woman and fall in-love with a man who finds her, she doesn't force the man to love her in return. She becomes aware when she truly finds a man who genuinely loves her with all his heart, he'll do what it takes to show her!

A father's advice also expresses commitment and loyalty to his daughter. Her dad's words can protect her from knowing that domestic abuse can be seen as a red flag in the early stages of dating and it's not the sign of love. A dad can protect his daughter's heart from detecting the difference between a man loving her versus a man being in love with her. Last but surely not least, a dad can teach his daughter to know the difference between lust and love and not be blindsided by desperation and not being vulnerable to the games that some men play. Having a father's love and presence doesn't always mean that his daughter is 100% safeguarded from being hurt or being cheated on but it can allow the daughter to be forewarned or become aware of knowing what signs to look for in a man and even through his imperfections. If a young lady is in a relationship and if the man she is seeing is emotionally abusive towards her, she may not see the abuse as dangerous to her life but because of her insecurities and low self-esteem of not believing she could do better, she sees this abuse as a language of love. She even start to feel obligated to not leaving him for various reasons. This could even reflect the abuser's insecurities and pain. Insecure people can attract other insecure people, just the same as spirits attracting other spirits that are alike. This is why toxicity attracts other spirits of toxicity. Unfortunately, when abusive and toxic relationships continue to break down the characters of men and women, unfortunately the results of death becomes the untimely factor. Currently, we read and hear about the rising numbers of domestic abuse, there are so many cases and factors where women are dying by the hands of men that gave them that false concept of love. Many women accepted and tolerated physical and verbal abuse and made it a part of their lifestyle where they couldn't find the courage or the confidence to leave and separate themselves from the dangerous outcomes. In many cases, they stayed in these abusive relationships for the sake of love, for the sake of that things might get better; more importantly they remain in these relationships for their kids or the fear of being alone, poverty or homelessness. Many times, they remain in unhappy relationships and marriages to prevent their children from being fatherless.

Many girls and women are looking for love in the wrong places and many times they seek love in broken boys and men who haven't found themselves due to their own loss of identities and the misleading behavior of what it is to be a man but sometimes they may never reach that stage of manhood maturity because they are grown boys who look like men.

The young lady couldn't find the strength to leave the mental, emotional and physical abuse, so they stayed and remained in these broken relationships and many times they stayed for the sake of being wanted or for the idea of being loved by something they lacked earlier in their childhood. I assume it's the idea of just having someone even when that someone doesn't want you. Many times spiritual soul-ties trap the couples in living and dwelling in dysfunctional situation-ships. This means a relationship that's based on complicated situations where each person is challenged with the strength or courage to let go, like for instance, letting go of the past of not forgiving our fathers for not being in our lives or by not forgiving ourselves for the past relationships that broke our spirits in the first place. So, you unite in holy matrimony with brokenness you've carried from your past with someone else who has hidden brokenness. Unfortunately, this would explain the cause of so many divorces we see and hear about on a regular basis from celebrities to our next door neighbors.

HOW OUR PAST AFFECTS LOVE AND OUR RELATIONSHIPS

I can remember my very first experience of dating. I was sixteen years old and my mother gave me permission to date at this age although there were boundaries set in place and I was definitely going to respect my mother's boundaries. A clean-cut and handsome guy from a different high school had asked me out on a date. I was a little hesitant, nervous, and a little shy at first, but I had the courage to take his offer in the midst of my emotional walls of guarding my heart and the insecurities that were never healed. This was a dinner date to be exact. My heart was pounding in deep fear, wondering what I would wear and how am I going to fix myself up. Better yet, how am I going to manage enough courage to be myself around this guy. I had been rejected so many times and I just didn't know if this would be another episode of being rejected for being me or is this guy just wanting me for sex. I got so worked up for this moment…..well, that moment that I was so excited for never happened. He stood me up! Prior to the date we had planned, we had talked on the phone for many months to form a close relationship. Well, I thought that the relationship had developed into a closer bond because I really liked him and he would talk as if he were excited to see me with expectation of the days nearly approaching for our big date. I was starting to really like him but reliving my past pain of rejection flooded my heart once again. To make matters worse, weeks later I found out that he was dating someone else. Life has a way of showing a person's true character with every passing time, life showed me that this handsome, clean-cut guy wasn't as serious as I desired him to be. He had his girlfriend wear his jersey to school on a particular day. This was a trade school program that his girlfriend and I attended during my high school years and I thought he would have had enough sense not to allow her to wear the jersey that was very noticeable! I thought that I was special to him because he let me keep this particular jersey months prior to us planning our first date. When I reflect on this, I smile and think about how you're we were. We had no clue about being in-love. I was young and naive and it felt so good to feel noticed by a nice looking guy. It was heartbreaking to discover that I knew that it was his jersey shirt being worn by another girl because of the unique style and his initials of his name were printed on the back. How dumb was I, to allow myself to believe that this guy was seriously committed to starting a relationship with me. We were only sixteen years old but I didn't allow my age to make me believe that this was only puppy-love. I knew that I was seriously desiring a commitment with him and I felt dumb for believing it. It was one of those moments I'll never forget. I questioned myself on how he could lie to me and tell me it wasn't his jersey when I questioned him about it. The games that guys play show the lack of consideration on playing with young girls' emotions and their minds. He was too immature for me and I was too naive to accept it. The emotional betrayal and feelings of being embarrassed by close friends that knew about me and him, and feeling disappointed by being stood-up on my first date and his lies about this jersey not belonging to him was my first experience of developing a relationship with someone who I became fond of but developed not trusting guys. This betrayal and emotional abandonment felt so similar to my childhood feelings of being stood-up by my father when he had promised to pick me and my sibling up to spend quality time with us on many weekends, and that feeling of distrust left me feeling so cold inside. The broken promises, time after time led me to believe that I wasn't worthy of being accepted or worthy of being valued. This feeling of abandonment was a punch in the gut and a blow to the heart. Every time I would feel this pain, my heart would feel like it had stopped beating and it became difficult to breathe. This feeling was all so real. I remember many years of feeling like this. This pain of rejection and abandonment was rehearsed pain. The disappointment I felt brought up negative emotions again and left me feeling like my chances with trusting the next guy would be very slim. Trusting males was very challenging! If struggling with trusting my father was difficult, how much more difficult would it be trusting a guy that I desired to date? This rehearsed pain developed the seed of rejection, anger, bitterness, fear and insecurities and the need for me to isolate myself from everyone around me. I was living my past over and over again. It was like my past would always find a way to haunt me as if it was in close proximity to attack me. For this is what I had buried deep down in my soul but this time, I promised myself that it'll never happen again and I never talked to this guy anymore. I lost his number on purpose, his constant calls went unanswered until he finally gave up and got my indirect message of silence and never seeing or hearing about him gave me a sigh of relief. I'm sure he knew where I had lived and he knew that he could not come to my house either. My mother wasn't having it, especially seeing me distraught from abandoning me on my first date and not giving me any explanation as to why he did not show up. My mother felt bad for me and I was too embarrassed to even talk to her about it. So, that first dating experience at the age of sixteen was an embarrassment and horrible experience that planted the spirit of shame in my heart. I became sensitive and so fragile. I felt like broken glass on a picture that hadn't shattered; you could only see the cracks. I felt distrust, fear and expected that the next future relationship would be the same outcome. I became hopeless for love!

As months went by and the situation was clearly out of my mind, once again, I found the courage in my heart to try it again. But this time, I was maturing and really liking guys. It had been a while since I had the courage to date. I was seeing how my friends and schoolmates looking happily in love. So, I felt that I'm willing to try this dating thing but this time my guards were up! I really hoped that this next relationship would be different and not a repeat of the immature guy who disappointed me the last time. I desired someone older, someone more mature. Someone who would seem stable, intelligent and a desire to be in a long-term relationship. Some relationships turned out to become serious and long-termed and some were not so serious. In both experiences, I gained the strength, hope and courage to have the desire to find that right guy. The problem that I discovered was I was looking for long-term relationships that would turn out to be short-termed. I was seeking love in the wrong places but I wasn't desperate. I wasn't drooling over guys like a thirsty, dry-mouth animal. I knew what type of guy I desired but they would turn out to be the "bad boys", unfortunately! I was attracted to intelligent men with a little street-knowledge in them and they had to be mature and a bit older. I assumed the older they were, the more mature they were. I started to believe that the guys a little older than me would have more experience with knowing how to treat me with respect and like a lady. I didn't have time for no immature, spoiled momma's boy. The guy I started dating this time stole my heart. He was my first love and the guy that took my virginity. I didn't have the desire to date guys from the same school I attended. I felt it would be better to date someone that I didn't grow up with although, I was naive to follow my heart. My heart was so pure and opened to desiring love but the man I had loved so dearly, and had dated for nearly three years would yet disappoint me and break my heart. After high school graduation, he left for the military and we had a long-distant relationship. It was very complicated being in love with someone whom you couldn't spend time with but I was hopeful that time would change our situation. We planned to marry someday and I knew he was for me. I allowed someone to steal my heart and it wasn't long before I noticed the red flags. I saw jealousy in him, I saw anger issues in him but I ignored these signs because as always, I felt that he would eventually change with time. It made me accept my brokenness as my normal character. Weeks were moving by fast, I would hardly hear from him. I started to believe he had met someone else but it was so hard to accept it. I needed closure but I still loved him. I was ready to accept that this distant relationship would soon end. It was that one and last phone call I received from him. I had called him and left many messages but he wouldn't return my calls, I was disappointed and yet excited to hear his voice this last time. He didn't sound the same this time, it was a sadness in his voice. As I laid stiff on the sofa and afraid to hear what he had to tell me, it would be that familiar feeling of rejection. He said, "Angel, I just need to tell you something." I could tell from the sound of his voice that this wasn't going to be good. As I lowered myself on the sofa with watery eyes and couldn't breathe to say a word, he said those words that placed a terrible ache in my chest. He said, "Angel, I think it's best that we remain friends". My mind was screaming, "REMAIN FRIENDS". I couldn't believe what he just said. I couldn't believe that he broke up with me. I didn't deserve it but I should have known that a long-distance relationship would soon end. I gasped for a few minutes in silence but I sat up as if I was too strong to make him think that I was in so much pain, I said, "Okay" with strength and with a calmness in my voice. He said, "This would be best for the both of us." "I'm sorry for the way this had to turn out." I couldn't believe what I was hearing, so I lied and said, "naw, I'll be okay"! "I'll be just fine." I wasn't okay! Nor was I just fine. I was a sorrowful wreck. He broke my heart. All of those vivid memories we shared and all of those dreams I pictured of sharing my life with him would turn into a pale dream that faded away in thin air. This was a pain that made it difficult to walk to my bedroom. I couldn't wait to end this call with him. I went to my room and shut my door. I laid in my bed and allowed my heart to sink. At least he called to tell me that it was over instead of just ignoring me completely, I thought as I was lying there with tears in my eyes. I had to take a moment to digest what I just heard. I cried and cried and cried until I became exhausted. I refused to ask him why. It wasn't worth the question. He had already made his mind up before he called me. The best peace at this point was to allow these weary eyes to rest and sleep away this pain. It would be a pain that I couldn't explain but this painful feeling was not so strange. It has been my lifestyle. It was a part of my past. I started to normalize pain. This is what I felt about life, in general. The only good I could see in this experience was the ability to feel my heart. I had to endure and face it in order to move forward with my life. Pain was what I felt and it was all I knew and I needed to close this chapter in my life and move on!

WE ATTRACT WHO WE ARE IN RELATIONSHIPS

By this time, it was nearly two years after my high school graduation. I was in my early twenties and yet experiencing another heartbreak from a broken relationship with a guy I considered my first love, brokenness, unfaithfulness and disappointment was all I've experienced with men and young teen guys. Here I am, entering into my early twenties, in this male-dominated society, I really needed my father's advice, support, protection and fatherly guidance. There were so questions on my mind and many times in my life where I felt that having a father could have really helped me make better choices, especially when it came to loving myself enough to make better decisions with men, in addition to not losing myself for the sake of making a relationship the priority over myself. Most importantly, seeking the affirmation of love from a guy due to the lack of affirmation I didn't receive as a little girl. I failed to accept my value for loving myself for who I was. I needed that validation from a man. This is where I had it all wrong! My goal in life was to maintain a healthy and happy relationship by making the right choices in men who sought after me. I was blinded by the red-flags because the love I thought as genuine and real, was only my imagination. It's like listening to the sounds of the

Temptations singing, "It was just my imagination...........running away from me.............It was just my imagination running away from me." In reality, I was attracted to who I was! I overlooked so much just to see the goodness in the guys I had dated. Although, we are planning all not perfect and whoever we decide to date will never be perfect either, I had to make sure not to overlook the red flags! Let's be truthful, when we don't consult God in a relationship with someone, we are destined to ignore the red flags! However, sometimes those red flags can be detected but I was clearly blinded by the toxicity of the false concept of love. Did I really know what love was? Later in life, I understood why I didn't. When you first start dating someone, you really just don't know whether a person would do you right, simply because they start off with a great personality. They can seem like the perfect match and later the real person usually comes out of them. When I say the "real" person I truly mean that their true character and behavior eventually reveals itself. One of my biggest failures was that I would lose myself in the relationships. I think that when we become a people-pleaser, we can lose ourselves and abandon our own needs for the sake of desiring love, attention and affection. If you're not careful or become unaware of your needs, you will find yourself lost and seeking out the wrong person repeatedly all for the sake of love and companionship. Once again, you keep attracting the same types of men. This is a red flag itself! What I needed the most was to discern whether the person would be a good match for me. I learned a lot by making bad choices when it came to dating but I also learned that those bad choices could make me a great expert when it comes to the experiences.

As my grandmother would say, whatever doesn't come out in the wash will come out in the rinse. Those sayings that my grandmothers used to say would make more sense for me later in life.

However, in my next phase of dating, I would find myself having the courage and hope but yet carrying the baggage of insecurities. The new guy I met, the ambitious, high-spirited, charismatic and a street-hustler to his heart, meant the world to me. It was his style and charisma that caught my attention when I first met him. His energy and vibe made me inquisitive about him. I met him through my cousin's boyfriend at that time. It was a mutual connection. We started out getting to know one another and everything felt great. Our conversations would go on for hours. We decided to start dating to see where our courtship would go but it was those red flags again. Many times, I would hear about his unfaithful behavior of being seen with other women in public from time to time, and yet denying every bit of it or hearing about him being a father to children that I would never see or never hear him mention. He would be so quick to deny these rumors. Yet, I knew that he was a father to a couple of children and I loved how he interacted with some of his children because it reminded me of what I had missed growing up without my father, I was still seeing those red-flags but I ignored every red flag because I was hoping for better, yet I knew that there was no perfect guy. I was finally feeling the need of being noticed and being desired. Yet, I was hoping deep down inside that he would change into a better man. Seeing this man as being a father to his children was surely not the red-flag in my eyes. In fact, it was the most impressive part about him that I'd love the most, but finding out that he was the father to many other children that he denied was one of many red flags that worried me and brought discouragement to my heart the most. I didn't want to judge him for being a man with many children. Honestly, I really couldn't see myself raising another woman's child at such a young age, yet alone, raising other women's children.

Withholding information was the biggest red flag of not being truthful with me from the very beginning and I thought we were better than that as our relationship grew and our conversations became more serious and personal. We would communicate on many subjects and he seemed to be very candid and open-minded about his thoughts and beliefs. My intuition kept telling me to stop and listen, although my heart didn't want to believe the truth, it gave me the reality I had to accept. I decided to remain in the relationship but the feeling of distrust would intensify. I didn't know if it would be my insecurities of not being confident or my intuition trying to warn me. I was torn with mixed emotions. I believed that it was my own insecurities from my past and that these insecurities would cause me to lose out on loving someone and being loved by someone who truly was in love with me. I had fallen in love with him and I didn't want to break up the relationship. I believed that he was in love with me. He and I were planning our wedding. Yes, it ended up getting serious. Despite him having a lot of children, I overlooked the responsibilities and it was frightening because it really seemed overwhelming. I was blindly in love and he had soon proposed to me with a beautiful ring. It was one of my most happiest moments. I was so excited, yet so afraid and nervous! I had good reasons to back out of this marriage proposal but I just couldn't help the fact that this man desired me. He loved me and that's what I desired!! I had it all planned out. I was so excited and nervous and couldn't wait to marry him. I bought my wedding dress and even had my bridesmaids buy their dresses. It was difficult to shake that gut feeling deep down inside. I just couldn't understand that feeling I kept ignoring. I didn't want to respond to that gut-wrenching feeling. I didn't want to let go of the idea of being a wife. I was in love with this man but the reality became clear, he was not the one for me. This was the bomb-shell of yet another disappointing experience! God gives women that special intuition, that feeling on the inside and it's more like that nudge from your gut that just won't leave, it's the truth that God wants to reveal to you but sometimes we tend to ignore it and believe what we want to believe. The truth will usually come out with time and after being tired of seeing and discovering signs of disloyalty and infidelity, it was time to close this chapter in my life. I needed my father's presence like never before. I needed my father to tell me that I could do better than this but I had to believe this for myself, even when it felt like a part of me had to die. I was in love with toxicity, a part of my past that I had a hard time shaking off. I had to believe that I was worth more and that there was more for me in life. Lowering my standards to find acceptance was not a healthy choice. Feeling betrayal and disloyalty is a pain that is indescribable when you love someone and it's genuine and your expectations are high for that relationship. The lesson I had to learn is to stop having high expectations in men when in love, especially when you love hard, when I say loving someone hard, I'm talking about that unconditional love where the magnitude of hurt leaves you feeling crippled, unable to eat, and desiring isolation and not having any energy to do anything. On the flip side, there are others who may respond in the opposite behavior to this type of pain, which may cause an increase in appetite to help deal with coping with the pain. For me, it caused me to lose my appetite, to eat less. This break-up was disheartening and very heartbreaking because I was loyal and waited for this guy for nearly two years when he got in trouble with the law and was locked up in prison. His street-hustling days had come to an end and I wanted to prove to him my loyalty, genuine admiration, sincerity, trust and strength in the midst of my own challenges. I wanted him to see that I truly had his back. I would visit him occasionally and write him letters to keep his head up and for him to stay strong during his incarceration. While he was locked up, it was very difficult for me! I truly felt lonely and discouraged;

yet I kept myself busy and focused by attending a community college to earn an associate's degree. I just didn't want life to stop for me. I needed to make an accomplishment and start focusing more on my future; so I kept my mind busy studying to help me to stay focused while making an educational achievement. I refused to wallow in sorrow because of his mistakes. This was my chance to get focused career-wise. This allowed me to focus on my goals and to strengthen my skills. I remained in solitude and at peace during this difficult time but I felt a sense of strength as well. I studied in college and worked two jobs and did hair on the side. Staying busy really helped me during a two year wait. When he was released from prison after serving his two years, I was so excited because I felt that this was our time. By this time, I was preparing to graduate from college and I was looking forward to him seeing me receive my degree during my graduation ceremony. This would be an exciting moment to see the guy I had waited for, now celebrate my accomplishments with me.

As I walked through the halls of the school with my cap and gown on, I called his phone, there was no answer. It kept going to his voicemail and I became worried. I knew something wasn't right. I wondered if he was sleeping? Did he forget? I had so many thoughts racing through my mind. "I knew he couldn't have forgotten about this big day for me because we'd just discussed this yesterday." This is what kept coming to my mind. As time moved on and getting closer for the graduation ceremony to start, family members and close friends were walking in and getting situated to take their seats and a few had asked, "Where is your fiancee?" Why isn't he here to see you graduate?" My response was blank. I just had a blank stare because I couldn't muster up the words to answer. I could barely say a word because my heart was filled with fear and disappointment and not really sure how to respond. I wish I had an answer for them. I was worried that something happened. So my response was, "I don't know where he is!" So, I took my place and I had to line up for the ceremony to start. All I could think of is where is this guy? Minutes passed by and I thought he would be walking in through the doors by now. Still, he was nowhere to be found. They called my name, "Angel" I walked across the stage to receive my degree. It was bittersweet. I was happy to receive my degree as this was my reminder of all the hard work, many nights of studying and time I invested into those two years and working two jobs during this time was a challenge but I made it through! I was hoping that maybe, I would still see him walking in the building or maybe seeing him sit in the audience would have been a great surprise. Yet, I was still saddened and devastated that this man still never showed up! I was trying to smile when I wanted to cry! I'm supposed to be celebrating and excited but was bothered because I truly believed something happened. I didn't really know what to think or how to feel. After the ceremony ended, I made one last call but still, he never answered. By this time, I was worried out of my mind because I knew that something had gone wrong. I made one last call to his relative's home but there was still no answer. Hours after celebrating my graduation with family, I went home and changed my clothes and decided to take a visit to his home. I went to his home to see if I could find him. As I knocked on the door to wait, I heard the footsteps coming. My heart was racing as I'm now desperate to hear some answers. It wasn't who I expected. It was his relative. I asked if he knew where my fiancée was. He replied that my fiancée had been home all day but he just left. I said okay and thank you. Then I walked away and left. As I drove home, I could hear my heart beating very rapidly! I couldn't believe that this guy didn't show up and he had been home all day. I was confused and I felt sick to my stomach. He didn't even answer any of my calls and didn't bother to return them. As rage filled my heart, I wasn't paying any attention to how fast I was driving. As I drove pass stop signs, it was as if my mind just went into a daze. I really couldn't think straight! All I could think of was memories of the many conversations we had concerning this event and thinking on how there could not be an excuse for missing one of the most important days of my life! Resentment and bitterness could have been my new name because I was wearing it well at this moment. I had to compose myself to keep from crying. It was hard being angry and in pain at the same time but yet trying to hold it all together and remain calm. It was obvious what happened to me. I felt this type of pain many times before. It reminded me of those days and it took me all the way back to that little girl, standing by the window once again, watching every passing car to realize that my dad wasn't going to pick me up for that weekend and the same situation weekends after that. It seemed as though my past pain just wouldn't allow me to enjoy my present life. It just wouldn't let me be great! I felt like a victim of my past. As this was a reminder of being broken-hearted by men in my life. This was yet another reminder of being stood up on my first date. This was just a reminder of why I would suffer the experience of not trusting men. Now, I had to accept the fact that this is the way men are. They play with your heart, mind and soul. My bitterness became bittersweet because at this moment I knew that payback was coming for him and with a force of vengeance! I was mad!!!

As I curled up in my bed like a fetus in a womb, I cried and cried for days. I fell into depression and couldn't shake the pain. I didn't bother to answer any calls. I ignored every call. I didn't want to talk to him or anyone. I didn't care to hear his voice or to listen to his lies. In my weakest moment, I began to pray. This was a short little prayer but it was what I needed the most. I can remember saying as I whispered, "God, give me strength to make it through" and "why isn't any of these relationships working out for me?" "Why is my life always full of disappointments, rejection and abandonment?" "Am I good enough for someone to love me?" My face was wet as if I had emerged my face in a bowl of warm water. My eyes were swollen and tired and I couldn't control the tears from flowing until I became physically weak but I managed to get myself together and pull myself up because I had to go to work and I had to keep a smile on my face when I didn't want to smile or be around anyone. I had to keep living in spite of how weak my body felt. I had very little contact with my father and he wasn't cognizant of my well-being. I needed someone to talk to. I was too embarrassed to open up about how those depressed moments I had been struggling with throughout my life. I started to believe that this was all because of me. This was all because of my own inabilities of not letting go of past pain. I just didn't have the confidence I really needed. I felt used and abused but there was something on the inside of me that wouldn't allow me to give up! As much as I wanted to give up, there was just a little dose of fight in me that wouldn't allow me to remain down this time.

As weeks passed by, I gained some strength. Everyday seemed hard but I was determined to keep striving. So, on this particular day, I decided to do some cleaning around the house. As I struggled to put on the latex cleaning gloves, I stared at my hand. I gazed at my hand as if a snake had bitten me. My heart started to race again. It was the engagement ring on my finger! I immediately stopped what I was doing and removed the ring from my finger. I didn't have the desire to wear the ring and I placed the ring on my dresser to prepare to return it to him. I made up my mind that there will not be a wedding, although I hadn't made anyone aware of it. I didn't want to keep or hold on to anything that reminded me of him. Hours later, someone knocked at my door. As I slowly walked to the front door, I quietly walked towards the door to look through the peephole and saw the familiar vehicle parked, there he was standing there looking handsome as ever. I let him in and before I could say anything, he responded by saying, "I know you're mad at me for not coming to your graduation." " I'm very sorry that I didn't come!" I asked him why he did not answer any of my calls and not show up? And he couldn't answer why. I told him how disappointed I was and how furious I was and that I could no longer be with him anymore. This relationship was over! I told him how embarrassed, hurt and disappointed I was for him not being there and how this was an important day for me. I even reminded him of how I was there for him during the two years he was locked up and that he couldn't be there for me on one occasion. "The wedding was off and we were officially done!" I gave him back his ring and told him that we were no longer going to see each other again. I didn't want him to come near my house. He tried to hug me but I pushed him away. It was a bit hard to say everything I told him but I had to say them out loud just to hear my voice reaffirm my reality! I had to accept the truth and the truth was, I wouldn't be a better person with him. I had to pay attention to that gut feeling this time and this time I had to pay attention to all the red flags. All the red flags were there for a reason. This time I wasn't ignoring them too! It was that moment where I made the right decision based on that gut feeling. It wasn't easy because I was still in love with him and he didn't want the relationship to end as he was begging and trying to make me think that I was just saying this because I was mad and that I would soon get over this but I could no longer trust him anymore. I told him to leave my house and he was out of my life that day. When he left, I took a deep breath as my eyes would become watery and my heart filled with sadness. I knew deep down in my soul that I had made the right decision, even when my heart didn't want to let him go. I was broken and mad at the same time! After a few weeks of moving forward with my life, his whereabouts were revealed on the day of my event. I finally learned the truth. He was spending some quality time with a young lady on the day of my graduation. After receiving the news from several reliable sources, it was my confirmation that the decision I made was one of the best decisions I've ever made in a relationship.

In the midst of brokenness and sadness, I knew that he was a broken soul trying to escape his own battles, struggles and the secrets he shared with me about his childhood and growing up into becoming a man, but I couldn't heal him or complete him and he couldn't heal or complete me. When a man or a woman depletes your soul, you should never tolerate him or her. You must let that relationship go. Run fast and run as far as you can! The brokenness in our spirits was the attraction of our toxicity of our own past lives that caused our insecurities as a couple to excessively cripple our hearts even more. Things would have became worse had I stayed. We were attracted by our weaknesses and our struggles, yet our spirits were no match for one another, so that chapter of my life ended for good.

THE REPERCUSSIONS OF BROKEN FATHERS

In this society, there are 19.7 million children living without their father according to the United States Census Bureau. This is more than 1 in 4 children without a father in the household.

The repercussions of fathers with broken souls can become the painful cycle of characteristics developed in children from the impact of being fatherless.

"A father of the fatherless, and a judge of the widows, is God in his holy habitation." Psalms 68:5 KJV

Although I focus on the heart and soul of the woman, the man plays an important role in the woman's spirit, mind and soul. Whether this man is her father, her son, her brother, her uncle, her companion or her husband, there is an effect he has on her and it's either a positive or negative influence or impact. As this chapter focuses on relationships, my personal experiences, and the struggle of repeated pain throughout my life with men; I can't leave out the important facts of what the male child experienced or how the young man was affected growing up and the psychological, emotional and spiritual impact men endured. The first question would come to mind: Did these young men have fathers in their home? What were the relationships like with their mothers? A majority of these social implications derive from the fact that fathers aren't in the homes in the lives of their sons growing up to become men. In other cases, the fathers who are at home with their sons may have not been healthy role models themselves.

Many would agree that there are many males living in single-parent households without their fathers being present in their lives. For centuries this has been a globalized crisis in societies and in countries in which, at this present time in our lives, it places a major impact on young males growing up into becoming young men today. The absence of fathers has an impact on the sons and daughters. The effects of this may vary and differ in girls and boys. It also places a strain on the family structure. A strain that breaks down the family unity. In many other cases, it is unfortunate when children grow up without both parents being in their lives, having to be raised by extended family members or grow up in homes of strangers through adoption. Whatever the case may be, the absences can trigger different types of father wounds and broken spirits and the effects are different in every child growing up. Each child copes with these father wounds and deficiencies in various forms, the characteristics and mannerisms are outwardly shown through conditioned behaviors and personalities. The problem is -- to what degree does it impact or influences each child and how does it affect these children developing into men socially, physically, emotionally, spiritually and psychologically?

BROKEN SONS BECOMING BROKEN MEN, HUSBANDS AND DADS

So many fatherless boys who became men lacked positive role models in their lives, struggled with the oppressed emotions of their environment through depression, anger and fear, in which caused guilt, shame, violence and self-destruction to themselves and to the lives of their children, this also includes their families around them. Unfortunately, this can negatively impact relationships in the development of their manhood and could possibly cause the vicious cycle of another fatherless generation of our sons and daughters.

Sons of broken fathers may someday experience becoming fathers of their own. Whether the young father is carrying the spiritual inheritance of brokenness, or whether he is carrying his father's spiritual inheritance of faith, strength and/or blessings, he is carrying what his father has left him but it is up to the son to decide how he must use what his father left him. Whether it's a great thing or a bad thing, the son must make a decision in his heart, soul and spirit on where it will take him for the rest of his life.

The great things that a father can leave to his children is the inheritance of his legacy, honor, faith, fortune and blessings from God. On the other hand, the bad things that a father can leave his children is his absence, influence of negative behavior, dishonor, his own baggage, debt, emotional deprivation and broken spirits. These are some examples of what children can inherit from their fathers. I know that there's more.

From this perspective, let's examine how it affects the heart, mind, soul and spirit of the fatherless child becoming a man. Through his mental state of mind, this deficiency can cause him to lose his sense of self-identity and purpose in life. We generally understand that identity comes from your father and your character comes from your mother, in most instances. Boys look up to their fathers as role models, living in their culture and society. The lack of paternal presence causes lack of guidance, financial support, instruction, advice, discipline, input, security and protection that the young male will need for proper development, mental growth and proper grooming that gives him a foundation in his formative years. Without the attributes for development, the young male suffers and this can create the case of arrested development in our male youth today. He lacks the guidance of proper responsibility, proper masculinity, healthy emotional growth and many other factors, yet his desires in life and what he seeks become tarnished from, toxic promiscuity, reckless behavior, and a life of chaos, confusion, and dysfunction.

What our father, mother or grandparents may have struggled from, doesn't determine our future but it may have had an impact, shaped or influenced our perspectives and misled us to believe that we may somehow, genetically face the same struggles and birth the same seeds of baggage as they have through social conditioning and generational curses through spirituality.

My story sheds light on a society of fathers and expresses a direct and indirect message on the importance of fatherhood. Why are fathers important in the lives of their children? Especially their daughters. We have many generations of fathers who are emotionally, mentally and physically incapable of being a father to their children due to their own broken past, seeds of rooted-baggage and deficiencies from their past, their childhood and/or the lack of paternal love, guidance, instruction and/or positive role models, in which developed misguidance, fear, unforgiveness, and the distorted perception of how they see themselves through their own failures and disappointments. Some young men see the influence as a normal way of living and a normal way of being because this is all he sees and all he's ever seen.

Children need both parents in their lives. However, this doesn't mean that the child(ren) can not live healthy and functional lives later in life due to the absence of either parent but there are different effects of not having parents, and how the effects can follow a man or a woman later in life. We would never have the ability to predict the extinction of how it will affect them later. There is an important ingredient that each parent imparts into the child's life. One parent can't fill the gap for the other parent, no matter how hard they try or how well we can debate this, it's just impossible. This doesn't mean that the child will grow up to have a terrible life if he or she lacks the presence of either parent. It just means, there may be some challenges along the way when a child has lacked an important part of their development, that is crucial and essential for their adulthood, from the perspective of a man and a woman's view. We all can agree that men and women aren't alike. There's a message that only a man can convey to another man and there's a message that a woman can convey to another woman. Most importantly, there's a real-life talk that a father can share with his daughter and that's understanding the character of a man from a man's point of view.

This is my story as a fatherless daughter! As I can only express and remember the impact of being a fatherless girl since the age of seven, I have seen what a male and female child had to endure during the growth and developmental stages into their adulthood lives without the deposits of their father's presence, instruction and guidance. In my years of development, I've observed how these same father wounds have affected family members, peers, and others, in general. I have seen how this impacts young men culturally and psychologically in their development of how they perceive themselves and are strongly influenced and impacted in a male-dominated world where their manhood is guided by factors, such as society, education, culture, music, media, religion and other aspects. Unfortunately, this causes society to raise young males into men, which can pollute the young man's mental state of mind with the perception of how he should live, behave, think, and respond to others around him. It tarnishes his beliefs, morals and perspective of who he is, what he wants in life, what he values, what he envisions, his dreams, hopes, purpose of life, his ambitions, his goals, his education and career choices, his personal health, his financial plans and wealth, and what he desires in a relationship. As he matures into manhood, his mental state of mind solely reflects on how he respects women or what he should look for in a wife and his desire for marriage. Sometimes, the way he may perceive his mother, plays a major role in how he sees or respect women, in general and/or what to look for in a wife, his help-mate. The lack of fatherhood leaves the male son challenged by his manhood and his self-identity and leaves him seeking manhood from where he doesn't see positive manhood modeled around him. He's challenged by his decisions, so he's grasping on to what it feels like or what it looks like a real man should become. Many men won't admit that they need help or someone to talk to, so they suffer in silence! They suffer in pride! I believe that 99% of men, perhaps, may have not been told face to face by their father, those three words. "I love you" or "You make me proud son!" or even "You're doing well, my son!." Most men won't express themselves to even discuss the topic in general. Many men cope with these implications in silence and coping to deal with it on their own.

I'm sure that a large percentage of problems in our youth today, are the absence of their fathers. Many young men don't know what to do. They have lost their purpose in life and have lost their definition of manhood. Some have been feminized because their masculinity has been scrutinized by the loss of their identity. Many don't feel the power of self-confidence or self control and they have lost their role of being a man in society and in their home. They lost their value to live. They feel that they are not important to the world anymore. They don't have spiritual connection or affirmation of God's love, they don't know what their career path is, or they just survive without a clear plan by not creating a vision, so they move from one job to another, drink heavily from their poison of pain, or become functioning alcoholics, joining street-gangs, committing senseless murders and domestically violating their family because they have no sense of value or moral conscience. When I speak in terms of "they", these are the groups of men who are hurting inside but are afraid to seek help or are numb to know what help really looks like or maybe their pride of seeking help portrays as being weak. I'm speaking for the man that has no vision and no sense of authority, so he doesn't feel respected and he doesn't respect himself because of the loss of his manhood, the loss of hope in which is where his true identity becomes broken. This category of men are struggling struggling with his purpose and his place in society. He doesn't know what it is to be a man. He doesn't know what it means to have authority. He hasn't seen authority from a positive male perspective. He struggles with his self-image and relies on imitating others in his surroundings. He tries to define his image. He doesn't feel the power of his masculinity and many don't feel that they are wanted by a woman by the time they leave the home or that place of shelter.

The crisis of being a fatherless son, can result in an increase of early pregnancy in young girls and imprisonment or death in our young boys. From the emotional affect, the male child becomes angered by the lack of his father's presence. He is angered by the fact he's been abandoned and rejected as a young child and young man. His anger becomes his manhood. He's angry because he has developed a lost sense of hope, self-esteem, loss of self-conviction in life of self-love. He has no self-conviction and this may explain infidelity in relationships and in marriages or why many men sleep around with many women. He's trying to fill the hole in his heart to find wholeness. In marriages, some men struggle to feel important to their wife. He may be afraid to challenge or conflict with her because the root of his own problem hasn't been fixed. The root of the man's problems results to self-concept of how he sees himself in the world around him; self-image of how he sees himself, self-confidence of having characteristics of being timid, very shy or very angry; a loss of self-worth of feeling worthy or valued to himself and to others. When men are faced with this crisis, they become confused and unable to communicate and express themselves without feeling misunderstood. This father wound of emotion can unfortunately cause violent behavior, uncontrollable emotions with a callus heart and a contrite spirit.

Men who are very angry due to frustration can develop self-hatred in which they manifest depressive behavior and they will quietly carry their anger and keep it concealed due to pride, shame or fear. Concealed fear in males can create a violent man. This could explain the increased cases of domestic violence and how the root of resentment grows in a man's soul. There are angry men living in silence! They are angry at the situation they were forced to be in. They feel trapped in a cage mentally and spiritually and feel the need to release all that has been trapped inside and when their anger is released, it can bring a life of imprisonment. Many bad decisions are made because there wasn't a positive outlet to breakthrough or to release the build up that kept them in solitude. So, the anger is deeply concealed and many men in prison are angry today. The anger is built up so strong that they blame everyone else for their own anger. What your father or your mother didn't do for you or what they did to you can become the blame for why the anger is so intense. This corresponds to resentment. Resentment is transferring your own feelings on other people or blaming others for your behavior or for the poor choices that lead to your misfortunes in life. Examples are: "I'm the way I am because my father left me or because I was abused. This results in social abandonment, meaning I blame this on why I gave up on myself and my life. Men who have social abandonment issues sometimes tend to need the approval of people and this affects them in relationships. They will tend to feel that the person doesn't make them feel like a priority or they will become inferior to how they were treated from their past. When there is an inflicted pain of emotional abandonment, that feeling can trigger the lost of not feeling motivated or determined and to better themselves, or have the need or gain the drive to attend school or earn an education, a job, or improve their current situation or believe that they can use their creativity to create the opportunity in their life. If they don't believe in themselves, they can't find their path. I've seen this growing up in teen boys growing up in school when fights would break out and I've seen this in my own personal life of peers in my neighborhood and in some cases in my own family.

When I observe these effects of the father's wounds and how young men react from feeling rejected or abandoned, I think about the story of Joseph. His brothers became jealous and angered because their father Jacob favored him over them. In the New King James version of the bible from the book of Genesis 37:3-5, "Now Israel (the father) loved Joseph more than any of his other sons, because he had been born to him in his old age; and he made an ornate, robe for him. When his brothers saw that their father loved him more than any of them, they hated him and could not speak a kind word to him." They were deeply jealous and angry. Isn't this the example in our society today, where being rejected and feeling angered due to favoritism among siblings or feeling overlooked from the father or both parents can cause emotions of anger, jealousy, malice, and family discord of conflict, which can create a multitude of problems within a household. Would you agree that this is an example of how father wounds feed toxic masculinity in men?

The seed of anger is yet built inside of him from the rejection of his father. He becomes more angered by the sufferings of his absence or the feeling of neglect when the young man's expectations aren't met or when things do not go in his favor, even when his expectations aren't favorable, the outcome can become detrimental to himself and to everyone around him.

As I speak more about the brokenness in men, men manifest this hatred through domestic application. Application, meaning he makes the decision to leave home. This domestic application brings diversity among families, separation from children, broken relationships and marriages. This may explain why divorce rates are so high, along with abandonment in families and infidelity in marriages. This can also result in why some men spread their sperm around and have babies with multiple women. This is clearly how their past can affect their present life because this is how they were reared growing up in many cases.

THE INFLUENCE OF SINGLE MOTHERS RAISING SONS

Many young men who grew up in single-parent homes and were raised by their mothers, were sometimes impacted by the pressure of being the man of the household. In some men, it caused the young man to feel the pressure to take on responsibilities that weren't designed for him, whereas he was pressured to make choices that compromised his dreams, aspirations and goals. His choices were pressured by the intense need to survive! He observed the struggles of his mother or other dependents and took on roles that he was taught in the streets of his society. In other cases, toxic behaviors become the seeds of despair when they are planted into the spirit of these men. When single mothers feel the need to overcompensate for the lack of the father's presence, the overcompensation is the mother's need to feel that she must protect and nurture for the sake of her child's lack. The lack is felt physically, emotionally and most times financially. Now the mother is impacted in these cases. It's clearly a domino affect. We as women are affected in many roles we become, whether we are the man's companion, wife, daughter or mother. We are impacted by men in many ways we can't imagine.

Some mothers unconsciously and consciously overly pampers the male child, where she feels the obligation to fill in the gaps from where the father left behind. This call of action in her spirit can bring a sense of helplessness, sadness, disappointment, shame, guilt and fear because she sees how it affects her son in many areas of his life. Unfortunately, the mother can feel a sense of hopelessness because she can't be the father and the mother too but in her eyes, she believes that she has earned the rights of the responsibility because of the pity and sorrow for her fatherless son, she may overcompensate by overly-pampering and spoiling the young man. She may not be aware that this can create an expectation in him to feel a sense of entitlement or temperamental issues that could develop characteristics and traits of a narcissist. She is not aware that this could do more harm than help her child. This is not to say that all men who are overly-pampered by their single-parents will turn out to become narcissist or become a bad person but overdoing anything has the potential of becoming dangerous!

A narcissistic personality disorder is the behavior that involves a pattern of being self-centered, arrogant thinking, a lack of empathy and consideration for other people, and an excessive need to be admired by others. This is the act of being superior over everyone else. The personalities and behaviors mimics someone that is often demanding, bossy, arrogant, cocky, manipulative and very selfish. As this behavior is seen in men and women, we are speaking in terms of males. A narcissist man may have difficulty respecting women and expecting women in relationships to treat him as his mother raised him and that is by being entitled to being overly-pampered as he was raised. Once again, it's the disposition of the male's past that may have caused him to behave in this manner. Some call these men, "Momma Boys" or call them "Superior-minded". He lacks having the real model of becoming a man because he has been overly pampered by his mother's treatment towards him. He is

116

considered a "grown boy" because he resembles the appearance of a man and engages in manly activities but he thinks and behaves as a child because he has not matured in taking accountability of the responsibilities of those activities or choices he has made. The way that he has been treated is the treatment he expects from others around him, especially in relationships. In the movie film 'Baby Boy '(2001), is a story based on an African American young man, played by actor Tyrese Gibson, who struggles with life and the responsibilities of a grown man who is not mentally ready to face the challenges and commitments of life through through poor choices in toxic relationships with women, fathering children by different women and trying to cope with of what it is to be a man in the hood of the street-life. He's a dependent on his mother and his baby momma for his needs and expectations while living at home with his mother and experiencing the conflict of demanding his territory of being the man of the house when his mother's live-in boyfriend becomes the man of her house. This affects the young man's sense of pride and manhood. It depicts the young man's aggravation, frustration and anger as he becomes stuck in a society of a vicious cycle. This would be the example of a "grown boy's" mentality who can't see his way out of his own crisis. When it comes to living a life where you feel stuck by the cycles of crisis. You become a product of your past. You become angry because you can't understand how your choices and decisions have caused failure and you become powerless and incompetent towards improving your life.

Do not misunderstand this point of view I express, I do not judge neither do I criticize single mothers for raising their sons in this manner because many are raising their son(s) in fear and in love but unfortunately, they aren't always psychologically aware of the poor and negative outcome in raising and over-saturating their son's desires by the cares and tangible things of this life, by allowing them to receive EVERYTHING in life and not having to teach them the importance of earning it, in which causes the misunderstanding and misguidance, yet not allowing them to understand the value of a dollar and not making them accountable or responsible to learn the necessity of taking the initiative behavior and accepting the reality, that life does not owe you one red cent. Not one!

These are life experiences that don't chastise the mother but it gives us an open perspective and understanding on how many single women who are raising sons at their best and to their best knowledge are yet learning, growing in strength and faith in the midst of their own personal struggles and lacks. I highly applaud them for taking this challenging role in the midst of lacking the help they need. Whether spiritual, emotional, mental or financial, many times, our mothers have no other choice when support or resources are not present in families or in our communities. Our communities can bring support to this crisis in our young males by taking them off the dangerous streets of crime and the unsafe streets of being targets, whether racial profiling or peer pressured into gangs for survival or the need for acceptance. I applaud single mothers and single fathers who are showing their sons positive alternatives of life and how making good choices can be the outcome of making better decisions down the road. Positive male figures that bring a call-to-action can allow the fatherless son to create a vision for positive thinking and to teach our sons about proper etiquette and direction on what is being a "responsible and mature" man. A call-to-action is needed for positive male figures to help many young males who lack their father's presence by becoming a better person than what the dangerous streets will teach them and/or how the streets can misguide them.

When we think about our parents, some of us are only reminded by the love, guidance and support we received from our parents even through their own shortcomings, faults, struggles and failures. On the other hand, it is unfortunate that others are only reminded by not being or feeling loved due to abandonment, neglect, and mistreatment, even in their own parent's shortcomings of life, their faults, struggles and failures. Our perspectives are shaped on how our family upbringing, social environment, religious beliefs or traditions, and influences gives us all individual opinions of how we perceive things and we see ourselves. We all have different views. We all have different pasts and there's only one direction we must take and that is to move forward if we want to see change as parents. Moving forward is the positive action to equip our sons and our daughters for a better future. We must accept that regardless of the choices that our sons and daughter make, we know that we have done our best as parents.

Parents didn't go through special training or courses to become parents! Parenting our children can be difficult if we, ourselves didn't receive discipline, proper training and guidance and/or didn't observe or inherit positive modeled behavior or receive the love, support and nurturing that was needed for our own development. Your mother and father may have not been the best at raising you because, maybe they didn't have the example they needed growing up or received what they had lacked in their childhood development. It becomes a cyclical broken family structure from generation to generation where broken fathers and broken mothers of their past become broken parents to raise children who become broken souls who inherited the seeds of brokenness, in which individually impacts and affects society as a whole. Regardless of how we see our parents, in obedience, we must still honor our fathers and mothers as it is written in the word of God, "Honor thy father and thy mother: that thy days may be long upon the land which the Lord thy God give thee." Exodus 20:12

As children, we see our parents as our providers, protectors, problem-solvers and as our tour guides of life, but when we don't receive the love, discipline, support and guidance we need as children, we aren't able to present the positive results that society expects us to possess because society doesn't see what goes on behind closed doors in our personal lives, in our environment and in our minds.

On the other hand, there are many mothers who are women of strength and honor and are not plagued by the seed of fear, grief, shame and guilt of overcompensating the needs and desires for their child(ren). They are not overshadowing the child with gifts and or spoiling their sons rotten due to the lack of their fathers absence because in the end results and consequences, they understand that they cannot be both of the parents

Great queens are women of strength and honor and are not filled by the seed of fear, grief, shame and guilt that their child's father left behind. They are not filled with the obligation of guilt or pity to overcompensate by overshadowing or spoiling their sons physical and mental desires due to the lack of their fathers absence.

From the biblical perspective in the book of Proverbs 31:8-9, this book speaks briefly on a mother who raised her son who soon became a king. His name was King Lemuel. The book never mentioned that the king had a father but spoke gracefully and profoundly on how a mother's wisdom of good advice, counsel and instruction created a man to become a great king. She taught and warned him not to fall for immoral behavior, not to chase and lust after women because if you do, they will swallow your strength. She warns her son about the dangers of drinking alcohol, (Proverbs 31:4-7), "A drunken king is never a good king. A ruler who craves beer and wine will pervert justice and act lawlessly". In addition, King Lemuel's mother also instructs her son about the necessity of true justice. "Speak up for those who cannot speak for themselves, for the rights of all who are destitute. Speak up and judge fairly; defend the rights of the poor and needy" (Proverbs 31:8-9).

When studying this brief story from the book of Proverbs, it reminded me of single mothers who have raised sons in the midst of the fathers absence, who later became great leaders in our society and great husbands and fathers, in the midst of their mother's own struggles, challenges, and poverty-restricted conditions and environments. But in the face of destitute and gloom, there are many sons who were raised by mothers of strength and in the face of their grief on behalf of their sons lacks, they managed to do the best they could with little they had but encouraged their sons through consistent and repetitive discipline, faith and prayer. Their faith in God and strength to not blame themselves for their son's absent father, but to instill responsibilities, values, morals, and to gain the mobility of being supportive in their sons lives through academics, sports, after-school curriculum and allowing them to think outside of their environment, outside of the box of the limitations they naturally see and to explore that all things are possible to those who believe, even in the most unimaginable situations or circumstances! Single mothers as well as mothers in general must instill the true factor of creating that "belief" system. They must speak the life of affirmation into their sons and daughters lives to allow them to gain the spiritual faith and a spiritual perspective that will give them the opening portal to God's divine grace, mercy and His purpose into their lives. Women are queens before and after they have been broken-hearted, broken-spirited, and with heavy hearts and restless minds. They must act as a queen to raise a king. Kings only strive when great queens are in position and King Lemuel mother's story gives us hope and divine empowerment that our sons can become great fathers to their sons and daughters in the midst of their own father wounds of being absent from their lives.

This also helps us to understand that in life we must roll with the punches and become and do the best we can with what we have in our possession and that is our love and support, determination, our strengths and abilities, and more importantly, our faith to not allow our past to dictate our future. Our past must remain in our past! Our past is just a reference to remind us of the lessons we have learned in life. Whatever we may have lacked from our past, whether it was companionship and love, honesty and faithfulness, our parent's presence, the guidance and support we needed, those needs and desires we never gained, the hurt and the pain that we are struggling to heal from, does not nor should it destroy our vision, goals, dreams, ambitions and our strive to thrive in our present moment and our future. There is hope at the end of the tunnel and the gift of life is our present moment! Don't beat up on yourself. I had to learn to find the beauty in myself today and stop living from my past and enjoy my present day! Rough times will come our way but joy helps us to always see the brighter side of everything.

Section 2

Better Days Are Coming

CHAPTER 4 - THE INTENSIVE CARE UNIT OF GOD -

LETTING GO AND LETTING GOD

It had been hard to let go of the past that scarred me. The past of not allowing me to emotionally and mentally heal due to holding on to the hurt and pain. I was becoming my own enemy from not letting go. I had too much pride to talk about it and I felt that I needed to own my pain by keeping those who had hurt me the blame. I became a victim of my past and I did not know how to let go, although I really desired to let go of my past. My past became who I was and it was because I had buried so much, so deeply within the reservoir of my soul. I couldn't admit that I needed help because I couldn't feel the pain anymore. I buried it so deeply because I didn't want to feel the pain ever again. It became numb. I became desensitized, so in my mind I thought I had let go of it all. I thought that I was healed because I had survived by moving forward with life. Little did I know, my past was still living in me because it was buried inside of me and now it was time for the root of the past to be dug up. It was time for me to become aware that I needed to be healed. It was time to accept and to admit that I had not been healed from the past. In order to do that it made me face the things that I didn't want to accept. Remember our past is our reference to a lesson! A lesson of learning what we need to heal from is the reference of our past but we shouldn't reside there. As I reflect during my late teens, I carried heavy bags in my soul and spirit that weighed me down. It took a toll on me. These were bags of fear, anxiety and abandonment that I developed as a child, in which developed more bags of low self-esteem, insecurities and rejection. My experience in middle and high school were not enjoyable years because I had become a functioning depressant filled with distrust, wounded by betrayal, angered with resentment and unforgiving and pessimistic with sadness and suicidal thoughts. These were supposed to have been my best moments of life and I felt robbed of the best times of my life.

Now let me take you further in time, years later after I graduated from high school and matured into a young woman, I struggled through several failed relationships and regrets of wasting my time through the disappointments.

It was a rainy weekend and as I laid in bed, I thought about all the times I had invested in relationships in hopes for real love, yet an experience that had to be lived, in order to help me face my own brokenness. I laid back in bed to listen to the calming sounds of the rain and to feel the teardrops roll down from my face. My heart hadn't healed but I was ready to face a new chapter in my life. My body felt cold as I wrapped myself in the blankets to keep my body warm and once again my soul felt that void from depression. This feeling was all so familiar. At this time in my early twenties, this felt like the rehearsal of pain. Those feelings of rejection and emotional abandonment from the past were memories of pain but this time, I was no longer a child but facing the child inside of me that still never healed. I couldn't release the bags of my past. I was spiritually tormented as a child and still haunted by my past. Twisting and turning in bed, unable to fall asleep, I was in deep thought, thinking about the life behind me and the future in front of me. I was in deep fear as my limped body laid in bed, feeling weak and debilitated, I was unable to speak. My heart questioned why would someone so close to me, who portrayed love so real, so genuine, and knowingly knew how pure, loyal and genuine my love for them, deliberately made me feel like trash, made me second guess my self-worth, my values of life and my identity of purpose.

I thought I was improving in life because I was still alive and breathing! I thought about those relentless pleas of begging for forgiveness, I thought about that one particular ex-boyfriend who still wouldn't admit to his cheating ways. His apologies for not being present at times when I couldn't find him and not having an explanation for not being present to see me receive my degree at my college graduation was enough for me. I felt that same pain of disloyalty and betrayal by his absence and his loyalty to someone else who was less deserving of the love and faith that I showed him with all the sacrifices I made and the patience of waiting. I could ha e easily dated others guys while waiting for him. It was like feeling stupid for waiting for someone who I wasn't married to! It was hard to forgive myself for being loyal to someone who didn't deserve it. I couldn't forgive myself for the decisions I had made!

It was the rehearsed rejection and pain I've always felt. Another man had emotionally and physically abandoned me. It was too difficult to accept why he had been loyal to another young lady after all that I've done for him and I didn't receive the loyalty I had deserved from him. I wasn't receiving what I had invested in this relationship. In fact, I was on the losing end and I'd come to the end where it had exhausted my spirit. My spirit to love again became heavy and resistant. I became angry and the numbness of my pain grew enormous and the best way of coping through my problems was to remain isolated again, to remain alone and away from people. I became bitter and more resentful! This pain left me secluded from desiring to be around my own family. I didn't want my family to see the bitterness inside. It wasn't that I didn't love my family, it wasn't that I didn't know how to live, although I knew that I had to survive. I had to move on through my brokenness, the embarrassment of thinking that this man would marry me, thinking how much of a fool I had been to someone I had been so loyal to, and waited patiently for while he was incarcerated for two years. I couldn't understand how he could do this to me. I wrote letters, drove miles to visit him and accepted all his phone calls. I was his support system and I thought that he would have been my support system when he was released. This pain was too familiar. I felt betrayed! There I was repeating this thoughts in my mind and those cycles of pain that I thought would be my way to escape. I wanted real love and loyalty from a man who could help me believe that a real and loving man existed, one who could help me release the emotional baggage that I suppressed. In reality, he was a broken man too. How could he treat me the way he explained his painful childhood past? He knew what abandonment felt like. I had to accept that I was attracted to who I was, a broken woman who kept living in the past and who couldn't let go.

My bitterness became my strength to give me the determination to live, although I knew that I had to survive this time. I had to move on the best way I knew how, moving on was making me bury baggage of pain during that time. Thoughts of why do I exist? And what am I good for, were questions that I would often ask myself. Being isolated and alone became my comfortable and safe place. I didn't have to face my pain from the disappointment of anyone coming through my safety zone; so isolation became safer as the years would pass. This place of isolation made me an introvert, as I felt this is a characteristic of who I am, it was peaceful for me. It kept me bound and in solitude for the sake of my strengths, my sanity from within but it didn't allow me to heal. It was my safe place and safe way to survive the fire around me. This was the best survival method for me. Yet, my heart sunk through depression, yet I had a determination to live beyond those moments of depression. I had always prayed to God throughout the moments of my despair to heal my heart and relieve me from my troubles. I would never hear from God but I always knew that God hears prayers whether he would answer them. I knew that there had to be a reason why I was still living and breathing.

In the late 90's, on a warm autumn night, it was a weekend to remember. I just got off the phone to quickly fix my hair to meet my blind date. I met this new guy through my sibling's acquaintance at the time and during this time in my life, I was very content. After coping through the disappointments and heartbreaks of past relationships that failed, I was living the single life and enjoying it for a change. I was alone but not lonely! I accepted being solitude of not having any worries of someone else's whereabouts or unanswered phone calls or trying to determine a truth from a lie. I was in a new season in my life and found a peaceful and happy place of contentment to love myself. I was beginning to enjoy peace! I didn't have any concerns for any particular person or issues. No dramas! I had been single for 3 weeks from a consecutive short and long-term relationship that felt like roller coaster rides of ups, downs, twists and turns. Of course, I was surely saddened by the way the prior relationships had ended, yet I was happy for a new chapter in my life.

I met my blind-date on a weekend. It wasn't easy persuading me to talk to another guy. I had made up my mind that I wouldn't put myself through the misery of liking someone and having high hopes in a man. I turned down so many offers to talk to guys because I really enjoyed being alone but this case was quite different. We talked on the phone for one day and he desperately desired to see me in person. It felt exciting to meet someone new and although I was very hesitant to give someone new a chance, I decided to welcome this new person into my life. I didn't know what outcome this new beginning would be, but I was comfortable with knowing that I was going to be just fine, despite whatever direction it would go. Before I left my house, I reassured a friend of the family and my mother that I was going to be fine meeting this new person for the first time. They were a bit concerned but I told them where to find me if they didn't hear back from me. It's very dangerous nowadays meeting someone you don't know, even though he was related to an acquaintance and relative. When I drove up to a particular area where there would be crowds of people, I didn't think to ask this new guy what car he was driving and it's amusing that he didn't think to ask me what car I was driving too. After coasting the area in my car, I parked to the side and I heard a voice say, "I hope you're Angel!" I looked up to find the voice and to my surprise, there he was! This guy was handsome. He was fine! His voice, very deep and distinctive and his physique was very stunning. He was very muscular and his physique reminded me of a well-groomed stallion. Once we became acquainted, we were very satisfied and excited to see one another and we drove away from the crowd to talk and to get to know one another in a private area. Our relationship grew stronger every day and we made a connection. We couldn't wait for the weekends to come because this was our time to see and to spend time with one another. I was falling for him but at the same time, I was extremely nervous. I had my walls up in fear, hoping that this relationship wouldn't turn out like my past relationships did. I remained positive! There was something different about this guy. He was very mature, a gentleman, very pleasant and respectful, generous and outspoken, and he had that sexy and cool charisma with a bit of humor all in one. At this moment, I was glad that all the past relationships didn't work out because this guy was surely worth getting to know. He was fun to be around and he made me feel secured and safe. It wasn't long before we started dating. We went out every weekend, enjoying each other's company and dining at restaurants from average to upscale. We made a great couple and as time passed, I found myself falling in love with him. I didn't think that I could open my heart again and trust anyone. I felt that I had reached a point in my life where I left the past behind. I felt like I was complete. This was that season in my life where I felt that I had moved on with my life, despite the bags I buried that left me broken, insecure, fearful, depressed, pitiful, resentful, bitterer and isolated. I felt like I had survived all that I had been through; although I had not healed from all that I had been through, our relationship was still going strong. As time passed, we experienced our ups and downs, yet we were still happy in our relationship. At that time, my then boyfriend settled into a cozy apartment in the suburbs of Illinois and I had taken a job offer nearby. It seemed ironic how things happened with timing because it was such a coincidence to work a job nearby his new residence. We spent more time with one another and after work, he would make some tasty home-cooked meals. He was a great cook. He's especially great at grilling and I enjoyed the pleasures of being spoiled by his tasty dinners and serving me meals after work and making me feel special. On many occasions, I would spend the night with him and head to work in the mornings, and some nights I would take that long ride back home to Indiana after long days at work. Our relationship took a whole new shift in the summer of 1999, we were surprised to receive the news that I was pregnant. We were having a baby! I was in denial after taking so many pregnancy tests because I couldn't believe that I was actually having a baby. The nausea, gurgitation, and sensitive smells to everything around me, made me think I had a terrible flu. It became reality after seeing the paperwork with positive results being handed to me by the nurse. This became the reality of a lifetime. The thought of becoming a mother was so exciting, yet I was so afraid and nervous. Months later would show a growing belly, weight gain and the flutters inside me would move stronger. The flutters became kicks and the kicks inside me grew harder and stronger. I was enjoying this moment of becoming a mother for the first time and I was excited that my boyfriend's feelings were mutual. This would be his second child because he had his first child from a previous relationship.

During my pregnancy, my first and second trimester was challenging, as morning sickness felt like I had the flu every day. It took a toll on my body and I would drag myself to work and hope to get through each passing day. My heart was full of joy, yet my body was struggling with the changes. At this time of my life, I still didn't have a relationship with my father. We would talk in passing and that was if we were to bump into one another and/or when I would visit my grandmother, on my father's side. However, we never developed a relationship. I reflected on how many times I had tried relentlessly to communicate with my father but I felt his rejection towards me as his behavior seemed nonchalant. When we had brief moments of conversations, it felt like he wasn't listening and he would jump to a new conversation that would completely dismiss what I was trying to discuss. There always seemed to be a disconnect between us and he seemed mostly interested in his clothes, cars and his highly paid job. These were his prized possessions. At this time of my life, I felt like I didn't need him as much as I needed him as a little girl and teenager blossoming into a young woman. I never understood my father's ways until latter years would bring me closure to unanswered questions. Life has a way of putting us into circumstances we aren't prepared for and yet God has His way of showing his love and how real He is when he allow us to see the outcome of those circumstances. Revelations of life have a way of filling in the missing pieces to a puzzle. The puzzles are the blueprint of our lives.

On a rainy, icy and slushy dark road, in December of 1999, I was driving home from work. I worked as a legal specialist for a bank at this time. This particular night I worked several hours over to earn some overtime pay, and as I was driving on this dark road, I immediately was struck by a vehicle from the rear of my car. The impact was so powerful, I lost control of my car and crashed into a semi-truck where I blacked out! I was 6 months pregnant at this time and when I finally woke up out of my unconscious state, I was looking up at doctors at a hospital in the trauma intensive care unit. The first thing that came to my mind was my baby! "Is my baby okay?" I asked the nurse standing over me. She said your baby's heartbeat is fine and then she said please rest. Minutes later, my boyfriend came to my bedside, the look of torment and distraught was all over his face, he called my name and asked if I was okay. I was glad to see him and he was relieved that me and our unborn child were okay. Over several months, I was under doctor's care and I had to stay bedridden until the baby was born. This was a setback for me to struggle with the trauma from the accident, lose my vehicle from being totaled by the insurance company, and get fired from my job because they didn't agree with my doctor's orders to not return to work. I'll never forget the day I told my doctor about how unfair my job was and how they gave me a warning, despite me being 6 months pregnant and unable to work, they denied my doctor's orders. My doctor said, "What's more important, your job or your baby?' "Of course my baby was more important to me than my job. As time always reveals, years later, the company ended up closing its doors for good. I stayed bedridden for months until it was time to deliver my baby. She came very early before her due date and I was very nervous and beyond excited to take on a new role as a mother. She was our little beautiful preemie. She was only 4 lbs and 15 oz. Our family was excited to welcome our new baby and I was overjoyed that she was healthy, strong and survived the accident months

132

prior. Despite all the setbacks, seeing this bundle of joy was our comeback. A comeback of life. As I looked into my baby's eyes, I was so proud and she was our blessing from God. She had to remain in the hospital for a couple of weeks due to mild medical care but when we brought her home to our apartment we shared together, it made home much sweeter.

The following month in April of 2000, the blind-date I had met over the phone, who was the mature gentleman, spontaneous and respectful, generous and outspoken, sexy and cool, humorous and charismatic guy would later become my husband. We had a small marriage ceremony with close family and friends.

It was a new season filled with joy and celebration! My days of being single transformed into being a new wife and a new mother. It all happened so fast! My heart was overjoyed and full of love and in my mind, I had survived my past. This felt monumental for me because I was finally enjoying my present life! It was a dream come true. Throughout the course of our marriage, it was an adjustment taking on new responsibilities of being a wife and a mother, however it was the best and is the best feeling in life. It's an experience like no other and I desired to have more children but the many attempts had failed me. I had several miscarriages and one of the miscarriages were life threatening.

I can remember in the year of 2003, getting ready for work one morning as usual, while my 3 year old daughter was up watching TV and eating breakfast, I had just finished showering and suddenly I became weak, fell to the floor and screamed for help. My 3 year old ran to the room and screamed, "Mommy!" She had always been very mature for her age. She immediately dialed the phone to call for help. I was thankful that we had taught her to dial on the phone in case there were any emergencies. We provided her with numbers to call. She had always been a quick learner. This was an unforgettable moment! As I laid on the floor, I could hear her voice and the sounds from the TV started to fade away. It was like I was drifting away very slowly, minute by minute. During this experience I had, I heard a tick, tock sound and soon my daughter's voice would no longer seem near, her voice would echo and I became unconscious soon after. It was like a deep coma-like sleep. Next, I would find myself seeing a blurred face where I could hear, "Ma'am can you hear me?" This person's voice seemed muffled. It was paramedics. Somehow, they were able to gain access inside the house, rushed my body to resuscitate me. It was a strange feeling of not being able to respond to them and move my body but I could hear them talk to me. I felt trapped inside my own body. Moments later, I could hear the familiar voices of a few family members coming into the house. They waited while the ambulance prepared to lift my body into the stretcher and place me inside the vehicle. One of my relatives rode with me as I was rushed to the nearest hospital. The doctors ran several tests as quickly as possible. They used certain methods to stabilize my conscience but I kept passing out. They couldn't figure out why my blood pressure dropped significantly and my vitals were low and unstable. By the time more family members showed up at the hospital, my husband rushed in. He had received an emergency call from his job to come to the hospital. He was very worried, upset and shocked by all that had happened. The doctors spoke to my family and said we must do an immediate surgery! They stated that if I would have been 30 minutes late on arrival, I would have died. My appearance, skin color had immediately taken a form of death, it was frightening to my family to see me this way and as I laid in bed, limp and feeling lifeless, everything was in slow motion and my sight became very dim. I was closer to death than I've ever been. I couldn't see everyone as clear. Some of the family members prayed over me. They were praying that God heal me and restore my life. Moments later, I was taken into surgery. It went well! I made it through the surgery. I was told that I had an ectopic pregnancy and sepsis had developed into my body and this would explain why I had minutes to live before the sepsis had settled into my bloodstream. I felt sad that I had lost another baby. I felt like a failure once again but I kept telling myself, this was beyond my control. I wondered, what did I do to experience this ordeal? I didn't even know that I was pregnant. The baby had developed in my fallopian tubes and sepsis had settled into my bloodstream. This was such a traumatic moment for me and when I reflect on this moment of my life, I'm forever thankful how God's hands were on my life. He allowed me to live. My 3 year old daughter was horrified. She didn't understand what was going on but she knew that I was in trouble. Later, I was told that she wouldn't leave the house. She was very adamant about not leaving, so the family allowed her to stay under their care. This was a traumatic experience for all of us, but most of all it was an experience that would leave me thanking God for saving my life and thankful that my 3 year took the necessary steps to help save my life by calling for help. It was God's savings grace. Situations like this most times turn out with unfortunate results. God's hand was surely on my life because so many women have experienced ectopic pregnancies and many have died from this near fatal incident. I was blessed to be in the rare surviving percentage. At this time of my life, it had become a challenge to get pregnant again and I felt my chances of having a baby was slim but the experiences I had endured was God grabbing my attention, it was a bittersweet feeling as I went through motions of depression, feeling broken, worried, and losing the faith. As a member of the church I had attended during this time, I would humbly receive God's message, love, and prayers over my life, I started to have a new perspective of life and in the experiences that came with being a wife and a mother, I needed all the prayers I could get. The experiences of life are those that are unforeseen, and those situations that we have not prepared for, but yet are those experiences that allow us to grow, develop and mature for the sake of ourselves and for the sake of our family. Prayers change things and having faith in God and trusting God, despite your circumstances, you must remove the stress and worry to receive what God has in store for you. I didn't know what road was ahead of me but I knew that God was allowing me to know that he was ever-present even when I wasn't seeking him like I should have. Another breaking moment in my life came when God blessed us with another addition to our family. I gave birth to another beautiful daughter in 2006 and although I endured many complications to have her, God's hands were still on my life. Between that six year gap of having my first child and having my last child, we tried to have children and feelings of sadness, depression and shame filled my heart and soul with every miscarriage I suffered. It was a test of my faith and a test of my perseverance of prayer. My prayers became persistent although the waiting period was challenging. The doctors knew that the complications would make me high risk for having babies, but I knew that God would give me the desires of my heart, if I just believe! I had no choice! I knew that God's power is real. He's the same, yesterday, today and forever more. God is always faithful to us. His love for us never changes. Through the tests and trials, God allowed me to endure the pain of what I had been through and he allowed me to see his power and miraculous works to know that there is power in prayer and in faith.

Being a mother to my two daughters was very rewarding beyond the burdens and worries we must go through as mothers to ensure that our children have everything they need and that they do not lack. Being a mother also gave me a new purpose to live. It gave me a new perspective of life. It also gave me the willpower to discover my strengths even in my unforeseen and suppressed feelings of brokenness. I was yet not healed from my past wounds and the joy and love of giving birth to my babies helped aid my past wounds, although it did not heal my past wounds.

Once again, in my mind, I believed that I had moved on in my life, I had survived the test of times. My baggage of emotional pain was invisible, it was buried beneath my spirit, soul and mind. I was too overjoyed to feel it and I was determined not to face anything that I believed had disappeared. I ignored my past because I wanted to live in that present. I was in a new place in my mind, body and spirit. I felt that I had overcome my brokenness and I was grateful for my new family. It was not being that single woman but it was now me, my husband and our children. We were a family and it was what I had desired to have as a child where the mother and father would be in position and presently active with their children. I would often reflect on my childhood years and pray to God, "Lord, allow my children to always have their father by their side and always in their lives because I didn't have mine". This prayer was important to me. I'm raising young girls and I do not want them to have to experience any of my emotional abandonment, rejection or the feeling of not being loved by their dad. I want them to have what I didn't receive and have. I prayed to God to strengthen my marriage and to keep our family, during the good and rough times of our lives. In marriages, there are those bad times too. There's not one marriage that is perfect. I don't believe in the 50/50 rule of marriage where each partner gives 50/50. If one partner can only bring 20% and the other partner can bring the 80% at a particular season in that marriage, so be it. It goes either way.

In the same aspect, if one partner can bring the entire 100 percent when the other partner can't bring anything, due to whatever reason or many unforeseen reasons, either health issues of physical, emotional or mental disabilities or through a tough financial period, you must have each other's back and stand in the gap to carry the weight. You must be in it for the long haul. This is love! Marriage is based on the foundation of love. It's a partnership of love and unity. Seasons weren't created to remain forever. Seasons change and people change in marriage! The challenges in the marriage is weathering the storms. Marriage makes me think about the song I've always enjoyed listening to, "Can You Stand The Rain" by R&B group, New Edition.

Marriage is a teamwork effort and there are many seasons in a marriage. Marriage is a ministry and it is divinely designed for the two unique people who God has put together to love, help support, encourage and bring loyalty to that unity. When one of the partner's give their life to God, their unequally yoked partner, is their first ministry. This is why marriage is a ministry because it is our ministry to pray without ceasing and having faith that God will bring our partner closer to Him. Him refers to our Lord and Savior, Christ Jesus! Whether, you are equally yoked or whether you are not equally yoked, meaning (you and your spouse are on the same spiritual level of faith). It's what you invest into your marriage. Marriage is work, yet rewarding, considerate and selfless of your partner's needs. The most important factor that many should learn and be reminded of, is knowing that marriage doesn't heal you from your broken past, it doesn't complete you, it doesn't fill the void you have lacked from your childhood and it doesn't fill your voids from broken relationships you have endured. It surely doesn't validate the fact that you don't need help because although marriage is an important part of being married to the one you love, it doesn't give you life and it doesn't mean that you were created just to marry. You must be complete in your spirit, mind, body and soul before joining your life with someone else. It is not healthy going into a marriage full of baggage! Bags of brokenness that you may have buried in your soul and spirit for many years, these bags are bags of bondage, bags of shackles that have depressed you and when baggage is buried, it will soon cause you to suppress negative behavior on people around you, people who love you and people who want to help and bless you, especially when you have a spouse that didn't create those bags in the first place. Many tend to suppress negative behavior in their marriage. These broken hearts need mending! My broken heart needed mending! I was that broken woman who refused to let my guards down. I mentally and emotionally was seeking help quietly! I desired to be complete inside and I desired for a man to complete me! My heart lacked love and I felt that the love of my life filled that void.

Many who have never been married, need to always keep in mind that you must keep "dating" a constant part of your marriage and you need God to heal, transform you, renew your mind and to restore you back to your original settings. The original settings, which is the person you were before life's circumstances broke you down and created scars. Stop looking for marriage to fulfill your voids and needs. Marriage wasn't designed only for that, Marriage is an assignment!

I went into my marriage with a broken soul. The child inside of me never healed! The success of a great relationship and the reward and blessings of motherhood led me to believe that I was healed, restored in my mind, healed in my heart, body and my soul. I hadn't healed or been delivered from my childhood past because I had buried my pain for so many years where I couldn't feel the pain anymore. I felt since I couldn't feel my brokenness, I had survived my past. I was desensitized and numb by the fact that I had normalized my pain. I was too stubborn and too prideful to accept pain as a weakness! I could not admit that I needed healing. My internalized wounds became a part of my life for years and brought invisible baggage into my new season of my life. This took a toll on my marriage and on my children.

MY SOUL, MIND AND SPIRIT UNDER CONSTRUCTION

On a sunny day, where temperatures were in the mid 80's, as I walked through the warm sand in my bare feet, I walked alone and watched my daughters enjoy the waves of the water rushing back and forth. Their laughs and screams were sounds of joy that gave me a sense of comfort. During this time, it was a weekend and we rarely took trips to the beach although many years before my youngest was born, we used to live a mile away where we could walk to the beach from our home. I could count on one hand how many times we took visits. It was totally different as a child. In my youthful days, I would go to the beach many times and I couldn't count how many times that was, but I used to enjoy playing in the sand and enjoyed the sounds of the waves, the birds and all of God's precious creations. Memories came back and I realized that the beach had always been one of my most peaceful environments. It had always been tranquil for me. I could remember on my worst days, taking a short ride to the beach and sitting there to get my thoughts in order. It's a place where peace and tranquility has always been a special place and this time it was a special experience that surrounded me for that moment. It has always been a place to calm my spirit. As the girls played and enjoyed getting wet where they would barely allow the water to reach as high as their waist, I decided to lay the towel on the warm sand and I sat there for a while gazing into the beautiful blue sky. There weren't very many people out that day and I stared into the horizon and enjoyed the beautiful and pleasant sight of the lake and staring far in view as if I was marveling at a painted mural of downtown Chicago. It was refreshing and it was what I needed at this moment. I wanted to enjoy this day to the fullest because I knew that Monday at work was right around the corner and I wanted to get away from that thought as far away as I could, so I sat there and just relaxed and gazed into the hot sun in deep thought. As I sat there, I said a prayer. No one could hear me. This was a prayer to God in my mind. I remember praying to God to give me peace in my heart, to allow me to feel his love and to allow me to stop all of the self-infliction of worrying about life, all the stressors and anxieties that I was keeping and holding in silence. One of the worst parts I hated about myself was the problem of worrying about things that never ended up happening. I would worry about everything! I would worry about what tomorrow would bring. I would worry so much where some of my closer family members would even comment and say, "Girl, why do you worry so much?" I worried about the fact that it felt like I was worrying myself to death. I really never understood why. It was always something I dealt with as early in life as I could remember. As much as I attended church and as much as I would pray, I didn't understand why worrying would come back not long after a good prayer with God. I would pray to God and yet try to fix the problem on my own. It was like I had to find the answers and I just had to figure it out. It was like believing I had faith when I really didn't. I hadn't allowed God to take full control of my life because I had to be in control. It was like I had to know how God was going to fix my problems. I had over-analyzed how God would work it out, so the peace of God was not with me because God couldn't do the work for me because I couldn't allow him to be in control. This was a spirit of double-minded which is the struggle of believing and doubting during my prayers.

That warm sunny day sitting there praying was a moment where I realized that I had made myself unhappy because I worried too much. It would be those moments at the beach where I needed that type of environment to clear my thoughts, to clear my mind and just think about the present moment of life and how the sounds of peace, the feelings of peace and the sights of peace were all around me. The physical effects of peace on the beach is how I wanted to feel on the inside all the time. I would often look over to watch the girls and to ensure that they were well and safe. They were in plain view and as a mother I always kept my eyes on them no matter where I was. That was the overprotective part of me. Yet, gazing into the air, I thought about my life and thankful to God to experience life and to breath the fresh air for a moment, to take a deep breath, inhaling and exhaling and just absorbing it all in. The fresh aroma of the waters and the warm wind was perfect, it was not too windy. It was just right. The temperature, the atmosphere and that quiet time made this moment easy like a Sunday morning. It just couldn't get any better than this. No matter how beautiful and perfect this day felt, I had desired to feel this way all the time, every day. It wasn't like home-life wasn't good. I had a peaceful home. I was blessed with a loving husband and beautiful daughters. I attended a church and I loved God but something deep down on the inside just wasn't quite right within me. It just wasn't clear to me why I couldn't find the fulfillment of love, joy and peace within myself. Something was missing! I just couldn't seem to understand it. Something was wrong! It was hard to admit it.

In my late thirties, I became well adjusted to the life of being a married woman and a loving mother. It was a life I had dreamed, yet I would still find myself suffering in the silence of depression. Even on my best days, that feeling of depression would come over me. I couldn't understand why I had a feeling of sadness that wouldn't allow me to be great. It was that baggage that had been buried for years. It was still there. It was like a reminder that wouldn't allow me to ignore it. I was depressed because I had suppressed so much pain of not letting go of my past. I was always one for reminiscing about my past. I actually thought about my past a lot. I thought about what I had experienced and tried to make sense as to why I was quietly suffering. As eager as I tried to ignore it, there would be something or someone's that brought it back to my mind. Music from the past always recalled memories of my past. It was my own pain to face but yet I was still suffering from the days of my young adulthood, teenage years and the days of my childhood. I couldn't let go! I was flawed in different areas of my character, yet I always kept a smile on my face from my external appearance and treated people kindly. However, I wouldn't allow anyone to see beyond my smile. They say smiling faces tell lies! I was telling lies with the most beautiful smile as I was always told my smiles were beautiful. My smiles were my best mask! I was broken and needed to cover up my pain with my smiles. This was a true reality that I needed to be made whole internally. Emotionally, I was bleeding on the inside, yet my coping mechanisms were to convert the pain into energy and use the energy as fuel to motivate me to become a stronger woman in this predatory world, and to heal myself by meeting goals and fulfilling accomplishments which would measure up to my success. Yet, I was running on fuel that was burning gas, toxins and fumes. I had to find a way to love myself through the trash and chaos I've endured. I looked at earthly success for my healing and deliverance. Yet, all of my accomplishments and goals in life never filled the void in my soul. Self-accomplishments and self-righteousness was not going to heal me. They were all counterfeit affections. None of these affections could fill my pain until I really had that one encounter from God. In fact, There had been many encounters from God but I was too deep in my own mess and misery to realize Him or to even know Him. If I really knew Him, the true and living God, I wouldn't be feeling those moments of depression, stress and fear, especially those moments when doubt and wiry would seep in. I was raised and grew up in a semi-Christian environment and I knew about the Father, the Son of God and the Holy Spirit, and I knew that giving our lives to God is accepting Jesus as our personal Lord and Savior. It would be a personal experience for me. There could be no other way! You can teach me about God until your lips turned blue but I had to get this for myself! I had to experience a true commitment with my heart. I couldn't have trust in God one day and be in unbelief the next. God had to show me how real He was in my life.

So it took a leap of faith but in small increments in my life to allow God to come into my heart. These encounters from God came through tough situations that forced me to go to God in prayer because it was my last resort to live and I really didn't get to know Him for myself until God allowed me to see how real He was in my life. I made something simple become so complicated and time after time, God was merciful and patient with me. I would pray and later watch how God intervened in situations that seemed unexplainable. Things were so mysterious! Those encounters from God were those moments that God had to remind me that his love is never changing. I would then feel that conviction to know that God was knocking at my door waiting for me to open it. He was now waiting for me. He had already shown me what a merciful and faithful and absolute loving God He is and it was through all my hardship and pain and His spirit that kept drawing closer to me to open my heart to Him and to surrender with a humble heart and in peace.

During these times when God was calling me, I was battling with commitment of faith. I wasn't an alcoholic but there were a few times I would take a few glasses of wine and maybe a few cocktails to help clear my thoughts. Although, I was battling these vices in my life, I felt it was okay because I wasn't drinking hard liquor and I wasn't drinking heavy. Yet, I was a functioning depressant where in those lonely moments, my spirit was drowning me into desiring my life to end.

My spirit desired to commit to God but my flesh was comfortable with the lifestyle of not letting go of those false medications to soothe my inner pain. I wasn't fully ready to commit and I knew that I was not the one to play with God. You cannot play with God. I feared him too much! I wasn't going to live a hypocritical life as the imperfect person I was. I was either going to live for God or live for the world. I had to give my all to one or the other. I had to make a permanent choice! The Bible states, "Watch and pray so that you will not fall into temptation. The spirit is willing but the flesh is weak." Matthews 26:40 KJV

Indeed, my flesh was weak! Although I was full of the baggage that kept me bound, my spirit needed and desired to be made whole. Knowing what was right but not responding to God's call, made me feel like I was trapped with being double-minded all the time because I knew what was right but my motives to do right couldn't make me strong enough to make that commitment to God.

I knew that I had to give up the baggage in my life in order to gain peace, love, hope and faith. I really didn't know how to give up these things. It felt like they were a part of me. I felt like this was who I was and how could that be changed. How could I be changed? How could I be healed if I didn't know how or if I didn't believe that I could?

I would often ask God why am I so broken in my spirit when someone would probably desire to live in my shoes. I have a loving family, a beautiful home, luxury cars, decent paying jobs, my needs are being met and most of my desires in prayer are being answered. Why or how could someone like me become so broken when God has been nothing but good to me? I'm sure many people would ask the same question. This might help to explain why some celebrities or famous people around the world, have the fame, the money to buy anything in the world they desire, beautiful mansions, the stardom, the special perks and many favors, the freedom and pleasure to travel across the world, to meet and to engage with famous people, enjoy the best of fine dining, to win awards and to be called the greatest in their talents or gifts but at the end of the day, they are personally and privately battling with their own demons, those things that money can't fix. Money couldn't buy them their peace and joy although it bought them what they idolized. They don't find peace within their soul because they are battling the demons inside that no one will ever know but them and God. Many become strung out on substance abuse, alcohol, sex or whatever counterfeit affection and the vices of sin that can sooth them temporarily. As I've said in the previous chapters, you have to start at the root in order to fix the problem and most of the problems come from something of the past. Those spirits that come to haunt us from our past traumas, the scars and bruises of disappointments, the pain, or the sacrifices that got us there to the plateau or the feeling of having to sell our soul due to deception, yet to find ourselves in more agony or feeling like a dead-man walking, even while achieving success. Success can become the deception because it will have you thinking, you have achieved it all! Unfortunately, when you hear about people who have succumbed to their final end, either by drug overdoses, suicides, domestic abuse, homicides, alcohol poisoning or of a sudden unknown or mysterious death. How do we answer those questions of why did it happen and when did it all start?

When we hear about it so often in the public eye and when I think about my life, I must face the fact that it started at a very young age for me. Most times, it starts at a very young age in most of us where those issues that broke our spirits and made us feel like we had lost our souls, keeps us trying to find a solution like a dog that chases his tail. I really believe that in these dark moments, you really want the help you need but you become in denial of believing that help isn't available or even possible for you! Although I didn't want to relive the past for the process of healing, I had to accept reality that that's where it started for me. You have to face the dark area of the past in order to fix the dark area to uncover the mask. When facing the area that needs to be healed, we must feel those emotions and be honest with ourselves. Be honest that we are hurting. Be honest that we have been greatly disappointed and being honest with what we feel is the only way we can start the process of healing. You have to feel the pain in order to heal. This is the beginning of reconstruction! Second, you must admit that you have a problem in order to receive healing. You really have to desire it! It started with me as that little girl who was filled with fear of the unknown physically, mentally, spiritually and emotionally and I was that little girl who just couldn't seem to heal from being a fatherless daughter. I just couldn't seem to heal from the fact that I was unloved by him because I wasn't good enough to be loved, even being a part of him. That was still not enough for him. That was something that I never accepted and I didn't want to face the fact that I was hurting inside and therefore I couldn't be honest with my feelings. I couldn't and didn't

147

because I never confessed that part of me. It was too painful. All I knew was I had to be strong while burying what I couldn't face. If you really want help you have to be ready to do the work. I had to be ready to take that responsibility. We are responsible for our peace, joy, healing, and our happiness! We must accept what it is by making a choice to not self inflict our pain! Let go of those who hurt us! Continuing to talk about the pain will not allow us to heal if you don't do anything about it! That's feeling sorry for yourself. What good will that do? It will have you in a mindset of self-pity, pettiness and negativity. Why should we retell our story of our pain? Stop making your pain your comfort zone and start talking about the things that will bring you healing. People who want change, make moves! People who don't want to change, make excuses!

God wants to help us but we have to understand that we must take the necessary steps to show we want the help we need in order for God to supernaturally intercede on our behalf. Remember, we must first admit to needing help before we can desire to want help!

In the intensive care unit of Christ, He knows we are hurting inside. He sees our broken souls and spirits. This is why the word says, "Cast all your anxieties on Him because He cares for you." 1 Peter 5:7

Christ just doesn't want us to survive this life of pain. He wants us to live His plan. He wants us to know that there is hope and being broken in the arms of Christ is what brings us healing and wholeness. It will seem and appear as difficult and very challenging but there's not anything in this world that Jesus hadn't overcome. I can remember one night praying to God and as I prayed in private, I began to focus on God and I started thanking God for all the miracles he had performed in my life. Those many prayer requests that God answered and the many times I had prayed for loved-ones, it was clear that God answered those prayers. I thought about if God did it for me in my past, he can do it for me now. I began thanking God like never before. It was those moments of prayer when I could feel God's presence. It was frightening at first but I knew that it was God's spirit. I knew that the Spirit of God was real and God was gradually and repeatedly showing me how real he was in my life because there was a peace that would come in my presence of prayer. I could finally breathe this time. It was like I was starting to release. My release of tears were the flow of what I needed and my healing had come. My cries were louder and stronger during my prayers. Something was happening to me on the inside and this time it became a reality. I knew that this was a start to a new beginning. You must let go of where you've been because God will lead you to where you're going. I knew during these moments of prayer that I was in the process unit of healing. God was the hospital and Jesus was my doctor. The Holy Spirit was the IV going through my bloodstream. This was the intensive care unit of my mind, body and spirit.

There was that one thing I noticed and that is God moves according to our faith. It was in my trying times where I began to rejoice in God where I felt that my breaking point became my breakthrough. A joyful, cheerful heart brings healing to both body and soul. But the one whose heart is crushed struggles with sickness and depression. 17:22 Proverbs TPT

OUR HEALING IS OUR RESPONSIBILITY

We must agree that the person or that time in our life that created the pain is our truth, it's our story nevertheless, our healing is still our responsibility. Christ restores the broken heart, mind and spirit. All love, grace, mercy, peace and rest comes from God. We have to begin to create an environment for our peace and we must create and control our thoughts in order to disengage from the negativity. This is how we learn to take the chains off our brains. Our insecurities become our inabilities and this is why this is our responsibility to work at it on a daily basis. "Above all else, guard your heart, for everything you do flows from it. Keep your mouth free of perversity, keep corrupt talk far from your lips. Let your eyes look straight ahead, fix your gaze directly before you. Give careful thought to the paths for your feet and be steadfast in all your ways. Do not turn to the right or the left, keep your foot from evil." Proverbs 4:23-27 TPT

As I think about this passage, it reveals our intentions and shows us to change in the deepest place of our souls, our heart's motive. Our soul consists of our mindset, which is what we think about and how to control our mental health. It also consists of our emotions of how we feel when our souls are affected to feel what we feel. Most importantly, our souls are also the gift of freewill, it is our decisions we make. God gives us freewill to make choices. Once again, our freewill makes us accountable and responsible for our healing. We know that Christ promises us peace, love and joy when we seek him as we heal. I had to learn and ask myself, do I desire the promise more than the promiser, who is Christ Jesus? This question truthfully allowed me to examine my heart with Christ to desire more of Him than the promise. This is where desiring the relationship starts and this is how the healing process progressed for me. It was the applied knowledge to understand that our healing is examined by the glimpse of where our heart is postured. It's our decision which is our free will. God won't force himself on you!

When it comes to our mind, we must examine our mental and emotional health. We must think about who holds the keys to our emotions, feelings and perspective in life? When we know who holds our hands, we need to become stronger to have the fight to protect our heart. Remember, in order to maintain our healing progress, it is important to guard our heart. It's also important to think positive. This is why the passage states, "So keep your thoughts continually fixed on all that is authentic and real, honorable and admirable, beautiful and respectful, pure and holy, merciful and kind. And fasten your thoughts on every glorious work of God, praising him always. Philippians 4:8 TPT

Our mental and emotional health flows from our heart. We are often quick to guard our houses, cars, and material possessions but overlook our hearts. Physically, heart attacks occur when one or more of the coronary arteries becomes blocked. What unhealthy lifestyles are we living that is dangerous to our heart posture? God created the human heart to cast its cares on Him, not try carrying them on our own. It also states in the bible passage of Proverbs 4:23, "Keep thy heart with all diligence for it is the issue of life." We have to practice on a daily basis to have control over our thoughts and not allow the things of this life to affect our emotions. Guarding our hearts, destroys the walls of offense. We have to be careful that our responses are not influenced by our emotions. We must set boundaries in order to control our mindset. Have you been so upset and angry that you said something to someone you may have regretted? You were in the heat of the moment and what you said spilled out your mouth so fast that you didn't have time to filter your thoughts. It just blurted out. When we are moved by emotions, we must understand the posture of our hearts and minds. When I meditate on this passage in the scripture in Proverbs 4:23 that we should guard our hearts because everything we do flows from it. This explains how the conditions of our hearts and minds will suppress through our mouth. Since our mouth is the tool that gives our words power when we speak. We have to remember that what we speak has power over our lives and in the lives of others. Every part of our bodies is vital! Our hearts are like a well that continues to flow water daily. As our hearts actively pump blood and the blood flows to different organs in our bodies, spiritually our hearts also release and receive the conditions by which are affected, whether positively or negatively. What we say and how we say things reflect the conditions of our hearts. What are we holding in our hearts? What we hold is the condition or posture of our hearts and minds. What is on your mind? What is heavy on your heart? What bags have we've carried that have put weights on our mental state of mind or on our physical stature? Remember the weight of baggage wasn't created for us to carry. That wasn't God's design when He made us. So on a daily basis, this must be our exercise for the sake of guarding our hearts. This is for the sake of transitioning ourselves for transformation. This is for the sake of our personal development.

Proverbs 23:7 states,"For as he thinketh in his heart, so is he: Eat and drink, saith he to thee; but his heart is not with thee."

While our soul, mind and spirit is under reconstruction, we must let go of self-condemnation. This is blaming ourselves for what we have done wrong. This is the guilt and shame that we have carried in our hearts. This is yet one of those baggage of life that causes us to doubt in ourselves and to not believe who God says we are. This is what I struggled with the most. I had always been very hard on myself. I blamed myself and it became difficult to forgive myself fir decisions I had made. I held myself to higher standards. It was like whatever I did just wasn't good enough. I was critical of myself to do better. I blamed myself for all the poor choices I made in life but I hadn't forgave myself for it; so I believe this led to not having the peace of mind I needed and always over-analyzing everything made me a nervous wreck.

Self-condemnation can lead to stress, depression, anxiety in which can create heart disease. Walking around with pain in our bodies due to condemnation of ourselves can block us from accessing our purpose or discovering our purpose. Self-condemnation will cause us to reject and block the blessings that God has in store for us. The feelings of rejection will cause us to blame ourselves due to self-condemnation. We will start to make excuses for everything and then find ourselves feeling stuck. This leads to physical pain, which leads to stress, heart disease, stroke, fibromyalgia and other illnesses. Holding on to unforgiveness from people and family can cause physical illness too. Self-pity of feeling sorry for yourself by always being the victim is also not letting go of your past and it keeps you trapped and stuck from having a peace of mind and having the ability to heal. Pacifying your struggles is not healthy closure and when you are unable to forgive yourself, you become a product of arrested development. You start to wonder why things never get done or why you're hindered in improving your life.

You must go through a detox for spiritual restoration. This is a process of elimination. When your spirit is cluttered and empty, your spirit is full of stress. The spirit of insecurity is a seed. A seed that has been planted inside of you that has caused you to become fearful, inferior and the anxiety of uncertainty. Mental and emotional health isn't the most popular topic of discussion at the dinner table but yet is the most popular concern of our daily lives. It is the welfare of our being! It affects each and every one of us at certain degrees. If we are currently struggling in this area of our life, we must reach out to someone and someone who can cover us in prayer and impart God's love, peace and joy into our hearts and spirits. It is essential for spiritual restoration. I would recommend that if you are struggling mentally from depression and suicide, seek professional or medical help immediately, open up to someone you trust and ask God to give you a personalized strategy for your mental and emotional health but if that doesn't work for you, I highly recommend a godly spiritual coach or counselor to take you through deliverance. Deliverance is the children's bread. Deliverance is purification and cleansing to our souls. This is all apart if the intensive care unit of restoring us back to health. Reconstruction of our mind, body and spirit is restored hope in improving our lives day by day and step by step.

LOVE IS HEALING

"As the Father has loved me, so have I loved you. Now remain in my love. If you keep my commands, you will remain in my love, just as I have kept my Father's commands and remain in his love. I have told you this so that my joy may be in you and that your joy may be complete."John 15:9-11 KJV

It is important that we know that our Father in heaven loves us and is the answer to our every problem when it comes to the crossroads of relationships, situation-ships, struggling marriages and loving ourselves.

So what is love? Some people use this word and really don't know the meaning. The true meaning of love is an intense feeling of deep affection. If used as a verb, it is defined as a deep romantic or sexual attachment to someone. In the KJV passage, "Love is patient, love is kind. It does not envy, it does not boast, it is not proud. It does not dishonor others, it is not self-seeking, it is not easily angered, it keeps no record of wrongs. Love does not delight in evil but rejoices with the truth. It always protects, always trust, always hopes, always preserves. (1Corinthians 13:4-7)

We must love because God made us in his own image of love and he saw that it was good. Our soul longs for love because we are spirit beings created to receive love and to bring forth our love. Before we can really love someone else, the main factor is loving ourselves. When we love God, we love ourselves. This is our true healing. We can't make it into the kingdom of God without love in our hearts.

I remember those times of not loving myself and not seeing myself valuable! This was during the time of my depression. Those dark days of gloom that I buried and suppressed within my spirit caused me to experience other ailments of pain in my body. My broken heart was torn for many years and carrying silent pain is like drinking poison. In due time, if you haven't been healed from what you've carried, it will eat away at your soul. A broken spirit is deadly to yourself and you'll become toxic to others, even those who love you the most. Living this life, unfortunately I've seen and been around people with broken spirits and most times, it is seen through their behavior. Many people will not admit to carrying a broken spirit because many have made it normal as a lifestyle. Many broken spirits react and respond to brokenness and many attract others who are broken as well. Most times, we are who we are attracted to. I know this so well because I carried brokenness in my heart and spirit. I also attracted broken men who later would become my lover, guys I dated. When that significant other mistreats you or trigger those baggage of ill emotions that we haven't healed from, it can cause a domino effect of suppressed feelings, which consequently causes us not to love ourselves, endure deep depression, low self-esteem and sometimes causes extreme physical pain to our bodies. When we are emotionally affected, we are also physically affected. This is the domino effect of how we can cause illnesses and diseases to enter our bodies. Disappointment of those who have violated our trust, disorderly of not being able to manage our thoughts, emotions and behavior, discomfort of being in the mental state of sadness and disconnection of being spiritually separated from God, can ultimately cause Dis-Ease to our mind, body, soul and spirit.

This is why it is so important to receive healing and deliverance because you have to expose the things you worked a lifetime to cover up. Exposing the areas of our lives that have held us hostage in bondage is where the change begins because we are no longer in denial of needing the help and the need of support and love to get us through the pain. We can become uncomfortable through the process of our healing. We must feel the pain in order to heal from it. We can't take shortcuts by going around it and running away from it. Our hidden pain has a way of returning as an unwelcome visitor. When I endured my pain and the shame, it felt like God was punishing me. Consequently, I couldn't feel His love due to the deception of always feeling that I deserved to suffer and carry the heavy baggage of burden and the condemnation of not being or doing what God had called me to do and to become. I just didn't feel good about myself for a long time. No matter how I looked on the outside, it couldn't help what I was feeling on the inside. So, I accepted the faults and the failures of who I was, even though I wasn't happy with myself. This also can explain why we become so hard on ourselves to get better. Even when we are progressing, it seems like it's just not enough or we're not progressing fast enough or we feel as though we are failures and that it would be impossible to meet the standards of God because we just can't seem to get it right. This will have us believ we don't feel alright most of the time.

In my early twenties, living the single life and desiring to be married, I had always dreamed of being a beautiful bride and being taken away by my king where it was like envisioning this beautiful chariot with the couple smiling, waving and in love while drifting away into the horizon. That was what I fantasized about as a child, although I was very much aware that, that was a fairy tale most young girls dream of; but many who live a single life don't realize it because when you watch other couples together and they look happy and in love, you only get to see the view on the outside but you really don't know what it's like on the other side. Even in our singleness, for those who desire a mate, first allow God to become intimate and bond with you in a relationship. Allow God to become your portion every morning and every night. God understands your needs and he knows your desires. When you abide in Him, he will abide in you. When you make God your priority and focus, he changes your needs and desires and the feelings of loneliness and the personal emotions you are feeling won't become a void. God fills the void and becomes your desire. He creates the perfect companion for you when you become deeply rooted in his love. He will give you the patience you need to wait for the spouse that is seeking to be your help mate. God has to prepare you and your mate for the right season. God has to make you whole and he has to heal you from any open wounds before he can allow you to partner with whom he has made for you. God will allow you to become whole by allowing you to look in the mirror reflection. His purpose is to prepare you for the special person in your life. God's ultimate purpose in love and unity is for man to not be alone and he has that special person for everyone and any one who desires a mate. He designs the perfect fit like a hand that fits comfortably in a glove. Wait on the Lord and you won't regret the wait. The bible states, "Be anxious for nothing, but in everything by prayer and supplication, with thanksgiving, let your requests be made known to God. Philippians 4:6 KJV

Yet, we ought to have the fruits of patience, which is one of the fruits of the spirit. Many of us become impatient in our prayers. We want a companion and that is naturally normal. However, we want God to move and answer prayers on our time and on our watch, instead of God's timing. God's time is always the perfect time. That special person is not going to come early because he or she may not be ready and God is never late. Remember what many would always say, "He may not come when you want him to but he's always on time!" Maybe that special companion isn't ready for you because you aren't ready in your heart. Jesus is still performing surgery on your spiritual being. Could it be that you are in a season to wait to start loving yourself first? Could it be that you are waiting because you are still in the intensive care unit to love yourself for healing and to grow in perseverance? God's timing is not our time and just when you think you are ready to invite someone into your heart, God has to make sure you are healed and truly made whole for a healthy marriage in your future. Remember, His ways are not our ways and His thoughts are surely not our thoughts, so stop trying to plan the blueprint when God already completed it.

Self-love is the self-care and it's healing to a broken heart and soul. In the process of loving yourself, you remove all of the negative things that prevented you from loving yourself. You also remove those you have loved and have caused you to make them your priority over you. You can make someone more important to you than yourself. This isn't healthy when your broken soul is desperate for love because you become blind to what's really important. What's more important is that you need internal healing. There is a deficiency in your heart that you are trying to fulfill and you believe that it's this particular person who can only fulfill your soul. You find yourself loving this person to the point where it can become toxic because you are only loving them for the sake of your need to fill a lack but not for the sake of truly loving this person for who they really are. You become infatuated with the fact of being in love until you have lost your identity in this person. You have a false concept of what love is and therefore you can't understand why there are so many problems in the relationship or the marriage. You become in denial that "you" are really the problem, yet you blame your companion. Could it be that you really weren't ready for the relationship? Could it be that you are in need of healing and it may require you to be single for a while to develop a relationship with God? When you develop a closer relationship with God, you may be alone but you are not lonely, you learn to stop intimately loving and placing your values and self-worth in the hands of the one your heart yearned for, the one who couldn't love you, respect you, appreciate you or find you worthy enough. They didn't appreciate your total worth and have led you to believe that you were the apple of their eye when their eyes are in other places. I had to learn the hard way that I couldn't rely on people, significant ones to love me like I deserved to be loved. We must find our true happiness from within and not from the external places of our lives. We cannot find true happiness from tangible things and in people, especially when people don't live up to their promises and to your expectations. They only become your own personal desires and not needs. Many things we desire are not consistent with our needs. It cannot and will not satisfy the void. Your desires can not satisfy your needs! We are all searching for happiness. We all find happiness in different areas of our lives because what satisfies one person may not satisfy another. True happiness is defined as moments and experiences of love and expression that brings a contentment and an excitement of soothing the soul. Happiness has a close connection with love -- it's when you fully pursue happiness from your inner soul. When God is the center of your happiness, he becomes the joy that gives you strength. That's why it's so important to love God because you naturally start living yourself in a healthy manner.

Living a single life gives you the opportunity to take as much time as you need because marriage requires that your time is spent to also give to your spouse. You must understand that marriage doesn't bring you happiness. It brings you responsibility. You must be happy with yourself because you bring someone into your life spiritually and God must be the priority of your marriage in order to have a healthy marriage. Chemistry and compatibility won't be enough because when the chips are down; God has to intervene. Remember. A family that prays together stays together. Marriage doesn't define who you are and it doesn't make you more valuable or more worthier just by having a mate. When Christ is at the center of our relationships and marriages, He will do more than we could hope to accomplish on our own, even on our best day. So, we must take a step and vowel to put Him first. God is always first in everything!

Healing began the moment God allowed me to accept the true revelation of the man and in order to gain full knowledge on aspects that are difficult to accept and understand, we must have clarity about our pain. I believe that in situation-ships, which many relationships develop into, are considered "complicated". I think this has a lot to do with tolerating the issues and the baggage of others by accepting the toxicity of experiences, toxic environments and toxic behavior from others, which we feel that we must lower our standards

because we are afraid of being lonely; so we end will find
ourselves settling for or tolerating toxicity in that person
because we fear that it's the best that we can do. At the end of
the day, we know we're not perfect and we all have some
downfalls and issues and in some way or another we must
accept it as a legitimate truth but then we tend to think, since
we are aren't perfect anyway, it makes it only right to stay in
these types of relationships. I believe this is why so many
relationships become broken because we tend to allow fear,
low self-esteem and importantly, not loving ourselves enough
to create the desire to better ourselves or to believe in
ourselves to know that we are so much greater than our
circumstances or our current situation and/or being, dealing or
tolerating the drama and in our lives that robs us from our
peace. I've witnessed situations from people, some that I
know and some that I personally didn't know. These
situations were deemed as, "I can do bad all by myself." I've
seen where someone would date a person who had no goals,
had no desires or ambitions in life to improve their economic,
social and educational status. In general, there are people who
don't want anything in life or don't desire to grow and elevate
in life but will burn out your energy and use up your time and
everything you've worked hard to build until they have pulled
you completely down. If they don't have any hopes or dreams
in life but you have dreams of becoming or doing better for
yourself, you might become stifled or complacent and stuck
for settling for less. Not loving yourself will make you believe
that you cannot have anything better for yourself. Without a
doubt, you will allow yourself to become under someone
else's control and a sense of being powerless. People can pull
you down only if you allow them to. Not loving yourself or
finding your worth is a seed of impoverishment! This is how
depression, oppression and stress can seep into your soul and
that's where it begins. Depression, anxiety, and other forms of
mental health illnesses often causes people to live and think

more inwardly. Taking the time to evaluate yourself by looking in the mirror to examine what is causing you to feel the way you do, or to behave the way you do or allow people to come into your life who are toxic and brings drama or problems in you life are those who you will need to avoid as fast as you can and as far away from them as possible. We must all remember this one thing if we don't remember anything else and that is …. we must love God first before we can love ourselves! We have to create boundaries for the sake of our peace and for the sake of our healing and deliverance.

Self-love is defining our true identity of ourselves by stripping away every title of being a spouse, family member, title or position on the job, business or organization. Your domestic status, position or title doesn't define you or give you your self-worth. Your self-worth is your true character of knowing who you are, why you exist and where you are going in life. It's defining our true character and purpose through God, our creator. It's defining what we are in spirit and who we are in our mind and soul.

As I reflect on my past relationships with men, whether fatherly or intimate relationships of courtship, my perception of men became difficult to trust them and I harbored feelings of unforgiveness, fear and insecurities, yet I desired the integrity, loyalty, love, respect, kindness, caring and confidence and security from a man. As a little girl, I needed my father's love, care and protection. As a grown woman, I needed to affirm genuine love, loyalty, respect and security! It took time, tears and countless experiences from joy and pain to understand the nature of a man and to understand how society, environment and culture conditions a man's nature of being, thoughts, perception of how the world sees him and how he sees himself, his relationships with others, whether it's personal or professional. Most importantly, a man's true

162

identity and relationship with God, as it relates to his existence and being created by God of being a male, a man, a son, a father and a husband and how his divine purpose of existence affects his destiny and how it impacts the lives of women in the connection of love and relationships, is the true essence of receiving genuine love with compassion, integrity, loyalty and wholeness! It's a true companionship. A man that fears the lord, is a man who lives and enjoys life of being the better version of himself! A man who doesn't fear the Lord, unfortunately wouldn't know what that feels like or looks like.

The intent to allow God to heal me from my past experiences with men, I had to gain humility and patience to learn and to gain knowledge on understanding the man, to understand the way he thinks, his emotions, his behavior, his goals, his characteristics, his beliefs, his emotional and mental chemistry, his love language, his struggles, his pressures, his desires, his strengths, his weaknesses, his vulnerabilities and his " divine purpose"!

Many singles don't understand that being single is actually a great experience to learn more about yourself, especially when you have been in relationships most of our life. When you are living a single life, you are able to explore and educate yourself and take on new skills, hobbies and activities and you don't have to worry about any resistance to your decisions. For many, being single can be the best moments of your life because you have the opportunity to create a self-love that could allow you to focus on who you are and fall in love with the things that make life enjoyable and fun. While other singles may see this life as being lonely and experience the fear of desiring that day to join in unity with that significant other before the biological clock stops ticking. You must look at this time of your life as a valuable time to get to know God. You have an opportunity to spend an intimate time with God where you aren't distracted or limited with your time. Experiencing time with God is priceless and when you become closer with God, he becomes even closer to you and he is able to prepare the perfect match for you. You won't have to ever wonder if you're making the right decision during courtship or getting to know someone in dating. The intimate relationship with God can give you a discernment of knowing that he or she is not the one for you or if this is the right one you should spend the rest of your life with!

I've always acknowledged God and loved the Lord but there was always that void in my life of not having that peace that is without understanding. I knew that having God in my life would bring me peace that would take away all of my worries.

Beauty is skin deep and we all have heard the saying that beauty is in the eyes of the beholder. Being beautiful is not only appearance but more importantly, being beautiful is that, which is on the inside. Your inner beauty! It took me a while to fully understand what that meant to me and when I understood it, it made more sense because God already made each of us beautiful from the start but it's how beautiful we remain through the scars and baggage in our lives. So, just because I didn't receive the affirmation from my father on how beautiful I was, I also couldn't believe how beautiful I had become. In addition from the past relationships, it was a struggle and a big blow to my self-esteem that created the scars, bruises and baggage of life. I was blindfolded from the true beauty within. The internal healing of love is doing things to love yourself. It's not being selfish but self-caring. If that means you must take some quality time for yourself by fixing yourself up with a new hairstyle, getting pampered with a relaxing massage, buying that favorite lipstick color or treating yourself to a gorgeous outfit, do something for yourself to show self-love. Take care of yourself as you would do for someone who you truly love by showing yourself affection in what makes you feel good about yourself on the inside and on the outside. Self care for your inner-soul, is taking some of that quality time and spending some quiet time with God. That is self-healing. Now, please don't misunderstand me when I suggest that fixing up ourselves is a form of self-care, especially when some people over-compensate to fill a void. There always has to be balance in everything we do and there is truly nothing wrong with fixing yourself up and keeping yourself groomed and modest, as we should all do. We must ask ourselves what are our motives when we fix ourselves up? Is it for the need to bring closure for internal healing, is it for the need to gain attention from men, or is it for routine self-maintenance by maintaining to care for our needs and healthy grooming? Is this really making us feel better on the inside or on the outside? Is it truly loving ourselves? If our honest answer is to fix up our external appearance for the motive to bring closure to our internal deficiencies; or for the sake to impress others, or as I mentioned earlier, we are fixing up ourselves by overcompensating to fill an inner void, then we really need to be honest with ourselves? Please understand that this form of thinking and action masquerades and covers up the deficiencies inside of us. We are healing ourselves from the outside to the inner-soul. Self-deliverance is what we must accept and admit to in order for God to help us. Remember, we have to be honest with ourselves by admitting to it. Can we really accept the fact that we need healing at some level within ourselves when our actions and motives aren't naturally healthy? We can change our outer appearance, buy cosmetics, have plastic surgeries from top to bottom but will that alteration give us complete healing or eternal satisfaction to love ourselves? Sometimes, I can see how a really beautiful person will alter their looks and they not find satisfaction because they look for more ways to alter their body when in fact there's nothing wrong with their physical body because they have lacked and caused malnutrition to their soul and spirit. If we can't accept what God has made, there's not a man on earth who can satisfy us. A million compliments will never satisfy what's hurting on the inside. We must love ourselves and I don't mean this in a selfish way but I mean this in a way to accept the uniqueness in who God made us and not striving to be or to look like the image that we may desire for the sake of completing us. This can be challenging for many because we know the comfortability of what we've always lived through. We must accept that it's about loving our appearance but loving who we really are inside? Being whole and grounded with great character and knowing our worth is the healthy state of internal being. Our bare and naked self from the inside and out needs full intensive care. Our external posture cannot heal our internal condition. We might feel a sense of temporal satisfaction but it's not repairing us or healing us from what really needs to be repaired permanently. We must invest in repairing and changing what's on the inside before we can accept what's on the outside. I know what this feels like because this woman was me. Although, I've never had plastic surgery but I purchased cosmetics and wigs and hair extensions, and wouldn't leave the house without it. I purchased clothing that made me feel good for the sake of not being able to afford clothes in my formative years, and I wore extensions only for the sake of making me feel better about myself but it only helped me externally. The more I purchased things to enhance my appearance, the more I ignores my needs over my desires. I felt that I needed this to love myself. I claimed that it was just an enhancement but it never seemed as though it was enough. I still had wounds that were bleeding on the inside, that needed to be healed. Trust me, I'm not against enhancing your appearance. If you are healed on the inside, that's perfectly fine with what you do with your body as long as you are not causing harm to your body by contaminating or poisoning your bloodstream with dangerous toxins and chemicals that are being injected into your body or damaging your hair with wigs or extensions or bleaching your hair excessively that may cause baldness and permanent damage to your natural hair for the sake of being beautiful to complete you. God had to heal me internally before I could love myself and enjoy the beauty on the outside and this is why it's important for our mate to love us internally and not only love us based upon our appearance for his or her sexual or lustful pleasures. Our looks will fade someday and if the love was created on the foundation of our looks, then the love will fade away someday too! The naked truth is that there's more to life than just being beautiful and when God made man, he was pleased with his own creation. the book of Proverbs 31:30 says 'Charm is deceitful, and beauty is vain, but a woman who fears the Lord is to be praised. '

In the intensive care unit of Christ, the passage that reminds me of how Christ is our healer is, "Jesus said unto him, Rise, take up thy bed, and walk." John 5:8 KJV

This clearly reflects the power of God on how he raises us up from our dead or dying places in our lives and how his power restores our soul, reconstructs our mind and renews our spirit to wake up and arise! Remember, it is our responsibility to do the work so that Christ can perform the healing and deliverance to allow us to the path of recovery!

CHAPTER 5 - THE ROAD TO RECOVERY

WHEN GOD SPEAKS

Our journey of life is a temporal process and the testament of our faith through our wilderness. Only God can bring manifestation that sets us free in our hearts, our minds, our souls and our spirits to become a better person, physically, emotionally, mentally and spiritually. It's learning to humble ourselves and to trust God through the wilderness by letting go of those heavy bags and triggers and start by enjoying a new life of healing, transformation, renewed heart and mind and a life of restoration and freedom. God had to reset us to His factory settings. There has to be a transformation before there could be a new beginning. He gave us the affirmation of love, self-worth, confidence, peace and security to not just survive but to love ourselves, forgive ourselves, to heal every wound and to enjoy life.

From my personal experience, God had to uncover all that was bleeding on the inside and He had to heal me from my brokenness of being a fatherless little girl who needed that affirmation of love to a woman that carried lots of baggage to a road of recovery, a road for my breakthrough. It felt like a long walk through a very dark and wooded pathway but with faith, this journey became the catalyst to my purpose in life.

It was the year 2010, I had experienced some emotional and financial blows in my life as if I had been hit in the gut by the professional boxer Floyd Mayweather or maybe getting my ear bitten off by Mike Tyson. In other words, there were some painful and troubled experiences of life I endured but yet I was still standing. It would be one circumstance after another and these circumstances were those painful cycles but this time, they came from unexpected and unforeseen timing. Although my husband weathered the storm and we were ten years in our marriage, our children were growing up and doing well, I was no longer a member at the church I attended, me and my husband's financial situation changed due to the 2008 economic recession, but the relationship with my father hadn't nor did my spiritual life changed. Through it all, I still maintained my hope in God. I started visiting different churches to gain some peace within. Yet, It felt like my faith took a back row seat because I was emotionally breaking down and I felt like I had given up. Things just didn't seem to work out for me during this time.

One particular Sunday, as I sat in the fourth row of a church I had visited, it was my usual routine of being a visitor and observing the flow of the service, the pastor's sermon grabbed my attention this time. It was as if he was speaking to me. As I was in my seat trying to sit comfortably, it felt more uncomfortable because I felt like God was talking to me through the pastor. I couldn't remember the passage he spoke on but the point of the message was forgiveness. He basically stated that you must forgive those who have hurt you. "You must forgive the men in your life in order for God to give you favor in your life." God can not bless you if you have not forgiven those who have caused you pain in your life." As much as I wanted to prove him wrong, I knew that he was right. In fact, I knew in my heart that he was speaking the truth but it just seemed like he was talking to me personally. My heavy hurt was convicted. As he was speaking, I thought to myself, had it been my own disobedience that caused me so much pain and suffering? Had it been my pride to not forgive my father and a few others in my life that had blocked my blessing from coming forth and my prayers from being answered? I wanted to cry in my seat but I didn't want anyone to see my tears. My daughters came with me and I surely didn't want them to see me cry. At this moment, God was speaking to me. At the end of the service, I received prayer to ask God to help me to forgive. I didn't know how to forgive my father when the sting was still there. I didn't want to say that I forgave my father when I really didn't, so I just asked God to help me to forgive. On my way home, I held back tears. I waited to go home to release my cry in private. The sermon was so powerful that it gripped my heart that entire day. All I could do was think about forgiving but what was preventing me from making the phone call was not being sure if I really meant it. Am I forgiving my father because I was convicted by God or was I really ready to forgive him from the bottom of my heart? For nights I couldn't sleep. The message from God was that first encounter of God really speaking to me. I always wondered how God speaks to us privately and this was that first experience of knowing that he spoke to me. It was that sermon that touched my heart and gave me an urgency to pray and ask God to forgive me.

As I began to pray more and more, I felt that urgency to call my father but I didn't call him. In the following year, I enrolled in college due to a need for a career change. I had worked administrative and management jobs for years and I felt the need to embark on a career path that I desired. I believed that a teaching degree would allow me to fulfill a passion in life. I thought about how well I worked with children and how much I enjoyed teaching. I felt that it was time for a change. I had earned a computer science degree many years ago but I felt the need for change. It was May 2011 and that is where life seemed hectic. I was under a great deal of stress trying to work a full-time job while in college full-time and balancing this with family life took a toll on me. I felt like I had sacrificed four years of family life to finish college and work. I was beat down mentally and there was no spiritual time for God. During this time, I occasionally visited a church on Sundays and I started visiting a different church, a much larger church because the church started services promptly on time and service ended at an expected time to make it home to cook for the family for dinner. In addition, no one would notice those days when I would be absent from church. It seemed to work perfectly for my busy schedule, yet I was mentally stressed out. I had no peace within because I felt guilty for not being able to spend time with my family, how and when I wanted to. I felt robbed of my time although I knew that in the end it would all pay off. In May 2013, I graduated Cum Laude with honors. It was one of my greatest accomplishments to earn my bachelors degree. I was thankful to God for sustaining me for four years because many times I felt tempted to give up. Many times the pressure was too overwhelming and typing up 10 to 20 page essays were sometimes more than I could handle. I was grateful that my husband stood in the gap many times to help by cooking meals and making sure our daughters homework was complete. It not only took a toll on me but it took a toll on all of us. The bittersweet moment of graduation came as a shock when I was called to the office at work to receive the news that I had been laid off from my job. This happened a few days before my graduation. I was nearly in tears but I had to accept that the unfortunate happens and it's beyond our control, all you have left is faith to believe that it happened for a reason. There's a purpose behind every suffering situation! Days, weeks, months passed and it became difficult to find a decent paying job. I was fortunate and thankful to obtain unemployment benefits but it was just not sufficient income to meet my financial needs. At this time of my life I would find myself in those moments again, fighting the weights of worry, stress, fear and those feelings of uncertainty and depression.

SEEKING GOD IN THE LOW VALLEYS

"You will seek Me and find Me, when you seek me with all your heart." Jeremiah 29:13

"I call heaven and earth to witness against you today, that I have set before you life and death, blessing and curse, Therefore choose life, that you and your offspring may live, loving the Lord your God, obeying his voice and holding fast to him, for he is your life and length of days, that you may dwell in the land that the Lord swore to your fathers, to Abraham, to Isaac, and to Jacob, to give them." Deuteronomy 30:19-20

As we are on the road to recovery, we are seeking God in those low valleys. In those low valleys, that's where God's divine glory and anointing is carrying us. That's a place in our life that gives us the strength to carry on when life's trials and troubles have brought us to a place where we aren't able to do it or make it by ourselves. This is why our low valleys are our ministries. When I think about the low valleys and the scars of life, God's love, grace and his mercy allowed me to understand how my broken soul of affliction was what strengthened me. While I was enduring the pain and submerged in the floods of my tears, it was too difficult to see and to feel the power and the glory because I was too busy being broken. It didn't feel good and it didn't feel like hope was a step away but in the aftermath, those difficult days and those dark moments became my healing for a breakthrough. It was those moments that shaped me and molded me into something greater. Sometimes when we're being molded and undergoing the process of change, it's those moments that don't feel good. In fact, it feels like your worst moments because it feels as though you're not progressing or improving. Yet, with God being with me every step of the way, it was Him that carried me even when I didn't know it and it was Him that was molding me even when I couldn't feel it. Sometimes we go through seasons where it feels like we're falling apart while God is putting us together. It's the transformation process that's molding us when we are seeking God to deliver us and to heal us. We must understand that before things come together, it generally has to fall apart. Broken areas are those that will soon become repaired when we humble ourselves by tearing down the walls and dropping the baggage that keeps us bound. Once we decide to make that decision of desiring to be made new, God has a chance to show who He is and what His plans are for us! Just know, He was and will always be there for us. Jesus meets us in our broken places because He knows what a broken heart feels like. He knows what it feels like to be rejected by his own. He knows what it feels like to be betrayed by a friend. He knows what it feels like to be beaten and called names. He knows what it feels like to be accused of something he hadn't done or hadn't been. He knows what it feels like of being accused. So, when he sees and feels your sorrows, he can empathize the pain.

He allows us to know that He is our rock when we are rock-bottom and broken into pieces. Just because you are feeling low and broken doesn't mean you aren't a king or a queen. Every king and queen had to go through tough moments in their lives because life isn't always perfect. God reminds us how he heals our broken hearts and He takes care of our wounds. KJV- Psalms 147:3

Only God can meet us where we are but we have to put our trust in Him. He knows what individual needs. What a mighty God we serve where He can meet the needs of millions of people on this earth simultaneously and love us back to life. He picks us up when we are weak! He makes us persevere when we want to give up! Who can match that? Nobody!

I can remember as a child being so afraid, tormented by the presence of evil and living in deep fear by the trauma when I lived in the home where I was tormented in fear where the atmosphere was demonic. It was a horrible experience for me and the enemy's (the devil) plan was to instill fear in me. His plan was to attack my mind with evil images that were not pleasant for my innocent eyes to see. The experiences planted the seed of fear that would haunt me for a very long time. I can remember not having peace and always being fearful, especially at night when the sightings and the spirit of fear were heightened and were felt the strongest. This would explain why I do not watch any horror movies this present day. You are being entertained by these demonic spirits that enter into your eyes and into your spirit when you watch these types of movies. During those times, I can remember someone telling me to read the passage in the bible and to always read it every time I felt fear or torment.

"The Lord is my shepherd; I shall not want. He maketh me to lie down in green pastures; He leadeth me beside the still waters. He restoreth my soul; He leadeth me in the paths of righteousness for His name's sake. Yea, though I walk through the valley of the shadow of death, I will fear no evil; for Thou art with me; Thy rod and Thy staff, they comfort me. Thou preparest a table before me in the presence of mine enemies; Thou anointest my head with oil; my cup runneth over. Surely goodness and mercy shall follow me all the days of my life; and I will dwell in the house of the Lord for ever." Psalms 23 KJV

This passage carried me through the tough times in my life. I would read this passage almost on a daily basis, year after year until it saturated my heart. By the time I became a woman, I didn't have to read it anymore because it was hidden in my heart. We are walking and living in the shadow of death because this is the evil world we live in today. In Psalms 23:4, "Yea though I walk through the valley of the shadow of death, I will fear no evil: for thou art with me." Have comfort and know that God is still with you. There is no need to be afraid. God knows that the enemy rules this evil world but God is always protecting us. The end of that verse says, "for thou art with me; thy rod and thy staff they comfort me." God is always with you because He is omnipresent. He is an ever present help! He was with us in the very beginning and He will continue to be with us to the very end. His rod and his staff reflects how the shepherd boy in the bible used the rod, (a stick) to guide and to protect his sheep. We are the sheep and God is yet, guiding us and protecting us. As I reflect on the shadow of death, this is the wide path that is taken by those who do not believe in God or reverence Him. This is the most riskiest path we could ever take. However, this is the path that reflects the enemy's plan. This is the path that the enemy wants us to be on. He knows that the narrow path is the path to salvation but the wider path is the path to destruction. We must remember and continue to remind ourselves that the enemy's plan is to kill, steal and to destroy us. His plan is never to help us. Anything that God has created, the enemy wants to destroy it! God created you and me and yes, you got it! He wants to destroy us all! There is an anonymous saying that states, "The greatest battles you will ever fight in your life are between your ears." It is true, your mind is often your biggest battlefield. When you cast your cares on the Lord through prayer, the peace of God will guard your heart and mind.

In our minds, we tend to worry about things that we do not have any control over. We must take captive the negative and shameful thoughts of the enemy attacks. We have to make it a daily practice to focus on winning the battle in our minds. As mentioned early in this book, "Be very careful about what you think. Your thoughts run your life." Proverbs 4:23

Don't think about what tomorrow will bring, tomorrow isn't promised to us. Don't think about how the past has affected you, the past is gone and became history. Think about the present. This very day. Focus on winning the battle today and remove our characteristic of self-control, which can become our deterrent of not allowing God to be in control. We have consciously and unconsciously been programmed in our lifestyle due to the accountabilities and the responsibilities of always being in control of how we bring results. We tend to take God out of the equation by always trying to figure out his plan or create a vision in our mind of how our prayers will work out. That's none of our business on how God will do it for us. It's our peace to allow God to take control. It's our trust in God to depend on Him. So focus on God by thanking him in advance and make this a mindset lifestyle.

WHEN WE KNOW BETTER WE DO BETTER

The devil's plan was to keep me bound in fear as he tormented me in my early childhood days by keeping me frightened by the terrible and unearthly sightings in my bedroom almost every night, and the horrible nightmares that took away my peace and trapped me with the spirit of insecurity and fear. The enemy's plan was to try and make me believe that I was mentally crazy and incompetent because he knew that if I would tell others about things that I saw, things that I had experienced, they wouldn't believe me and they would consider me crazy. I was afraid of being rejected but I was too intelligent for anyone to misunderstand or discredit my truth. Even as young as five years old, I knew that I was intelligent, creative and brilliant. The enemy couldn't take

176

away my strength and he didn't play fair. He tried to break down my emotional state by separating my family, which caused brokenness within me to disconnect me from my father. This was a specific love I lacked. I didn't know the magnitude of the lack and how it would bring damage to me over a course of time. The enemy also tried to keep resentment, bitterness and distrust in my heart by repeated discouragement and disappointment from the actions of my father. I became angry at him for the emotional, physical abandonment, rejection, and the feeling of not being loved by him. This created the spirit of depression, walls of offense of keeping me isolated, building walls around me to protect myself from the repeated and the rehearsed pain from other people, that I had already felt as a child to teens and young adult life. I didn't have the courage and the confidence to trust anyone or to allow people to become close to me emotionally and physically. The enemy tried to break down my spirit through an identity crisis of low self-esteem, not having confidence, not knowing my self-worth, and believing that I had to accept these deficiencies due to the brokenness of generational curses that had been passed through the family bloodline.

The silent pain that my parents endured, as this pain was the device of the enemy's plan to destroy the family and the next generations. It's a spiritual attack that starts through ancestry. The enemy's ultimate plan was for me to rehearse these weaknesses of my past throughout my adolescence, teenage years and early twenties. The spirit of anxieties, depression and suicidal attempts were the enemies ultimate plan because as I look back over my life; the enemy was intimidated by the seed that God had planted in me. His plan was strategic toward breaking me down and by using what caused my breakdowns to become my shortcomings and my weakness to take me to those dark days. The enemy will use the closest person to you to try to attack you spiritually, emotionally, mentally and physically. These are sudden and counter attacks of the enemy!

When the enemy comes against our mind, he will make us think that we deserve everything that happened to us. He will make us doubtful and unworthy. His plan is to desensitize us from the truth. This is called deception because he forces you to believe lies. I can remember in my earlier days of dating and not feeling valued, or not having self-worth, and lacking the love that I needed from that significant other. I would find myself repeating the same cycles over and over again because I kept attracting men who were not compatible with me and while my intentions were to seek real love like that happily-ever after love-story, I would find myself starting all over again, repeating the cycles of being more broken-hearted from relationship after relationship. I desired to be loved and have companionship and a relationship that I thought would be promising but it would turn out to become emotionally and mentally draining, the sense of feeling hopeless, and never believing that love could ever exist. I couldn't believe in true love because I could not experience it and it felt like false hope. The enemy would often remind me that I wasn't worth being a keeper and that I didn't have what it took to be loved, so I believed it. I started to believe that the rejection I received from failed relationships was what I deserved. These bad relationships would often remind me how it felt when I was a child and lacked my father's presence. I kept reliving the pain and didn't want to feel it or be reminded by it. So, I believed that I wasn't good enough for my father to be in my life, therefore I believed that I would have to be content without it but I wasn't content. I tried to ignore it and the more I tried to ignore it, the more I would bury it. The enemy wanted me to believe that since I couldn't receive my father's love, I would never receive genuine and authentic love from a companion.

This is why it's so powerful how a daughter sees her father, it gives her a perception of how she sees men, in general.

Any negative fight attack that influences our thoughts is the fight against the mind and the enemy will come into our thoughts to make us believe a lie. The KJV of 1st Peter 5:8 states, "Be alert and sober minded. Your enemy, the devil prowls around like a roaring lion looking for someone to devour."

The roaring lion is literally not the enemy but the roar in the lion are the storms, issues and problems that we deal with in our lives and the enemy will use these problems as tactics, devices, and plans to distract us, to harm us or to enter into our minds and our thoughts and try to entice us to not believe or to not have faith that our Lord and Savior is the problem-solver, a miracle-worker and the answer to what we are going through. His reign will only last for a short period of time but it won't last forever. The enemy will make us think that YOU and I are, and will never be worth anything. He will cause many to believe the many lies that were told to us are our reality. For those who were fatherless or motherless, he will make you believe that you deserved being without your father or your mother, being absent in our lives would insenuate that we weren't good enough to receive the love that we needed growing up from the abandonment, neglect, rejection, fear, impoverishment, homelessness or the insecurities of not accepting ourselves. The enemy will make us think negative thoughts about ourselves, that we weren't worth our ex-spouse or ex-companion's love, and that is why those exes were unfaithful and cheated on us. The enemy's lies will make us believe that we weren't worth a red penny on our jobs and that's why we were fired and the jobs never worked out, or maybe the business we owned failed because we were failures of life; we may have believed that being incompetent is what made our business fail because there are no sales, no profits being made or maybe we started believing that the product wasn't good enough to compete in an over saturated market. So now the enemy will whisper doubt in your ear to see yourself as a failure. These are negative thoughts that enter into the mind and if you don't take those thoughts into captive, you will start believing those thoughts are your reality. You will start believing the enemy over God. The enemy can use the most significant things in our lives to make us examine ourselves or second doubt ourselves by making us feel that since we do not have enough followers on social media, we are insignificant or irrelevant. He will use social media to affect how we believe in ourselves by making us compare ourselves with others on social media. The enemy will use social media as the stage to make you compare and believe that you are not as good as the next women or man you see, even in their own flaws that have been camouflaged and even in their own brokenness, we will start to compare ourselves to other characteristics and other identities that aren't us. We would copycat someone else's identity just to win acceptance with others we see. These are the insecurities that have been buried for many years and we've never faced them because either we believed that facing them would only make us worse because we don't want to feel the pain again, and perhaps it wouldn't help us anyway. That suppressed behavior springs forth from the insecurities as a child that can carry a personality trait known as the spirit of envy or jealousy. It is a trick by the enemy because everything we see is not always one hundred percent real but the enemy will use false perception to bring out the worst in us. There are so many negative thoughts that the enemy will place in our minds to steal our hearts to make us believe that it is our voice that is talking when in fact, it is the enemy who is talking to us. Nothing good comes from the enemy. Remember God brings goodness and truth and the enemy brings evil and lies.

We must understand and know the difference. We must not allow the enemy to steal our joy, desensitize the truth that God brings to us, this is why the Word of God says, "Therefore submit to God. Resist the devil and he will flee from you. KJV, James 4:7

The word of God is our sword to fight in the spiritual realm of evil. This is why God had to give us the ammunition and the tools to fight because he knew what we would have to deal with the evil on earth on a daily basis. We must live in this world when we have no allegiance to this world. It is our duty to fight effectively on this battlefield, in order for us to stand strong and be resilient in God's grace and mercy! We have to position and guard our hearts, minds and align our spirits with God in order to be in preparation for the tactics that are the plots to come against us.

The enemy will even use our own strengths against our weaknesses because I desired to settle down and I desired love more than anything. So, I became isolated with my emotions to love anyone and it was hard to trust anyone because I had built walls of offense to guard and to protect my heart. I had refused to allow anyone to break my heart into pieces, so I dug up the root of rejection, insecurities and vulnerabilities of not seeing myself as being pretty enough, or worthy enough, so I hid myself from people. I would create ideas in my head by judging a person's character or their perception of me based on how they looked at me or based upon their imperfections. I could only see flaws in myself. My strengths were the power to love others with a genuine love and a love of loyalty. However, my strength came against my weakness of insecurity because I couldn't be vulnerable enough to give genuine love due to fear of being cheated on. This created trust issues I've battled for years and yet it still becomes a battle. I created false beliefs that caused me to distance myself from people due to fear of rejection. I felt that I could never fit in and it really didn't matter if it were family, church, work, or any social function. I didn't realize that the problem was in Me. The insecurities grew deeper and increased as the years passed by and I couldn't seem to heal. The insecurities, trust issues and spirit of offense continued to increase. I became too sensitive and always offended and it took over my whole perspective of my thoughts, how I would see myself and others. I was broken inside and I was silently breaking down. I felt like a flower being trampled over. I was trampled by my own negative thoughts and false beliefs but I couldn't and would never think that I was my own enemy! I was a victim of myself. I allowed the enemy to enter into my eyes and ears to trick me into believing that I wasn't good enough.

Once again as I reflect on my high school years, no one knew how I was feeling inside. I didn't feel like I had true friendships because I couldn't really develop trust in anyone. I had a few friends that I would spend a little time with but I felt no one would ever understand me for who I was and what I was going through inside. I felt like it would be a waste of time trying to express myself that would make matters ten times worse. I knew that real friends are genuinely great supporters but they are not your saviors.

Who wants to hear about my problems and what I was going through? I didn't think that I mattered enough. So, I kept it that way. No one knew my ill thoughts and no one knew my desire to not live. Since I felt like an outsider and couldn't blend in with my peers due to the rejection, I kept myself isolated. My inner soul felt empty and being lonely became safe.

When I think of the grace and mercy of Jesus and all he had done for me throughout the years, especially my past, it's always been His love that never left me. It was always His love that surrounded me. It was His love that kept me, preserved me, and protected me from the worst of all the things that could have taken my life away. I always felt like I was a good-natured and loving soul although bitterness, anger, fear and resentment were the plagues of my life that I battled for many years. I knew that God's spirit was upon me. When I mentioned earlier how the enemy will use our own strengths against our weaknesses, my strength was the gift of encouragement but my weakness was to encourage myself. I always had the desire to help people, especially helping and inspiring children, yet I always felt rejuvenated when I would and could encourage others, whether young or mature family or friends. If someone shared their personal struggles with me of being stressed, discouraged or angered, I would have an encouraging word to say to them. I always found it easy to encourage others, yet it was so difficult to encourage myself! There was always a desire inside of me to provide encouragement, inspiration and gain the courage to comfort others. When others would grieve during their times of bereavement of losing a loved-one, my heart would grieve along with them and I wouldn't want to leave their side. I believe that the pain they felt at those moments quickly allowed me to discover God's love and a desire to bring compassion and comfort to them because I knew what emotional pain of losing loved-ones felt like and I also knew what emotional pain of discouragement, disappointment and being broken felt like too. My main desire was always to encourage those who needed it. It didn't matter who they were, whether they were a child or elderly, there were kind words of compassion to share with them and I felt that this was a gift from God because I wondered how did I have the strength to encourage others when I was going through so much in my life.

Only God knew what I was feeling and going through during my saddest moments of life. God's grace and mercy lifted me up even when I needed someone to encourage me but it was those moments where God gave me the power and an unknown strength to encourage others who were feeling down and sad. In those moments, I knew that it had to be God because there was no way I could help someone else when I needed help myself. While I was going through my own baggage, there is a verse in the bible that reminds me.

"Three times I pleaded with the Lord to relieve me of this. But he answered me, "My grace is always more than enough for you, and my power finds its full expression through your weakness." So I will celebrate my weaknesses, for when I'm weak I sense more deeply the mighty power of Christ living in me. 2 Corinthians 12:8-10 TPT

The bible states that my weaknesses become a portal to God's power. This was the mystery that I couldn't understand, yet God was always with me and I didn't realize it.

When the spirit of the Lord is inside of us, there's a void that is filled. There is a feeling of wholeness and a joy that is complete. I can remember many days in my teenage years and young adult life where I would feel depressed and sad and there was nothing that could comfort my grief. Sometimes, all I could do is quietly cry and pray to God in private to help me feel better and to change the way I felt. What do you do when you have those moments where those unknown feelings of sadness just come and linger? Where does these feelings originate and how do these feelings just appear when things are going great or when things are not so great? For we must understand that God has not given us the spirit of fear but he has given unto us, the spirit of power, the spirit of love and of a sound mind. 2 Timothy 1:7

With that being said, since these feelings don't come from God, where do they come from? It comes from our adversary, the enemy who comes to steal our joy, steal our peace, kill our hopes and dreams and to destroy our purpose and destiny. We must remind ourselves and we also must understand that the enemy doesn't play fair and is very intelligent in knowing your weakest link and will use your weakest link to break you down, piece by piece until you no longer have peace in your soul, mind and spirit. That is the enemy's plan. It's a trick to get you to see surface level attacks that will make you feel a sense of unhappiness, a sense of fear, worry or anxiety, that sense of vulnerability of always being offended or intimidated by the people but it's the enemy using the person(s) to attack you or to create confusion to make you believe that the person's intentions are to harm you. This is a surface level view. What you can't see in the spirit, is seen in the natural. Remember, we live in two atmospheric realms. The natural that we see with our natural eyes is temporary and the spiritual realm that we can only see in the spirit, which is permanent, when we are led by God or if we are to be led in darkness, which is the enemy. The enemy is a spirit and God is a spirit! The good news is that God's spirit doesn't compare to the spirit of the enemy! Why is that? God made everything, from earthy to supernatural beings. He made the angels and Satan was a fallen angel! So, whose power is greater? You already know!

We must be reminded that our spirits are much stronger than our flesh, which is our natural being. If God gives you the gift to see all that is going on in the spirit, you will have a keen understanding as to why things in the natural happen the way that it does. You must understand that the real world we live in is in the spiritual. This is the lens that we don't see in nature and it can fool you because the surroundings and environment looks absolutely different. We are only living in

185

the picture called life. A picture is worth a thousand words one would say but our lives are worth so much more if we can only see with our spiritual lenses. The trick of the enemy is to give you false hope that the surroundings in the natural is your permanent environment. One of the portals of your soul is through your eyes. The portals of our bodies are the openings. It's what we allow to enter in. Your eyes and our ears are the entry ways to what enters into our soul. Our soul is the container of our heart. That's how our emotions flow and that plays a major part of our character. What is poured inside our entry ways, sits into the container of our souls! This wins exactly why you must examine your company, those who you hang around! Make sure you're in good company with people who can pour goodness and godly things into your soul!

When you're around negative people, they pour negativity into your soul. The enemy knows that if he can get into our soul, which consists of our mindset, our emotions and our decisions, which is through the entry-way of our eyes and ears, he can plant roots of deception. This is the enemy's plot. His plot is the trick and it is wicked and he knows that deception is the abstract plot to lure us and to advertise what is desirable to us but his intent is to hurt and harm us. The beginning plot is always camouflaged to look good, feel good, and sound great but the end result is to hurt, harm us and to bring death and destruction to our souls.

In addition, another portal to our soul is through our ears. The sound that enters inside of us. Something can sound good but is it the sound that has our attention over what's really the truth. I can remember many years back when I used to go on dates and with all intentions, my heart's desire was to find love. A man who could solely love me for who I am and not whisper sweet nothings into my ear for his personal gratifications; Not whispering things that girls and women love to hear a man say. Women love to hear those three words, "I love you!" Those three words can be very deceiving when it's not meant for good and it's trustworthy. When those three words are used to manipulate a woman and when those words are not intently from the heart, those words become deceptive. This is why it is so important to ask God to give us the gift of discernment to test the spirits by the spirit of God. Testing the hearts of man for the sake of determining his integrity. Testing the spirits can help us to determine lies from truth. The enemy is going to make us think that it would be in our best interest to give our body to a man that may whisper in our ears, "I'm in love with you." "So show me that you love me too!" Many women fall into this trap when there are men who are into them for love but for sexual pleasures and alluring bodies. In the same manner, for example, there are women who would deceive a man into using him for his money and possessions. We've observed how there are women who would purposely use pregnancies to manipulate a man for personal gain. We have seen this a lot with professional sports players. It doesn't matter if it's a man or woman, we all have a spirit and the question is, is our spirit pure or perverse? Are our hearts positioned in the right posture? We must understand this thoroughly, in order to believe this.

This world is full of so much evil! Just look around, watch the news and think about how evil the world has become. It's almost like the world is getting worse with every passing day. As mentioned earlier in this chapter, "We wrestle not with flesh and blood, but against principalities, against powers, against the rulers of the darkness of this world, against spiritual wickedness in high places". Ephesians 6:12 KJV

Let's just examine this part, "against the rulers of the darkness of this world." Remember it said rulers. What rules this world? The answer is Darkness. In the high places of this world, what are we challenged with? The answer is spiritual wickedness in high places. Let me take you back to another part of the bible where the enemy tried to tempt Jesus by trying to offer him the world. The enemy is so evil and so malicious that he tried to test Jesus. In Matthew 4, it states, "Again, the enemy took Him up on an exceedingly high mountain, and showed Him all the kingdoms of the world and their glory and he said to him, "All these things I will give You if You will fall down and worship me." then Jesus said to him, "Away with you, Satan! For it is written, "You shall worship the Lord your God, and Him only you shall serve." Matthew 4:10

The enemy knows that he is doomed but he will try his very best to test you to see where he can trick you. His plan is to attack you in every area of your life to see where you are the weakest and to see where there's an opening to come in. Once he finds your weak spots, then that's where he plays dirty. He keeps attacking the weaker area of your life until you give up or give in. Once he feels he has you, then he attacks you to allow sin to consume you and then he accuses you of being the sinner that you are, so that he can kill you, steal your joy and every good fruit that God placed inside of you and then he wants to destroy you forever so that you can join him in misery. You know that misery enjoys company! When I think about the power of love, I think about how people can use the word love to manipulate, test, trick and control a person's mind and heart for their own advantage or self-gain.

It often saddens me how so many young and older women are yet struggling with not being or feeling loved and they will lower their standards, beliefs, morals and values for someone that could care less about them for the sake of being loved. Relationships have taught me what to look for in love. Many

188

times I was told, "I love you" by a companion and I believed it because it felt real and it would sound real and it would even look real but later it would be that unfortunate reminder of how love is misinterpreted and misunderstood. There are so many who really don't know what it means to love someone or to be in-love with someone. There is a huge difference! I used to believe that if a guy loved me that he would be loyal to me, treat me with the utmost respect, and not betray, lie or cheat on me but I learned the hard way. Just like you can love your favorite TV show, or you can love your favorite shoes or restaurant, it's an emotion of caring but not an emotion of loyalty. In contrast, I had to learn that being in-love is a strong emotion that is beyond caring for someone, it's that emotion and loyalty of being committed in love, meaning to never physically or emotionally cheat on your spouse, to respect and always be available for that person's needs and desires. It's also being supportive of that person's hopes and dreams. It's sad to admit that I actually know a few people who struggle in the area of accepting the disloyalty and being mistreated by their fiancée or spouse and considering it to be love when in reality this person doesn't love or isn't in love with them. They may treat their dog or cat better than they treat you. It sometimes may make us think a bit further as to why someone would remain in an unhealthy relationship when they know that love doesn't exist in that person? I think maybe the women who are struggling in this area are battling to find the strength, self-love or the belief that they can do a lot better by themselves. Let's keep this very real! There are women today who would rather settle for a piece of a man to avoid loneliness. The piece of the man that they are settling for is doing more harm to their mind, body and soul but yet they have listened to the voice of the enemy that has convinced them that they can't live without this piece of a man. The trick of the enemy makes them believe that the piece of a man is what makes them whole, but yet holding on to the piece of what they call a "man" is bringing more destruction, dysfunction and damage to their soul. When God blesses you with the "Man" for you, he won't be a piece and you won't be his piece. He or you won't be a side-piece nor a dime-piece. If you allow it, a piece of your soul will be tied-up and a piece of your heart will be tangled up in vanity! When God finds your mate, he will be the rib that matches your rib, a whole that doesn't leave a hole in your soul, and good peace that will never keep you wondering or second-guessing love. You will be far from a his side-piece. A side-piece doesn't fill you up like a whole meal ever will!

Furthermore, God desires us to be happy and he also desires us to be loved and feel loved but before God can give you the mate that you have been desiring, he has to do a new thing in you. He has to give you the healing and deliverance you need in order to enjoy the gift of the mate He has for you. He can't give you a gift that you aren't ready for. You must be whole with yourself, you must start loving yourself. You must find happiness within yourself. Most of all, you must find Jesus before you can start to find healing. It all starts with you! Another trick of the enemy is to make you believe that you don't need any help in the first place. You feel that you are perfectly fine! That is deception at its best. The truth only sets you free. Believing a lie doesn't set you free. The enemy will have you believing that you are not suffering from any pain so therefore you won't admit to needing help! You will continue believing that you are solid within your soul while full of dysfunction. The enemy will have you believing that since you have experienced a successful life by having a great career, educated and intelligent, an immaculate home, healthy children, years of marriage, charming personality, and gorgeous appearance; that you do not need any emotional, mental or spiritual help. That is a lie from the pit of hell too. The enemy will make us feel desensitized from our pain to the point where we won't feel that we need any help at all. We become self-righteous filled with arrogance and pride by our own intelligence and accomplishments. We become numb and deceived. You know why? Because the enemy is doing his job. His job is to numb the pain that we have buried years ago, allow it to become callus and put fear in our heart to face the problems that we doubt could ever be fixed. The enemy will take our minds and make us feel that the tangible things of this life will replace all the pain that we swept under the rug. The enemy will not allow us to not feel anything and to numb the feeling away with drinking alcohol and/or by smoking recreational marijuana or what others call "weed" and any other drug substances to suppress the pain or any other familiar wounds we have buried so deeply inside.

This happened to me but it's not only what happened to me, it happens to each and everyone one of us. The enemy will use certain people to trouble our hearts, minds, souls and spirits for His own wicked plan. He is deceptive by tempting you to present your weakness as a form of pleasure in the very beginning by making you feel like a failure in the end. He will use distractions to keep your mind from the truth and once you've realized that you have been distracted and tricked, he will bring condemnation on you for your sin. This would and could possibly make you doubt in your faith and allow your failures, shortcomings and downfalls to be your demise. Isn't this just how the enemy tempted Adam and Eve by eating from the Tree of Life in the garden. He knew that their disobedience would ultimately cause them to sin but his plan is always to kill, steal and to destroy what God has created. The enemy knows that the wages of sin is death and if he can use the smallest temptation to lure you in a deadly path, he would allow your smallest temptation and your biggest weakness to destroy you by all means necessary. He will make you an enemy to yourself. The enemy knows that he is doomed and he wants to take as many souls with him as possible. The plan of misery and we all should know, misery loves company! The enemy has already been defeated, so his plan is to deceive as many people as possible because he already knows he has lost the battle. His plan is to make us all believe we have lost the battle as well. The area of the body he attacks is our minds. Once he has our mind, every other part of our body follows. If he can make us believe that we will never make it, or that we will never be able to overcome and heal from our past struggles in life, we have allowed him to keep us in bondage. He allows us to feel the shame and guilt from our past mistakes to keep us in condemnation. It is a trick to make us feel that we have no hope in life, to make us accept that, it is what it is, as many people say. The saying, " it is what it is", is basically saying that I must accept what it is, but stop right at this moment and think about what you're saying! It may be what it is at that moment but it doesn't mean that it has to be this way for the rest of our lives.

We must not accept negativity as our normal way of thinking. Our setbacks and our struggles are at surface level,

view, meaning it's what we only see with our natural eyes. There is a spiritual realm of God that is seen through the spiritual lens. These are lenses that we view which are available when we spend time with God in a personal relationship, not a religion-ship.

There are stories that we have read about God in the Bible and there are many parables on how God's wrath was poured onto men due to their disobedience and sinful nature. These stories can make many believe that God is angry with us for our disobedience. We must understand that we are not His enemy but He does not like our sinful ways. Sin is what separates us from Him but He never stops loving us. However, His grace and mercy is what gives us the opportunity of a lifetime and that is what washes away our sins when we confess our sins and ask God to forgive us. Grace and mercy are gifts from God! He doesn't remember our sins when we ask him to forgive us! His love for us is so awesome because the gift that He gives us is eternal life and that is a gift bigger and much greater than any gift we would ever receive. When God gives, he gives with abundance! You won't have room to receive it. His goodness towards us overflows. What is bigger than the gift of life? God's love language towards us cannot be matched. It's our love language towards him that we must work on.

It's in those times on the road of recovery where we must vow to put our trust in him. It's in those times where change can become hard to adjust to. When our environment, family life, finances and career paths change, God brings transition. When we see things as falling apart, God sees it as falling together. God brings times of transition to create transformation that provides us with revelation to feel His manifestation and to take us to our victorious destination. This is why the passage was written, "Be transformed by the renewing of your mind." Someone has to tell you that you are greater than your present condition. You must renew your mind to understand your identity. Just look at it this way, our minds are the leader of our body. Our mind holds the brain to direct the body where to go and what to do. Without the brain, our body loses direction and function. It can't move. It can't stand and it surely can not walk. This is why the mind has to be renewed for the sake of change and restoration. We must arise to the occasion of letting go everything and anyone who creates a negative atmosphere that will distort and influence any type of negativity. Being around people who talk negative and behave negative, isn't going to allow us to change our mindset for the better. People and our surroundings can hinder our rise to evolve. This can be toxic friendships and relationships, procrastination and laziness are the keys to stunting our growth and sweltering our minds. Think about the passage and meditate on it, "As a man thinketh in his heart, so is he....." Proverbs 23:7

Even if you are in the right position, your mindset has been dispositioned because you need a renewed mind. You become what you think. This might explain how we attract who we are. When you're stagnant, you're stuck in a cycle and when you're stuck in a formal norm, it's like you're walking 100 miles per hour to realize you're still in the same spot. Your mind becomes stuck, stagnant and overworked because it will feel like you're walking a treadmill and once again, you haven't gone anywhere. Life is only as good as your mindset and your mindset is controlled by the conditions of your heart. You must take on the boldness and fearlessness to take on your purpose in the midst of opposition. You have to release it to go where God predestined you to go. When I reflect on the mindset of my past, those suicidal attempts as a teenager were one of my lowest valleys on the road to recovery. I knew there had to be hope nearby. Deep down and somewhere in my soul, I had believed that God had a purpose and destination for my life, that He loved me and that His plans were for good, not for evil. When those thoughts of depression consumed me in my adult years, I gained the strength to climb out of that pit. With God's power, I would soon climb out of that pit of depression. Psalms 147:3 states, "He heals the brokenhearted and binds up their wounds." My heart was wounded and my depression deepened.

Depression had compressed my mind. The tug of war was pulling for my soul in the middle of God and the enemy! This was the enemy's plot to pull as hard as he could. Yet, victory is possible because the battle is always won when we help

God help ourselves. Freedom is real! With God, you can overcome and experience proper mental and emotional health. You are not defined by your diagnosis, you are defined by your Heavenly Father's purpose. Do not give up on yourself when the road walk is difficult, even when you walk alone, God walks beside you! God calls you beloved, chosen, fearfully and wonderfully made and valuable. With God's supernatural help and taking wise steps in the natural, I walked up out of that pit and chose life. It was a faith walk! The good news is --- it is possible for you to experience victory from depression too. My prayer for you today, "Heavenly Father, today I decide to choose life. I ask that you would renew my mind and help me to see me the way you see me. Fill my heart and mind with your peace and give me wisdom and insight into the next steps towards full freedom and victory within my mental and emotional health. In Jesus name, Amen" - Deuteronomy 30:19-20

As I reflect on the portals of our bodies and what we allow to enter into our bodies, we must be keenly aware that the enemy isn't going to tell us something that represents the fruit of God's spirit. The enemy is going to tell us something that will tempt us and make us question or doubt what is good for our own personal gain or gratification. Think about the story when Adam and Eve were tempted in the garden. The enemy knew that Adam and Eve were not supposed to eat from the tree of Life but the snake, (the enemy) wanted to make Eve believe that God didn't really mean what He said by saying, "You can be sure that you won't die". The snake also told Eve, "God knows that when you eat the fruit of that tree, you will know things that you have never known before. You will be able to tell the difference between good and evil and you become like God" Genesis 3:4-5 NKJV

You see, the enemy tells lies and he will do what he can to tempt us and make us ignorantly curious to disobey God and to test God. God clearly told them not to eat from that tree but because they were deceived by the plan of the enemy and disobeyed God, they were thrown from God's paradise for their disobedience. In the same manner, when someone lies to us, to conspire or manipulate us to do something for their own advantage, they have used us for their own personal gain or advantage, even if it causes us to lose our lives, or even if it causes us to break our spirits; it was only for their greedy and selfish intent. Greed causes deception, distrust and destruction. In the same manner, the enemy will use us for his own advantage, even at the cost of losing our life when Jesus already sacrificed His life for our sins. The enemy's greed is to take our lives for the sake to gratify his evil plan. We have to always stay conscious by distractions and ask ourselves, "Is it worth losing our lives in eternity based on lies and deception?

REPENTANCE AND RADICAL PAIN

Remember, the plan of the enemy is to keep us from knowing who we are, and who we are to God. If we still have a beating pulse, God still has a working plan in our lives. God knew the mistakes we would make in this life. He knew the temptations, sorrows and hardships we would have to go through, and this is why He will never forsake us and never leave us because He died on the cross with the ultimate sacrifice for the sake of cleansing us from our sins. In this life, we are going to be challenged. We are going to go through persecution! We are going to suffer things we may not understand, but God's dying on the cross is our reminder that the blood that bled from the nails in his hands, the blood that he shed from the thorns pressed into his head while hanging on the cross, was the blood shed for our sins. The shedding of the blood is cleansing us when we humble ourselves to God and the blood will never lose its power! The blood has power to heal and to deliver us and meet us at our very place in our moments. It heals the mind, the body and it saves our souls. That's right! The shedding of the blood.

However, the enemy's plot is for us to not know who we are and what Jesus' death on the cross means to us. We must believe in the power of God to receive this new place that God has for us. We must allow God to not allow surface level attacks, sudden or counter attacks or distractions to trick us or to deter us from seeing what God's ultimate plan is for our lives. He gives us the spiritual lens to look beyond our setbacks and circumstances that weigh us down.

Remember, the blood of Jesus has the power to break every chain of bondage in our lives. It's a cleansing, a healing, a deliverance and a covering that God is faithful to transform us by the renewing of our minds. Remember, it starts with the mind. The mind is a terrible thing to waste and the enemy knows that.

Always keep in mind on a daily basis that the enemy is our accuser and he knows that sin is what separates us from God. So his ultimate plot on this battlefield on earth is to attack us in many ways unimaginable that would cause us to commit sin. He is the author of confusion and the accuser of the brethren.

"And I heard a loud voice saying in heaven, "Now salvation, and strength, and the kingdom of our God, and the power of His Christ have come, for the accuser of our brethren who accused them before our God day and night, has been cast down." Revelation 12:10 KJV

Did you know that every time we commit a sin, whether we are conscious or unconsciously aware of committing sin, the enemy comes to the throne of God to find ways to forfeit our blessings and our glory with God by accusing us of all the things we've done wrong and why he should be given the authority to punish us and to bring condemnation to our hearts and souls. Remember, he was already defeated at the cross when Jesus died for our sins and the enemy's goal is to cause us to fall and become defeated with sin right along with him. Most of all, the enemy desires for us to remain in our sins and to be condemned by guilt and shame. His plot is to take as many souls with him to a sweltering and burning hell that will burn in eternity. There's nothing good in hell.

Matthew 25:46, states, "Hell was prepared for the devil and his angels." So, that tells us that It wasn't prepared for you and I but many will go if they have not surrendered their hearts to our Lord and Savior, Jesus. We must be born again. This means we must accept Jesus into our lives and to believe in Him but the enemy's plot is to get us in unbelief. To have us believe more on our problems than on what God can do about the problem. The enemy's plot is subtle and will always go against God's word. God's word will never come void, but the enemy is the author of confusion and the accuser who comes to steal, kill and to destroy our faith and to get us to forfeit our blessings. He doesn't want us to have faith or to trust and to depend on God and to create an intimate relationship by getting in God's presence and when we think about misery loving company, just think about this being a part of the enemy's character. He already knows that he's doomed from the beginning, so his plot is to take as many souls with him as possible during his reign here on earth.

During this time of my life, I had no peace. I worried every day and this was when I discovered I had been in fear and suffered from anxieties nearly on a daily basis. I had worked several business projects and a business deal that spiraled downhill. The experience was many lessons learned and the true lesson of learning that all money ain't good money, yet I had become so weak in faith, I felt sick and ill. I had grieved the death of a close relative who had passed from cervical cancer. I grieved her death so bad because she and I grew up together as kids and we had so many great stories we used to reminisce on. We would just talk on the phone and laugh. It was always a joy to talk to her. To accept the fact that she was gone and recalling that last moment and not knowing that it would be our last conversation, we talked on the phone when she told me how seriously ill she was. It was heartbreaking! I will never forget that day she told me that she didn't want to die. She didn't want to leave her two daughters behind. They needed her and she was afraid. I remember telling her that she was going to beat this illness and I really believed it. I prayed and had faith that she would beat the cancer but she soon passed away in May of 2013. God had the final say! It was one of my worst experiences to lose a close relative who was more like my friend, a sister and someone who always understood me, someone who always had my back and who looked out for me when we were growing up. I was back to being depressed again and although my family would try to keep my spirits up, I couldn't find the power to move forward. I lost weight, couldn't eat and had no motivation to do anything. It was like I had given up hope for a while.

In the summer of 2015, one Sunday morning, I mustered enough faith to get myself ready for church. In the months of all the prayers, I was starting to believe that God wasn't going to get me over this hump. This was another encounter from God. This time it wasn't at the church where God had spoken to me back in 2011. It was at the larger church I had been visiting for several years where no one would notice whether I was there or not. It was a different message this time. This time the message was preached by the pastor of the church and that was the message of salvation, hope and repentance. For me, this was the message of healing and the message to answer prayers that God would change my life around. It wasn't so much about my disappointment of not working a steady job and the loss of my cousin. It was that state of my existence where I had become a failure of life and a question of how my decisions and the sacrifices that led me to a place of misery and misfortunes. I needed to be emotionally, mentally and spiritually alive for my family. It wasn't about me! It was about what God was doing inside of me. I was hungry and thirsty for God.

So, as I walked to the altar for prayer, I asked God to forgive me for my sins and to allow me to live again, to not just survive which is what it felt like but this time I needed peace, joy, freedom and the faith to believe that one day there will be a brighter day, a much better day, a much better me!

As I bowed my head and lifted my hands in prayer, tears began to flow down my cheeks. I had to surrender to God. I can hear the praise and worship music playing very peacefully and low in the background. It was a moment of letting go and letting God take away all that I had held inside. All that was eating me up had to be purged. It had to be pulled by the root and now it was time to let God inside my heart. I asked God to take anything out of me that wasn't pleasing to Him.

When Jesus died on the cross, he died for our sins. Our sins are what leads us to death. We are dead men walking when we have not accepted Christ. When Jesus arose from the dead on the third day, the reflection of His resurrection is a symbol of "Life". He arose so that we can "Arise" from our broken conscious, broken-spirit, broken-soul and broken bodies.

ARISE from the brokenness and become the best version of yourself, a transformed person who has been healed, delivered, restored and renewed. It's like discovering the new version of yourself, whom you've never met.

"The Spirit of God, who raised Jesus from the dead, lives in us. And just as God raised Christ Jesus from the dead, he will give life to our mortal bodies by this same Spirit living within." Romans 8:11

We must believe that he is the son of God. We must have the radical faith to believe in order to surrender our lives through repentance. We must be born-again as a new creature in Christ, recreated as we live a life full of purpose, renewed in our minds as this transforms our body and restored by our radical faith to just believe! God knows our beginning and end and yes, God will have the final say!

A RENEWED COMMITMENT

I was always a nice person and I enjoyed doing generous things for people but being a nice person wasn't enough to eliminate my grief, sadness and sorrow within those moments of my recovery. Doing good works doesn't earn us a ticket to heaven and being nice to people doesn't mean we have surrendered to God, although it is our righteous duty before God, it doesn't give us reward points to redeem a staircase to heaven. We must understand that salvation is a gift from God and we don't earn it through good works. The book of Ephesians 2:8-10 (NIV) states, "For it is by grace you have been saved, through faith—and this is not from yourselves, it is the gift of God—not by works, so that no one can boast. For we are God's handiwork, created in Christ Jesus to do good works, which God prepared in advance for us to do."

I was a God-fearing woman and I feared death. Sometimes, I would worry about dying and the scariest feeling was the thought of dying in my sins. Yet, in those moments of depression I desired my life to end because I was hopeless. I also feared that if I didn't get my life in order, I would die in my sins and go to a burning hell. Hell is very real and it's sad that many don't believe it. God doesn't want us to give our lives to him as an obligation or because it is the law of Christ. More importantly, He doesn't want to force fear on us to accept him. He's not a God to intimidate or to enforce fear on us by condemning us to accept Him in any way. He simply wants us to surrender at our own free will. I hadn't made up my mind to surrender on my own free-will but many times I did surrender my life due to fearing God and fearing Judgment Day and then there were those times where I felt myself going backwards. Right back to living and breathing those cycles as many saved folks consider as a "back-slider". I didn't feel like a Christian because I hadn't changed my life and made a 360 degree change. I would pray and sometimes read my bible and sometimes God would answer my prayers but I didn't commit to God faithfully because it felt like I was more religious than spiritual. There's a huge difference between the two. Some people religiously attend church on a regular basis because it gives them fulfillment and it become a formality, tradition and familiarity, unfortunately that's not having a personal relationship with God, Then you have those who are super-saved (legalistically religious) and are so arrogant that they believe they are the only ones who hears from God and become more critical on everyone else's life or what they're not doing instead of showing love and being humble with a desire to pray for others. This is a form of godliness because God is a God of love, not condemnation.

Fortunately, then you have those who are spiritual believers, where they hear and know God's voice by being in his presence, they become overseers of Christ, the have compassion for people, yet still attend church and don't act like they are perfect or better than anybody else because they once were delivered from their own bondage and they understand how the spiritual warfare is required through prayer, obedience and fasting. Their characteristics represent the fruits of God's spirit with a genuine, relatable, integrity and yet become your biggest supporter, inspirational and motivational advocate for Christ for those who are going through life's trials and tribulations. They are there by your side to help you, to pray for you and to push you in your purpose! They don't condemn but they do correct and coach you. They don't try to be anymore than who God has intended them to be. They have a desire to intercede and cover souls in their prayers and a love for you with the love of Christ.

I was one who attended church most of my life but didn't know God's voice and I couldn't hear his voice. I just believed in God as I was taught and grew up to believe and trust in Him. I didn't diligently seek Him on a consistent basis. I prayed to Him and would sometimes worship and meditate on His Word by reading the bible but would sometimes fall asleep and I would later find myself worried about what I just prayed for, even after reading the bible and gaining faith to not worry. It's like how do you pray, read your bible and still worry about what you have just prayed for? Isn't that contradicting yourself? Isn't that unbelief in God? When I know that God has performed many miracles and great works in people's lives, where I have heard testimonies after testimonies how he delivered people from drugs, alcohol, gangs, violence and revived people from their sick beds. When I have seen the hand of God move in my own family lives and his word is never changing. His living word is truth and his promises are yes and amen. His affirmations are my DNA because I am who God says I am, yet I still lived in unbelief many times and had not lived by the truth, even when it was staring me in my face. It was that I doubted him. I knew God was able to do anything but I didn't believe that he would do the unimaginable for me. I had faith for others but not for myself. It was like God saying to me, "Oh ye, of little faith!" I was troubled with the spirit of unbelief that had me going through cycles in my life. It would be those cycles to put me back into depression.

I couldn't shake who I was. One moment I was saved, meaning surrendering my life to Christ and on Sunday morning used a few choice words a few days later, on a Tuesday, then to go back to church to get saved again. I couldn't find that breakthrough of freedom for stability. I was wavering in my salvation and I couldn't find the power to keep consistency in my salvation! I was fighting for my life but I kept losing the fight to win. I knew God could perform miracles and I could surely use a miracle to turn my life around for good! Meaning, not wavering but being solid in my faith and grounded. I would hear the pastors preach and often say, you won't need to thirst again once you have a thirst of righteousness. I needed to really be planted like a tree by the living waters. I desired that taste! "Oh, taste and see that the Lord is good."Psalms 34:8

God wants us all to serve and to surrender to Him with an open heart. He wants us to do it at our own free will because He gives us a will, which is our choice to serve him or to serve this world. The free-will that God gives us is a gift and although it is a gift, it is very dangerous because that same gift gives us the freedom to also go against God and love the world, which the enemy presently reigns. The enemy knows that we are God's chosen people and he loves us with an everlasting love. Even at our worst, God thinks we're the best but you must believe that. Believing is knowing Jesus! Jesus is the way, the truth, and the light! When you have Jesus in your heart and on your mind, you are living in truth! You are living in the light and you are definitely going in the right direction.

"But you are a chosen generation, a royal priesthood, a holy nation, His own special people, that you may proclaim the praises of Him who called you out of darkness into His marvelous light." 1st Peter 2:9

So, our gift of free-will gives us the choice to make a decision and that choice can only be made by us. Our own individual free-will of what we decide to do with our lives.

Matthews 20:28 states, "Just as the Son of Man did not want to be served, but to serve, and to give his life as a ransom for many." This is a gift of life that can't be earned, purchased or deserved. It is a gift of eternal life which expresses the love, grace and the mercy of Christ. It is our renewed commitment to receive a gift and to receive it with an appreciation and with loyalty. God is your creator, not your father until you have invited Him in. "Seek the Lord while He may be found." Isaiah 55:6 KJV

THE TRANSFORMATION OF FORGIVENESS

In the book of Ephesians 4:29 & 30, it states, "And never let ugly or hateful words come from your mouth, but instead let your words become beautiful gifts that encourage others; do this by speaking words of grace to help them. The Holy Spirit of God has sealed you in Jesus Christ until you experience your full salvation. So never grieve the Spirit of God or take for granted his holy influence in your life. Lay aside bitter words, temper tantrums, revenge, profanity, and insults. But instead be kind and affectionate toward one another. Has God graciously forgiven you? Then graciously forgive one another in the depths of Christ's love."

When I was broken from the past hurts of holding grudges and blaming my father for not being in my life, I felt that I was doing the right thing! I felt validated because he was the bigger person who should have accepted me into his life by keeping promises! The promises that a little girl felt were so important in growing up. I felt that my father left a big hole in my heart because he chose things over me. The rejection I felt from him ignoring my calls and needing his presence but yet feeling abandoned by him on weekends where I would look for him with bags packed and he was nowhere to be found made me feel unwanted and unloved! My heart was aching for so many years and I had to put the blame on somebody. I couldn't and didn't know how to let go of the grudge because I owned what I felt and what I felt had always been familiar to me. It was my reality! I had to feel what was real to me. The first man I ever loved was the first man that let me down! I couldn't find a way to forgive him for robbing me of my peace, my security, affirmation, my trust, my hope, my joy, my courage, my expectations to believe that genuine love from a man could be real! All I believed were lies and I believed that most men were liars!

Throughout my marriage and motherhood, I had limited access to my father. I would bump into him from time to time in passing by. We lived a few miles from each other but I refused to accept him into my life. As I got older, I felt like I didn't have a need for a father in my life. I felt that all the love that I once lost was revived and restored through the love of my new family. My husband and children were something new and fulfilling. My identity of who I grew into was satisfied. I loved being a wife and a mother, so I felt that my family were all that I needed to fully heal inside and to discover a love like no other. There were times where I made some attempts to visit my father on certain occasions while visiting my grandmother. I can remember a particular time when I was pregnant with my oldest child until the time she turned 8 months and at that moment, a family conflict erupted and caused havoc and separation.

This particular side of the family has always dealt with conflict, havoc and separation, so this wasn't anything new. My father was involved in this conflict. This was the moment I decided that he wouldn't stand a chance in my life. I had enough! I know longer desired to have anything to do with him. I decided to erase him out of my mind and out of my heart. For so many years, I was emotionally worn from the disappointments of hoping that this man would change and start acting like a father to me, well, to all his children. I felt hopeless and despair and this time, I promised that I would never forgive him. I gave up on him and I also promised that he would never see or get to know any of my children. This was his punishment for what he'd put me through all of my life growing up suffering and wounded by his intentional and unintentional absence. I'd say intentional because I felt that he was an adult and I was the child. It was the parent's responsibility to be a father and not neglect his own child and I'd say unintentional absence because as humans, our negative behavior and bad decisions are based upon who we are and my father wasn't at peace with himself. He had bottled up resentment and anger throughout his disappointments with his own personal past. I believe that whatever is trapped in our hearts, will suppress the behavior and actions of what we hold in your souls for many years and it becomes who we are. It becomes our character! We attract negative thinking that can cause us to make bad choices that are based upon bad perceptions and distorted perspectives that could cause more problems to arise in our lives. It can soon become the worst version of who we are. This reflects the unintentional absence of me, not having my father; not having his paternal instruction, guidance and advice is what I lacked. He wasn't emotionally and spiritually capable to give me or any of his children the best version of himself. I carried bags of unforgiveness in my heart towards my father and this lasted for nearly over 15 years. Even those years when I would see my father, I resented being in his presence while trying to find the grace to give him chances to change. I felt that the only love I could give him was my time and patience. I felt that maybe as he got older, he would become more of a father to me and his children and change. I felt that he could change into this role he never was, but he didn't. I continued to carry bags of unforgiveness for so long, 15 years long and maybe even longer than that. So, I continued to keep my guards up. As long as I've been raised in church to love and to forgive people, I didn't know how to forgive my father. I didn't know how to heal and to let go of this emotional baggage. I did not know how to break the chains that had me bound for so many years of burying my pain. My buried pain wouldn't allow me to let go. I carried the weight of unforgiveness for so many years, where the weight became normal to carry but I was unaware that the weight on my soul, mind and spirit became a slow death. Unforgiveness is a slow death. After so many years of carrying this weight, it will chip away from life. It chipped away from my soul. Unforgiveness creates an enemy within ourselves. It created double-mindedness in me because I expected people to forgive me of any wrongdoings but I couldn't forgive my father? Being double-minded divides our soul and keeps our minds hijacked. Many don't understand that unforgiveness causes sickness to occur in our bodies. It's a physical and spiritual cancer that will cause us to rot or spoil if we don't get the help we need.

We all have to make a determined decision. We believe that we are pardoning the crime against the other person or freeing them from the offenses, when in fact, we are freeing ourselves spiritually when we forgive others and not hold on to the offense or hold the grudge. We must be free in order to move on with our lives. We have to let go of those past and current offenses. Forgiveness is a choice! You cannot allow the person another day to steal your peace! It releases freedoms and breaks walls. In order to gain power within, you have to stop giving this person your power! You're giving that person control over you when you won't forgive them. In your mind, you want them to suffer because you have suffered but in reality you are suffering the most because you are waiting for them to change. You are waiting for an apology that may never come. Forgiveness is a gift to ourselves. It releases stress, our mental health, our cardiovascular health, illnesses such as cancer, high-cholesterol, diseases, and in mental illness of depression and oppression. There is research studies on how there's significant positive results on how forgiveness and emotional and spiritual development enhances our physical conditions. It enhances us to live longer. Forgiveness opens up a pathway to a new place of peace where we can persist despite what has happened to us! Forgiveness is the key to evolve from our brokenness. We must dispose of the painful residue of our unfortunate history. From the gutter to the throne, forgiveness chains us to the gutters and down into pits of being stuck and imprisoned and most times we must forgive those who are the closest to us that brought the pain to us because those are the people and the experiences that detest the most because we least expected it from them.

Unforgiveness is what contaminates our soul and poisons our destiny. Our tears and cries are cleansing to our hearts. Our tears and our cries is a sign to show us that God removed the numbness from our hearts. He allows us to feel again. You cannot correct what you will not confront in this life. When people hurt you, God will heal you. When people humiliate you, God will magnify you. When people judge you, God will justify you! Our healing is not an overnight process. It's going to take time. Don't give up and don't get discouraged. Take each day one step at a time. Every step you take, know that each step becomes the pathway to your power. Keep in mind that forgiving is not for others but for you. Forgiving is not forgetting. It is remembering without anger. It frees up your power, heals your body, mind and spirit.

On our road to recovering, we must remember that as we walk up that road, Jesus walks with us. Those encounters from God would come to visit me at different times in my life to remind me that Jesus never left me. He was always with me. It would be that one day that changed the trajectory of my life. It would be that radical faith that would change the direction my life was going and would provide my soul with inner peace and freedom to soar. It was that day I forgave my father! That moment as I kneeled before God in my bedroom, no one was home that day. I closed my bedroom door to feel the privacy of peace as I began to pray to God. I felt a release from my soul. Loud screams were forced out of my mouth as the cries felt stronger. I was weeping aggressively before the presence of God to forgive myself first for all that I had blamed myself and for all the years for not forgiving my father. This time my heart and soul was healed and the Spirit of God was on me. I felt the deliverance! I felt the power of the Holy Spirit. The Holy Spirit is the spiritual feeling from God that comforts us, guides us, teaches us, and builds our character. Holy Spirit speaks to us and through us when we allow Holy Spirit to live in us. I recognized the presence of God. I felt an outer body experience because I felt a whirlwind inside of my stomach and all I could do was weep and cry and tears were streaming down my face. My soul was humbled. My body felt like a power charge, similar to feeling electricity. I had a peace that was indescribable. It filled my atmosphere. That very moment felt renewed from an intense prayer and meditation with God, I felt that urgency within to pick up the phone and make that call. This was a call of obedience and God knew that this was what I had to do to break those chains of bondage from my life. It's according to our obedience to God when life begin to change!

As I sat down on my bed and dialed the number, I started to feel a bit nervous because I didn't know if my father would pick up his phone. We hadn't talked in over a decade and I got his number from my grandmother. On the other end of the phone I heard, "Hello". I replied, "It's me dad, Angel". He was very surprised to hear my voice. He wasn't sure what this call was about because we hadn't spoken to each for so long and he knew how I'd felt about him. I immediately cleared my mind of all those things that happened years ago. I was now ready to utter those words. Once I said those words "I forgive you for all the pain you put me through and for all those times you left me and my sibling stranded on weekends and for all the resentment I carried towards you for not being present in my life and I have forgiven you and I can't hold my past any longer. I can't hold and carry this pain any longer. I must forgive you so that I can be free to love you again." My father was very remorseful. He knew that my words were from my heart and he felt the pain in my voice as I trembled to hold back the tears. He said, "Please forgive me" I'm sorry for the pain I caused you all those years and as we began to talk and discuss those years from the past. He shared much of his personal pain and his own demons he struggled through and faced from growing up as a child all the way through adulthood. He stated that he wasn't proud of all that he had done and he was very regretful for it. I knew that what he had shared were not excuses to validate all he had done but at that moment I became empathetic because I had to realize that I wasn't the only one hurting. He too was hurting. We both were hurting just like we both aren't perfect. We were both broken souls and did our best to heal the best we could. It was empathy that helped me through this forgiving process. The sting of the pain stopped. When Christ abides in your heart, he will give you the strength to forgive. He allowed me to experience the struggles of my father's pain. I never knew about his pain and his struggles and what he was going through at that time. Some of these emotional pains were similar to mine. He too, didn't have the love from his father although his father was around physically, his father (my grandfather) was absent mentally and emotionally. He never healed from the pain he had buried throughout his entire manhood, and would soon suppress later in the years of being a husband and a father. We must understand that we can't blame our loved-ones for what they did to us or what they did not do for us because we really don't know what they may have endured in their personal lives growing up. We really don't know the secrets that may have been buried and swept under the rug. We may never know the hurt or the pain but one thing is for sure, the wound might not be our fought but the healing is surely our responsibility!

THE NEW REVELATION

"Train up a child in the way he should go, and when he is old he will not depart from it. Proverbs 22:6 KJV

As I experience the impact of fathers in everyday lives, I think about how the impact of fathers can cause a positive or negative impact on male lives. I was blessed as a child to get to know both of my grandfathers, each from my paternal and maternal side of my family. It is considered a blessing these days to have a chance to know and develop a relationship with your grandparents because many do not, and have not had that chance. However, when I think about my maternal grandfather, I think about a man of honor, respect, integrity and a leader in the body of Christ. He was pastor of a church for over 25 years, whom he walked in his father's footsteps to preach the word of God and carried the legacy of my great-grandfather, who God gave him a vision to build a church in the Midwest. He left his home from the South and that vision that God gave him manifested and became a great legacy for over 5 generations. It was my great-grandfather's unwavering faith in God. It makes my heart full of gratitude to know and appreciate all of his great teachings and personal attributes in which my grandfather instilled in me as a little girl through my young adulthood years. Also, the legacy of my great-grandfather has always inspired me to use my gifts and talents that God has given me to activate my purpose and to allow my purpose to give God the glory. It is having that extra boost of knowing that if God can do it for my forefathers, he can do it for me as well. "For there is no respect of persons with God." Roman 2:12 KJV

In my grandfather's later years of pastoring his church for over 20 years, I've always been admired by his caring and compassionate personality towards his family, youth, community and his members. When he left this life to be with the Lord, I believe he died in peace and it gives me peace that his father's love, which was my great-grandfather's, guidance, instruction, anointing and the vision that God gave him in the early 1930's is what made an impact on my grandfathers' entire life as well.

In life, we are all influenced by someone, whether it's a parent, relative, friend, school-advisor, community-activist, church-leader, mentor/coach, godly spiritual advisor or neighbor. Whether the influence brings a negative or positive impact, it plants a seed into that person's spirit. We must be reminded that men who became fathers may not have the ability to be a father to their own son if they never felt like a son from their own father. The father's influence on his son, shapes the son's mental state of how he should become as a father to his son. This cycle repeats but the influence can either go left or right, meaning it can influence the son to become a broken soul just like his father or be great and become like his father or better than his father was to him.

As I think back from the time period as a child growing up into my early twenties, I reflect on my paternal grandfather. His life impacts me from a world of deep hurt and sadness. It breaks my heart that I now have a better understanding of what made him who he was. It's a reflection of the passage of Proverbs 23:7, "As a man thinketh in his heart, so is he!" KJV

My paternal grandfather lived a difficult life that caused him grief, shame, guilt and pain from his past that he could not find a way to heal from. He carried the burden and the root of unforgiveness in his heart due to not being able to forgive himself for something that troubled him for so many years as a child growing up in an unstable environment where racism, poverty, rejection, abandonment, feeling unloved and being fatherless, broke his soul and crippled his spirit.
Unfortunately, he became a victim of his past by allowing his past life to become his present life. He was living his past and not his presence.

As a child, I couldn't and didn't understand his demeanor and personality and what caused him to be the way he was. He was not happy with his life, but often very bitter and brokenhearted. He never knew how to love or heal due to his childhood past of pain. He struggled to numb the pain with alcohol, yet he was a very hard-working man with strong work ethics. He went to work everyday and financially provided for his family. There had to be love in his heart to work a laborious job under extreme circumstances to provide for his family's basic welfare, but yet, he was unemotional and desensitized to the affection of love. His heart was callus and isolated. I often wondered how he had the ability to start a family, due to the conditions of his soul, spirit, mind and heart that never healed. I loved my grandfather and will always love him, yet as a child, I always expected his actions of not having peace, yet I knew that there was a good person deep down in his heart somewhere. Only God knew his heart and how it had been covered up and buried underneath from so many layers of pain and grief over many, many years. He died from a physical illness. His body was afflicted as well as his soul and spirit. I believe that his illness was the result of the pain, guilt and the emotional and mental broken bags he carried with him all his life. However, deep down inside, I knew that he had accepted Christ into his life during his last days. I talked with him before he transitioned and as I stood at his bedside, I asked him had he accepted Christ into his heart. His frail body slowly turned to me and he gazed at me and became very annoyed and said, "How many times must I accept God?" "I already accepted Him!" His words took me by surprise and I smiled and apologized quickly and said, "Grand dad, I didn't know you had accepted Christ into your life and I'm glad you did." I looked at him for the last time and as tears rolled down his eyes, I was happy because at this moment, I knew that he would go to a much better place and a much peaceful place than what he had gone through his entire life. I knew that God had allowed him the time to get his life together before his last day on earth. God knew all the heartaches and pain that my grandfather lived through and all the bags of pain that he had buried and carried in his soul. Everyone in the family knew he was a broken soul but God had a better plan for him. He peacefully died one week later. Yet, as I reminisce about my grandfather and the impact he had on our family, I think about a man who was blessed with a wife for over 70 years and children who grew up to have children of their own, but he didn't have the love, courage and affection to give because he never received the love and affection he needed as a child growing up into his adulthood. I never heard him ever say, "I love you". I never saw him hug or kiss any of the family members with any affection. His words were always bitter and full of sadness and complaints. When I would hug him as a child, he would never say anything in return. He would always remain quiet. This impact of being unaffectionate and broken inside, carried the seed to his children. His children didn't feel his love and affection and it affected each of them differently in their own personal lives in many ways unimaginable. I would often wonder how it would have impacted the lives of his offspring, had he been healed and delivered from his deep wounds? How would it have changed the course of the entire family, and all the generations to come? Although my grandmother showed her love and affection to our family, how much more would it have impacted our family had my grandfather done the same and made a positive impact on our next generations?

My grandfather grew up fatherless! He didn't have any male figures in his life to give him positive instruction, guidance, security and protection, the morality and ethical standards of manhood, financial and emotional support, love, and the role model of being a father. He lacked the identity and courage of being worthy and valued and to feel that he deserved to be loved. He was wounded emotionally and spiritually and he should never be criticized for being a crippled soul. Many of us can relate to the human side of our own emotions, which can cripple and break down our soul and spirit. I must remind myself of the pain on how it feels to not have a father. My grandfather didn't have a father of his own to understand what it meant to be a father to his children. This is the pure example and the raw truth of what many men are facing in our society today. Many young men are troubled in their soul, spirit and mind and are facing these same struggles in many different ways as my grandfather experienced. If you don't get better, you will eventually get bitter and when you don't get healed from your bitterness, your heart becomes hardened from the bags you carry. If you don't face the problem and pull out the root of that spirit, it will rotten your soul, you will allow the root to grow deeper into your soul and callus in your heart. When there's a root, something is planted. Healing and deliverance is essential! It's a must. There are some children with parents presently in their homes but when the parent is emotionally and mentally disconnected from the child's life, they lack the same as the child who doesn't have their father or their mother presently in their home. Many may disagree with this belief but the premise is that they share the same pain of rejection, mental and social disconnection, neglect and abandonment. The struggle might be different but the feeling of pain is relatable. My father felt his father's rejection and he lacked the emotional and mental connection while yet being in his presence and living under the same roof. His shadows of his body were just a reminder that he existed but his soul, mind and spirit were absent all the time. This impact of my grandfather's wound planted a seed of brokenness in my father. For he was a fatherless child growing up with his father in the same household!

We must think about the root of the problem and not dwell on the surface level problem. The root of the problem is when and where did it start and what happened when it started? What happened when the root of the problem was planted? If you dwell on the surface level of the problem, you will not have the ability to understand the spiritual perspective of the problem and you will not understand why the problem, most times have a way of repeating itself from one generation to the next and how almost every family member becomes affected or impacted by their parent's brokenness. Would you agree that broken parents end up raising broken children because the parent's broken heart and broken spirits becomes who they are? A broken soul that produces negative characteristics and actions. A bad seed roots a broken tree. Doesn't the tree resemble the family structure? When a tree is planted on good ground, it produces good fruit but when a tree is planted on bad soil, it withers. We must reflect on how this impacts on our children, our sons and daughters who will later have children of their own. Children look up to their parents and learn by what they observe. They can either be guided in the positive direction and they become misguided by their parent's actions because of what the child sees in his or her parents can become his or her reality, morality or mortality. The new revelation that helped me on the road of recovery was the ability to forgive and that ability was the day I forgave my father. The moral of this lesson was the power that released the moment I became obedient to God. When I became obedient and trusted God's will to carry me through, it was God who allowed my heart to empathize with my father and his father for all that they endured in silence. It was the pain and baggage that they carried from their childhood through their manhood. Their behavior and actions were suppressed feelings that never healed, yet I was not forgiving of my father because I made it about me. I didn't understand this growing up as a child and wondering why my father couldn't be the father I desired him to be. I didn't have a clue that my father was only a sufferer because and a victim of his past and that he didn't allow me to suffer because he wanted to. I suffered because he suffered! His spirit of pain carried over to me with the spirit of pain. I'm sure it affected others but I can only share my story about my experience. Once again, it wasn't about me. The new revelation on this road of healing was liberating. God allowed separation for my elevation. This was a spiritual elevation for my spirit and a revelation for my soul I needed. The sting of forgiveness was removed. God had to heal me in certain areas and in certain parts at a certain season in life. There was supernatural healing in the midst of forgiveness. In the book of Luke 23:34. "Then Jesus said, Father, forgive them; for they know not what they do......." During this moment when Jesus was suffering on the cross, he forgave them that persecuted him, whipped him, cast lots on him, spit on him, called him names, when his own rejected him, when he felt alone with his arms stretched on that cross preparing to die. He was positioned to die. They were going to kill him but yet, his heart had mercy on those people, for his prayer to God shows how long-suffering he was to ask his Father in heaven to forgive because they simply had no idea what they were doing. This was my revelation! I simply did not know what I was doing for over 15 years of hating my father and not one bit having any mercy to forgive him. I simply had no clue what, how and why my father's behavior appeared to be his negligence but yet the truth was that he too needed healing and deliverance and we can not throw rocks and stones at anyone when we too, ourselves have not been perfect in God's sight. Forgiveness is an action of humility that we must act on. This is doing the work. We must do the work before God can do the work in us and through us. Give me an example of one perfect person living on earth right at this moment. Think about it. I'm waiting..............We have to understand that healing is our responsibility even though the pain we endured wasn't our blame. It simply wasn't our fault! God is faithful to forgive us! You need to fix yourself by forgiving yourself. The therapist can't fix it. You need to forgive yourself because you didn't do anything to get what you got. Forgiving doesn't mean we have to be around this person. It surely means that we must make the choice to let go of the pain and the harm that the person caused on us. Many times, the hardest person to forgive is ourselves!

Forgiving doesn't mean we have to forget because we need to remember how God helped us to forgive and how God will continue to bless us, liberate us and strengthen us as he continues to make us whole within ourselves. This is our road to recovery.

CHAPTER 6 - FINDING AND DISCOVERING A

RELATIONSHIP WITH GOD

WHAT IS RELATIONSHIP?

Relationship is a special bond, unity, connection and a chemistry or compatibility with someone. It's sharing goals, hopes, dreams, and fears. It's getting to know a person more and more each time you spend with them. Whether you talk on the phone or whether you are visiting and in each other's presence on a regular basis, it's what creates a relationship.

There are various types of relationships. These are people who you are related to. They are family, which includes immediate family members such as parents, spouse, children, siblings, aunts, uncles or cousins. Family could also be extended to friends who have a special connection and are considered family. Then you have friendships. This person allows you total freedom to be yourself. They more than likely are in your best interest as they are great for giving you advice or support that will help you and not hurt you. They will be completely honest with you if when the truth hurts. They normally have your back and are there for you through the good and bad times. Next, you have acquaintances. These are people who might be included in a circle of friends. They are someone you know little about, they are not your best friends and they are less intimate than a friend. Oftentimes, they could be an associate or someone of business. Lastly, romantic relationships. This person could be your spouse, fiancée or close companion. These types of relationships are passionate emotionally or sexually. There is a chemistry and a compatibility blended in this unity. Love, trust, respect, commitment, faithfulness and communication are essential for these types of relationships.

THE RELATIONSHIPS IN MARRIAGE

From my personal experience, I believe that for any general relationships, the main key ingredients are love, care, mutual respect, loyalty, trust, communication, support and the attention that is needed for both. In the journey of relationships and marriages, it can be surprisingly easy to find ourselves reacting defensively or angrily when the person we love most disagrees with us. Any topic of issues can lead to trouble. We can find conflict in our conversations about our finances, our jobs, friends or associates, our beliefs and/or our priorities. When tempers flare, it can heighten and become unnecessarily uncontrollable to the point of creating division. The next thing you know, your spouse becomes your enemy. Divisiveness is a characteristic of our spiritual enemy. It doesn't mean that every time you fight as a couple that you're still under spiritual attack from the enemy himself. We have to become mindful that the enemy would love nothing more than for us to view our spouses or companions as our enemy. The enemy comes to destroy relationships and our marriages.

Marriage is companionship! It is the institution of transformation. Marriage is made to transform us in ourselves. It's a transformation of maturity when we are married. We can't have a strong marriage without a wholeness of ourselves. We can't have a healthy marriage without a healthy mind, soul, body and spirit! In my marriage of over 20 years, I am not the same person now as I was back in my twenties. I had to develop and transform in the midst of my brokenness. You probably can't understand how a marriage has the capabilities of producing a better version of yourself because you're probably wondering how you can grow and develop in a marriage when there are those moments of tension and challenges? We often hear that we can't change a person in marriage and that is absolutely true. However, we're also not aware that as we grow closer with our spouse, and as we age together, change happens as our physical bodies change, our physical abilities change, our perspectives of life change, our finances change, and our desires and needs change individually. The individual changes within us and in our spouse causes us to transform in which forces us to adjust and adapt in growing together. However, one person can't do it alone. Both partners have to be willing to adapt to change even when it is beyond their comfort zone. In marriages, you will experience problems, challenges and difficulties. Marriage will also allow you to see yourself or it can also cause you to lose yourself depending on the type of personality your mate has. A mate who possesses narcissistic behavior is like feeling you are in a war or a battle that is always unpredictable on a daily basis. A narcissist is a personality disorder that demonstrates a dominating, controlling, manipulative and selfish personality. This type of person always sees things their way. This type of person only esteems themselves over others and isn't willing to consider the feelings of others because they feel that they are always correct and perfect. Their manipulative behavior tends to gaslight their partners' vulnerabilities, which intimidates and makes them and others believe that their mate is mentally crazy. This becomes emotionally and mentally abusive to the mate who struggles to know their self-worth and becomes more powerless and more vulnerable to believe that they are mentally insufficient. Most men who carry this behavior are egoistic and most times are male chauvinists where they are intrigued when they feel the power to rule or are in powerful positions of leadership or authority. When you are in these types of relationships, you must put on your track shoes and run as fast and as far as you can. This is not the person you would want to marry. If you are married to a narcissistic person, it can damage your self-esteem, contaminate your soul and cause you to become sick in the mind. In Proverbs of the KJV, it states, " Hope deferred makes the heart sick, but a longing fulfilled is a tree of life." Proverbs 13:12.

On the other hand, there are some marriages that last a lifetime and it's a beautiful sight to see older couples in marriages for decades where they can laugh, communicate, and enjoy the companionship of their partners and don't allow the small stuff to blow out of control. They are willing to ride the tidal waves of life together and they are committed to the vows they agreed to on that first day of marriage. In healthy marriages, the individual person can see the brighter side of things and it can allow them to improve in their own weaknesses and faults, especially when humility and patience are key factors of the both partners. Marriage can make you a better version of yourself because the closeness of you and your spouse allows you to see yourself through the relationship. It's being self-reflective for change. A change to become better and a perspective to accept change in a positive light. When God blesses you with a companion, you have an inward and accountability to progress for self-improvement. Through tight spots of tension and adversity in your marriage, it's the tension and the friction in the marriage that turns something that seems like hardship, converted to unforeseen courtship when we navigate and position our lives in God. We can never give up on what God has put together. Even when we have had it to our wit's end, we do not give up because we are still growing up. The best part of marriage is growing up because it requires change. Anything that you are connected to, develops you, defines you, sharpens you or shapes you, is forever changing you because without transition there is no growth. If marriage was perfect, how could a perfect day on a daily basis from a perfect unity allow growth? It wouldn't and it couldn't. It has to challenge you in order for it to change you! It is the fire that causes gold to become redefined, formed and shaped when it is soldered. Sometimes, when we feel the heat or a strain in our marriage, it can either cause us to give up or to gain strength when the pressure seems high. Marriage allows us to become something of allowing us to become the better version of ourselves by being reflective. Being reflective allows us to see our strengths and weaknesses. Looking in that mirror and examining our hearts, mind, and soul for the ultimate areas of growth. Think about it, you wouldn't know how to grow if it hadn't been for the sake of marriage. So, if you feel the tension or the pressure in your marriage or in a companionship, God is trying to mature you. He's trying to cause you to become something and a pure example for your children. So, don't give up on your marriage because your marriage is about "you." Ask yourself, "Who do you need to be to facilitate their growth?" God is asking, "Can you be a reflection of me through your relationship? Ask God to forgive you for being impatient, over-critical or a complainer. When your marriage is going through the hardships, say these words of prayer, "Lord allow me to be convicted, not condemned. I've been looking at my marriage in the wrong way. Lord, give me the fortitude, strength, and the determination not to quit but to embrace the growth that I need to become the better version of me. God I know that transformation is my destination. They are not perfect and neither am I dear Lord. God, all places where I have fallen short, forgive me, heal me! Let healing take place! Allow me to forget and leave those things behind me. Lord, take me to a place to love better, In Jesus name. Amen!

RELATIONSHIP VERSUS RELIGION

From the same aspect, in our relationships in our marriage, it becomes a reflector of ourselves. We want our spouse to love us, respect our feelings, our morals and our principles, showing attention, become intimate, be loyal to us, and be caring. Marriage is being mindful of how you treat your spouse and how God sees you in your marriage. We must ask ourselves do we really love our spouses by what love is defined by God? From a supernatural perspective, God desires the same relationship with him. He wants us to love him, show attention, be loyal and be mindful of God. God wants to be loved and he wants communication just like our significant other would desire from us and when I mention God, most people automatically think "Religion" which is defined by traditions, customs, rules, a particular system of how faith, worship or prayer is presented or the formalities. The truth is God has not called us into religion. He has called us into a relationship with him. As any relationship, as we must work on strengthening our marriages, God desires more time with him and the more time we spend together, the deeper and more fulfilling the relationship becomes. Having a deeper relationship with God is not about living this perfect life. God just wants our time. It's that simple! He desires us to journey with him. This is why trusting in God on the journey is so important. When discovering a relationship with God there are three important things to consider. First, we must commit to spending some time each day by reading our bible. This is when God talks to us. This is our daily devotion.

"For the Word of God is living and powerful, and sharper than any two-edged sword, piercing even to the division of soul and spirit, and of joints and marrow, and is a discerner of the thoughts and intents of the heart." Hebrews 4:12

This is how God talks to me the majority of the time. "All Scripture is God-breathed and is useful for teaching, rebuking,

226

correcting and training in righteousness. So that the servant of God may be thoroughly equipped for every good work." 2 Timothy 3:16-17

Second, we must pray to God and develop that quiet time when no one is around and when there is complete silence. This is when we talk to God. This is when we are ministering to God through our worship. Third, we must do both on a daily basis. Not only on Sundays but all throughout the week. We must pray and read our bible daily. Just like we would with someone new we're getting to know or to build a relationship.

This is how developing a relationship with God starts to form and grow. In Proverbs 18:24, it states, "A man who has friends must himself be friendly, but there is a friend who sticks closer than a brother." This is the characteristic of God. He is a loving and compassionate God and he will never leave us nor will he forsake us. When dating someone new, how will you get to know the person if we don't communicate or spend some time with them on a daily basis? As my husband would joke around with me and say, "act like you like me!" This is his joking way of saying to spend some time with me or show more affection towards him. In the book of Hebrews 10:22, it states, "We come closer to God and approach him with an open heart, fully convinced that nothing will keep us at a distance from him. For our hearts have been sprinkled with blood to remove impurity, and we have been freed from an accusing conscience. Now we are clean, unstained, and presentable to God inside and out." When I started developing a closer relationship with God, it was during the early mornings around 4:30 am where I would wake up from my comfortable sleep and make that sacrifice to spend time with God. I knew that if I were to wait any later, there would be many distractions coming my way. During this time in the morning was when I had that freedom by pouring out my heart to God. I talk to God just like I talk to that unbiased friend that doesn't judge me on what I say and how I communicate. I can be myself without overdoing it with fancy vocabulary words as if God only listens to a certain vocabulary. The more I began praying to God, the more I felt his presence. Feeling his presence was his love language for me. He allowed me to feel his presence by feeling a tranquility of peace and I would feel my stomach turn as if something was leaping on the inside and the warm feeling of peace that felt like an electric current would run across my body, especially in my hands. That's where I would feel his presence the most. Many times in the past, I would feel my face move as if a strong wind was blowing over my face. It was very rare when this would occur but it was when God's presence was at its strongest.

As I experienced these encounters with the presence of God, this is where it became a real deal for me. This is where I knew for a fact that it was my own personal experience and a personal relationship that couldn't be matched to any relationship I've ever experienced. I was spending time with my Abba Father. "My sheep hear My voice, and I know them, and they follow me." John 10:27 KJV

ON A PERSONAL AND DEEPER LEVEL

From the beginning, the first man that ever loved us was our Father God who gave His only begotten Son to die for our sins. How can you measure a love for a sacrifice that huge? A sacrifice for mankind! When you encounter and receive the revelation and the true and genuine love of how much our Father God loves us, you will never be the same again. You will begin to realize that the lack of your natural father's love can't compare to the love that your spiritual Father gives on a daily basis. This is getting to know the first man who ever loved you! His love fills the void and heals the open-wounds that have brought many years of suffering in my life. Getting to know Him is one thing and getting to know the magnitude of His love is another. Love is a being because God is love. When love lives in you, that's what makes you act in love. "I have loved you with an everlasting love; therefore I have drawn you with loving kindness." (Jeremiah 31:3). When we go deeper with God, we begin to learn the characteristics of God, we begin to learn the fruits of his Spirit.

God's love has drawn me unto Him. His love never fails! It was not fear this time from the last encounters I had with Him. It was His love. Sometimes, we tend to think that God's ways and thoughts are like ours but it's not. In my mind, I used to think that I wasn't great enough for His love because I wasn't obedient and didn't answer God's call many years ago when I knew he was calling me. I felt that God was angry with me because I allowed so much time to slip away from my life and in those precious years, I could have done so much more for Him. Trusting God is necessary, not when it's something that I decide to do. I must continue to remind myself that in the unknown that God has a plan. He is in control of everything! He has my best interests at heart. In the book of 1st John 4:18-19, it states, There is no fear in love, but perfect love casts out fear, because fear involves torment. But he who fears has not been made perfect in love. We love Him because He first loved us."

There were many encounters I've had with God and then there were moments where I doubted God because I wanted things to work out on my terms because I didn't take the time to get to know him but more and more God was so merciful on my life where he saved my life in many near death occurrences. I often wondered, why me Lord? What made me so different from others who had passed away but didn't take the chance to find God and to discover God for themselves. Their lives had expired before they had the time to and the opportunity to choose God into their lives. Being raised in church, you learn about God's goodness and you even sing songs about what a mighty God we serve. I did this all of my life. I knew about God from what I learned and how I was raised growing up in a single parent household with a family rooted in the gospel and the teachings of Christ. Learning about God is one thing but getting to know him for yourself is a totally different ballgame. My close encounters with God were those quiet and private moments in prayer. It was those moments where my prayers were being answered right before my eyes. I can remember someone asking me to urgently pray for someone during an illness and within days they would recover. There were many times where I would pray for a loved-one while they were suffering from physical pain in their body and they were seen by physicians who recommended surgery, I can remember putting my hands on that particular area of where the pain felt intense and as I would pray from my heart and in the Spirit of God, the pain would leave the next day and the next doctor's visit would make the doctor's questions their reports and wonder why the last visit's findings did not match the recent results where surgery would be ruled out completely. I can remember how many times I would get on my knees for so many things and yet, the answers were not always right away but I would have my prayers answered within months and a few years. Regardless, of how long, my prayers were being met.

THE POWER OF PRAYER

Many would ask, "Angel, what do you pray to God about?"
There's so much we can pray to God for. During my prayers, I
always made sure to first thank God for all the wonderful
things he's done for me and for all the prayers that were
submitted to God where I was still awaiting answers. Whether
these prayers were for my needs or for prayer requests from
others. God was always right on time by answering them.
How many times have you thanked The Lord today for all
he's done for you? I dare you to just write down all of the
prayers God answered for you during the span of your life and
if there is anything you can remember, write it down and I'm
quite sure that once you start writing, you won't be able to
stop writing. I believe this is when you will soon realize he is
compassionate, a faithful God who show you the outcome of
your prayers, this is when your faith will start to elevate. The
next time you get on your knees to pray, start thanking God
for that job you don't like, someone else would be happy to
get that job you don't like. Every job has its pros and cons and
not one person can say that their job is perfect and flawless
but when you complain about what God has done for you,
you're not being thankful, especially when you don't show
that you appreciate the job by coming to work late and leaving
work early, taking more than 3-4 breaks per day on a daily
basis, complaining all the time and griping all day to other
coworkers and not taking the initiative to do a little more than
what you're asked. If the job is that miserable, ask God for a
job that will allow you fulfillment or to start working for
yourself in your own business. Allow God to activate the
skills, talents, and gifts in you to open up your own business
or start a nonprofit organization. It's not God's will for us to
be unhappy and have stressful lives but always know that
there are always going to be challenges and trials in anything
you do and in those moments, those are lessons for growth
and maturity.

In our everyday prayers, be thankful for your food by praying over your food before you eat! Thank God for your food you can afford to purchase at the grocery store! Say your grace before you eat your food! God not only blesses the food before you eat it but He also multiplies your food. He blesses you to have more! He will supply your needs even when you lack the basic necessities! God will allow you to get the best deals and prices at the grocery stores even during those seasons of financial distress and hardships. I know this very well because God had supplied my needs in the worst financial seasons of my life when it seemed that hope was gone and I couldn't see a way. Whether we are on our knees praying, driving our cars, cleaning our homes, sitting back from a long and tiring day, just be thankful for life because as we always normally hear, life is just too short. We are forever reminded by every funeral we pay our respects to, by hearing and reading about the young and the old passing away. Every day someone passes away! We should be thanking God for every breath we take while every second is crucial because it's surely not promised to us. I, personally, had to thank God for helping me to forgive and to gain patience and temperance, especially working jobs where some employees can be difficult to work with and some family members had been difficult to understand and to be around. This was one area where I really got on my knees and asked God to help me. This is when God sees your heart and he knows what you need. I had to remind myself that the reward is being kind to those who are not kind to you! Be kind to those who persecute, betray you or hate you! This is an area that seemed to be my biggest challenge and I knew God was real in many times I had been tested in these areas where clap-backs were my normal response. God is yet helping me to respond in a more pleasant yet firm reply because God knows I don't tolerate disrespect but I must love as Christ loves us. My prayers are always sacred and from the heart. My level of

232

relationship with God is allowing me to know just how much he loves me and who I am to him. Even more so, God allows me to see who he called me to be and how much power is invested in me because as a child of God, I have a heavenly and spiritual inheritance.

One of my favorite faith based movies came out in 2015, "War Room". I remember the day I went to the movies with family to watch it and it was more than I had expected. The movie was about a couple who were struggling in their failing marriage. It was one of those typical days when the wife met up with her newest client, Ms Clara, an elderly lady who taught the wife the power of prayer. It was that movie that motivated me to continue my passion and faith on believing and trusting God. What really touched me the most was when Ms. Clara wrote all of the things she had asked God in her prayers to remind her of how God had answered her prayers throughout the years of her entire life. It was that moment when I realized how much God had performed miracles in my life too. We are soon to forget the many times we prayed to God about something and yet we tend to doubt God when a new problem arises. We must remember that if He answered prayers for us in the past and in several moments in our lives and another time in our lives and another time after that, wouldn't he do the same for us right now?

"Now to him who is able to do immeasurably more than all we ask or imagine, according to his power that is at work within us." Ephesians 3:20 KJV

During this time of my life, I was severely struggling through depression. It was as if those feelings came back, I had lost my job, a bad business deal went haywire and it stole my peace but left me suffering with anxieties and fear. I feared the unknown because my finances were the biggest challenge.

Wondering day to day how I will get the money to meet the needs and demands. I couldn't sleep. I couldn't eat but yet I wouldn't stop praying. This was a test of my faith. This was a test of perseverance. Some days I didn't know if I were coming or going and I suffered in silence. I talked a good faith talk but I was struggling in the faith walk. This was no walk of fame. This was surely the walk of faith. I felt embarrassed and ashamed and I behaved in isolation. I really didn't want others to see me in this sad condition and either I was going to die from depression or I was going to die fighting for my victory. When the tide and the roaring storms tried to consume me, I had to persevere and gain some muscle to fight back and declare what the Bible said. I had to put the Word of God to the test. This time I had to really know God for myself. It came down to the ringer. My prayers were passionate and filled with tears, my eyes in the brightest of bloodshot red and my face was pulled down as if I were in a mud fight. I had to get down on my knees and with the ugly face as I felt physically weak but strong in my spirit, I prayed like never before. Night and day, I prayed, I felt like Peter walking on water where he began to slip and fall. I experienced days like Peter because I would feel like I was sinking every time I would open up the mailbox to see another overdue bill or to receive a call to remind me that another bill was overdue. I pleaded and pleaded for God to not allow me sink but to stand and to stand in victory. To stand in faith and to not hold any doubt in my heart. I can remember that scripture in the bible, "Be still and know that I am God." Psalms 46:10 I began declaring God's word over my circumstances and months later the miracles were pouring in. I got several calls for job interviews, one after another. I interviewed for two jobs and God blessed me with the one I prayed that it would be his will for me to be placed with the job that was best for me. This time, I learned my true lesson. I made sure to pray God's will for the right job

234

to come along and it happened in November of 2015. I received a full time job, with great benefits and close distance to my home. Once again, it was the power of prayer that intervened and God showed me that my consistent prayers were surely not in vain. I just didn't pray one time, I had to pray without ceasing. It was nonstop! What did I have to lose?

Even to this day, I continue to thank the Lord for hearing and answering my prayers. I continue to thank God that I have breath to praise the Lord. We must remember that when we pray, it is our privilege from God. It is our gift from God and we can't take it for granted. We also have to be mindful that we have to pray without ceasing because God's timing is not our timing, so we have to pray that God gives us the patience and the strength to wait on his answer. Just because it doesn't appear like anything is happening doesn't mean that it won't happen. "For as the heavens are higher than the earth, So are My ways higher than your ways, And My thoughts than your thoughts." Isaiah 55:9 KJV

This is developing our faith in God. In the book of Isaiah 40:31 "They who wait for the Lord shall renew their strength; they shall mount up with wings like eagles; they shall run and not be weary; they shall walk and not faint."

As we walk this life of faith, we must remember that opposition, trials, temptation and challenges are always here to try to weaken us, this is why it is so important to develop that personal relationship with God by having the faith to obey his word. He talks to us through his word and we must obey. God is faithful to us in our walk with Christ. He is faithful to forgive us when we feel guilty or wrong. We can depend on Him better than we can depend on ourselves. Having faith in God is like knowing that God will and can do exceedingly and abundantly more than we can ever ask or think. We know that in God we can trust to know that our burdens, opposition and our trials are all in God's hands. We must allow God to take dominion over our problems even when we think we might know the answers, we will find out that God has the final say in everything we do. We know that when we are faithful to God with our sacrifices, obedience, our prayers, worship, fasting and serving others with the gifts that God has given us, He is faithful to ensure that our needs are met. When we delight ourselves in God by spending quality time out of our day, He provides for our every need and He will also give us the desires of our hearts. Obeying God's Word is listening to that still, small voice, and when you spend time with God on a regular basis, we will begin to communicate with Him in a form of two-way conversation. God is always speaking to us but we must be in alignment in His word in order to take heed to instruction and to his direction. This is when His divine favor becomes our reward.

So shall My word be that goes forth from My mouth; It shall not return to Me void, But it shall accomplish what I please, And it shall prosper in the thing for which I sent it." Isaiah 55:11

As I continued the process of my healing and deliverance, my relationship with my father progressed and it was different. My relationship with my father became new. It felt like a friendship. It felt restored. I no longer had that feeling of resentment, bitterness or sadness in my heart when I would talk with my father. I love my father for who he was and no longer what I needed him or desired him to be for me. God allowed my heart and soul to be healed and delivered to love him beyond his faults and failures and to not bring up his past. I was able to let my past go and he was able to sense that I had forgiven him. I truly cared for him and I didn't feel that I had to mistreat him for all the years I felt mistreated. I didn't and don't feel that he owes me anything. I had finally let go of a part of my life that allowed me to discover a new and refined relationship. Our conversations were on mature and authentic topics about life and even when we don't agree on certain things, we learned to respect each other's opinions and move forward. We learned that a disagreement shouldn't control the relationship by causing us to stop speaking to one another or become insensitive and emotionally out of control. For once, we can have a mature conversation of true honesty with a clean conscience of being able to support, respect, communicate, and to love one another unconditionally when love is not based on a price tag, terms, conditions, limitations and consequences. Our father and daughter relationship had been peacefully restored. Look what pure forgiveness can do when you allow God to get involved in your business and fully heal and deliver you. God is a God of restoration!

RESTORATION OF FATHER AND DAUGHTER RELATIONSHIPS

During this peaceful journey of a restored relationship with my father, I soon became inspired to advocate the importance of mending relationships of dads and daughters by supporting the movement by creating a brand new instagram page. I would post pictures of moments of fathers and daughters spending time with one another whether they were very young as babies or whether the daughters were grown women and many times they were celebrity dads spending time with their daughter(s). The new page immediately received positive responses and I was surprised to see that the audience and followers who supported my page were 50% women and 50% men. This movement is what inspired me even more to persevere through the challenge and countless hours to tell my story. This page allowed me to express my heart by allowing my pain to become my purpose.

I never knew in my adult years that I was hurting for many years of not having that relationship with my dad. I really had to dig deep to find the root of the baggage that I buried inside. Once I finally discovered the root, I was quite in denial but that was and is my truth. It was the little girl inside of me that never emotionally healed. More and more, I would hear stories from women around the world where they wished that they could have had their dads in their lives. It just wasn't me, there were many women who struggled like me. It's many women, famous, everyday women and women I personally know from family and friends.

The importance of spending quality time and bonding moments is monumental in a child's life. It is evident that sons need their dads and the need is important as the son will someday become the man of his household, therefore it is essential for the father to provide healthy guidance to his offspring in the same manner. There are men wounded by internalized pain from childhood to adulthood because they lacked the presence of their father or a fatherly role model. This lingering pain has caused problems in the lives of many young men and many have not healed from this pain or haven't felt the outlet or freedom to communicate with anybody, what has been affecting them all their lives. Many men won't communicate or express their feelings for many reasons. This could be due to self-pride or believing that this is a sign of weakness. However, as a daughter develops into her womanhood, there is a spiritual dynamic that makes a unique bond between a father and daughter very special. Just like there is something unique about the relationships of mothers and sons. However, the importance of the father's presence in his daughter's life starts very early. A baby growing up with her father reacts differently from a baby growing up without her dad. I'm not saying this to bring negativity on many who have not had their fathers in their lives. I can only be transparent with what I have witnessed in how my daughters' lives have been impacted consciously and subconsciously by the presence of their father being in their lives. In addition, I am a living product of a child who felt the pain of an absent father. I know what this pain feels like and many times when trying to cope through this pain, we by nature, find alternative outlets of finding love in the wrong places and looking to fill our voids from things and people to help cope through our struggles, whether it's a healthy or unhealthy experience. Unfortunately, finding love and desiring love that is not real but accepting it for what it is are alternative outlets which are quick-fixes. Fake love and counterfeit affections are unable to complete us. God can only complete us and it's a permanent fix! God can be everything that we need, if we allow Him to be. A woman who has dealt with father wounds as a child, will never heal until she faces those wounds, instead of burying and hiding those wounds for years. We must confront what needs to be corrected. It's not an easy task because I found it difficult to do. I hid these wounds most of my life. I just didn't want to relive those feelings again. A child growing up without her dad telling her that she is loved by him, that she is beautiful, brings affirmation to her life. This affirmation of love, gives her the courage, confidence, value, self-worth, self-assurance, identity and purpose to set standards for herself. She won't accept anything beneath her standards because she believes what her father has instilled in her is true. She doesn't have to second guess her worth or seek applauds and social media-likes for her acceptance. She can be vulnerable around her father and know that he will always have her back and she will never have to have her guards up against her father because this is the first man she'll ever love because he has her best interests from him! Her father will always be her first love and she believes who she loves! She believes that his love is pure. Therefore, she has a sense of security, protection, value and self-respect to make decisions by not compromising her hopes and dreams and making others a priority over her aspirations in life, for the sake to please a man for love and by seeking affirmation of what looks like love in the wrong places. When a woman is lost in this state of mind, she has lost her vision and sense of identity and she becomes attractive to who she is and what she has become. This becomes her reality! Her reality is her truth and she believes her truth. It's all she's ever known. It's her story of healing and restoration.

Before I ever thought about getting pregnant, I knew that one day in the future I would have children of my own and one of my dearest desires was to be in a marriage or in a companionship that would allow my children to grow up in their father's presence physically, emotionally and mentally. I never wanted my children to grow up and deal with the pain like I did growing up, whether son or daughter. What brought me so much satisfaction and hope was that God never forgot my prayers. He blessed my daughters to have their dad in their lives. To have their dad in the same home with them was very meaningful to me. This was what I lacked as a child growing up and developing into my teenage years. There are children who have lived or who live with a father in the home but there is still an emotional absence, detachment or disconnection. I was a child that felt that way when I did live in the same home with my father until the age of nine years old. I still felt a disconnection and emotional abandonment from my father, although I knew that he loved me. I just lacked that daddy and daughter bond. I wanted to be a daddy's girl. I never got to be a part of that role. As a mother, it is healthy and natural to desire your children to have better than what you've had growing up and experienced. Seeing my husband interact with our daughters, ensuring that they are properly provided for, being their protector, spending quality family time together, helping them with their homework and attending their school events and celebrations, emergencies and anything that is of great importance to their development, even through conflicting work schedules, going on trips together or even going to get ice cream on a beautify or rainy day meant the world to me and it means everything to them.

As I would observe the bond between my husband and our daughters. This relationship is very special to me. It reminded me of what I didn't have growing up as a child but it made me thankful and ultimately grateful for appreciating this relationship they have and seeing how it brings out the best in them. It has brought out the best in him as well! All men aren't perfect and all fathers aren't perfect. Mothers aren't perfect either. We are all not perfect but that's the beauty of being a parent. In a child's eyes, you don't have to be perfect. You just need to be present in their lives! The child sees this imperfectly perfect person and when the child becomes an adult and have children of their own, in a healthy state of mind, they can respect, honor and appreciate their parents because at this time of their life, they are now in the parent's role and can make healthy decisions on how to parent their children from an emotionally, physical, mental and spiritual approach. It's the little things that become great moments in their life. This gives them a new perception. Many times I can hear my mother's voice in me as I communicate and discipline my children, whether it's telling them to clean their rooms or do their chores or giving sound advice on a daily basis, I can't help but think about how I was taught by my mother when I was in the child's role. When my children become adults and have children of their own, this will give them an appreciation for their parents. In life, you appreciate the little things, especially when those little things are big things that become meaningful in your life. You don't think about them when you're younger, but as you mature, they become significant in your life. Those things that you never forget, no matter how old you get. Some people would probably consider those little things in life irrelevant or unimportant. When I speak on the "little things", it's those little things like a simple, "I love you's!" It's those little things of hearing your father or mother say those words or when your dad compliments how beautiful you are. These are words of affirmation. This was relevant for me growing up because my husband's relationship with both of our daughters is very special to me. The uniqueness of love is always shown with his interaction, affection, and his repetitive and different ways of showing them how much he loves them and how much they mean the world to him. The love is reciprocal. The love is genuine. The relationship is genuine because in the different stages of their growth and development, from babies to teens and adults-- their stages of life, has shown how their father's love for them has never changed. No matter how matured they have grown, they enjoy getting kisses and hugs from their dad. They love hearing their dad say those three words and knowing that when he says it, it's always at the right time. It's never a bad time to tell someone you love them. Over a course of time, I noticed how our daughters grew with high self-esteem and strong confidence. Their strong character of self-worth and high-spirited behavior showed their inner essence of beauty. They know who they are and know what they want in life, yet have the personality of humility and consideration for others. They are sensitive to the lack of others who have grown up without their parents or fathers in their lives. They understand how blessed they are and appreciative by having the opportunity to not only have a physical relationship with their dad but also an emotional relationship with him as well. This affirmation of love has allowed them to grow in the character of strength, courage and love, and when you love yourself, loving others comes easy!

A NEW LIFE OF COMFORT, PEACE, JOY AND LOVE

Finding and discovering a relationship with God has given me a new life of comfort, peace, joy and love. Even when the trials of life come to discourage me, I just don't react in the same manner as I used to. When I find myself going in that direction, I instantly stop and think…...I can hear God say, "This is not what you want to do." Trust in me as I abide in you." I immediately think about all the promises and what God had done for me. I keep telling myself that I can't go back to the way it used to be and this is why having that relationship with Christ and my heavenly father is so important because I won't have to second guess it, I won't have to wonder can I trust it and I surely know that His love will always cover me. In the book of Psalms 91, "He that dwelleth in the secret place of the most High shall abide under the shadow of the Almighty." Having a relationship with God has taught me to understand when God is speaking to me and God knows how to get my attention. Sometimes God will repetitively give me a message from different sources and I know it's God when it's the same message. Then there are those times when I can hear this small voice. In the beginning, I thought it was my small voice but more and more when I pray and read my bible, I begin to become familiar with that still small voice and it's that peaceful presence I feel. Sometimes, God is telling me to do something where I would feel this urgent feeling or the assignment would feel uncomfortable to see myself accomplishing the task, yet I am feeling joy and peace at the same time. Through this walk of faith, I am thankful that God has sustained my life by giving me that one more chance, I blew so many chances of salvation by turning back to the world, yet God was still merciful and gracious to strive with me to come back from sin. I worried that if I gave my life back to Christ, if I would have the strength to sustain salvation. I was hesitant about making that ultimate choice to never leave God again. I didn't and don't want to displease God but God allowed me to feel his

243

presence and peace and this is why he allowed us to remember our scars, our wounds, and our pain. It was good that I was afflicted to remind me that I didn't want to go through that pain again without God on my side. In addition, the affliction gave me the perseverance to strive and not give up! I know that living on this earth, we are truly going to experience trouble, pain and sorrow. That's just the way it is living on earth and that is why we can't get too comfortable with this temporary life but count it all joy when we don't have to experience the pain, the sorrows and the afflictions alone. Even when I feel alone, I'm not lonely because I have peace to know that my God is with me. God sent his holy spirit which is our comforter as our keeper. The holy spirit brings divine love in all various expressions. It gives us the peace that subdues, patience that endures, kindness in action, a life of virtue, a faith that prevails and gentleness of heart and strength of spirit. For me it gives me an abundance of joy that overflows. Even when I'm not at my best all the time, I have something great to look forward to. This is why the joy of the Lord is our strength. He is our protector. He is our personal security guard and he is our strong tower. I don't have to worry or stress and I don't have to remain discouraged when times of trouble come. When we call on Jesus to become our strength, we know that it is His strength that gives us endurance through the challenges. Sometimes it was those high-pressured moments in my marriage that kept me on my knees in prayer. It created a prayer-warrior inside of me. It gave me the tenacity to fight. When you seek God with all your heart and need him to come when you don't know what's going to happen next, it's those moments when God holds your hand and he starts to develop you by giving you the ability to endure and to do things that you could not do on your own. In those heated moments, "You're not telling God that you just can't deal with it anymore or that you can't put up with it anymore. It was those moments when God's presence would come and it was those moments when I knew God was real in my life. You've never been the YOU that you are BECOMING because you don't know what that looks like until you stop making the decisions and cast those cares and concerns to God. It's those moments of faith that sustains you, that keeps you and delivers you. It is those moments when you learn how strong you are and how mature you have come. When you put God to the test, he moves by your faith because you have given it to God and it is by faith that makes us new. It is by faith that makes us over comers. God is a rewarder of those who diligently seeks him. God said, "Do not be weary in well doing but faint not." You're going to reap so much more than you had ever imagined if you don't give up. You can not give up until you grow up. The challenges seem bigger than you but God will do a new thing in you that will enlarge your territory and expand your capacity and your tolerance. In the end you'll be glad that you stuck with it. It is God's grace and mercy that we cannot comprehend.

I believe that God had to keep allowing my heart to break in order to save my soul. I must admit that I've been broken most of my life, yet I've had the strength from God to hold it together. We have to ask ourselves are we enough. Ask yourself, *"Are you enough for yourself?"* Or, do you have to keep someone in your life who doesn't appreciate or respect you for the sake or the idea of calling it love? Yes, God had to allow my heart to break in order to grab my attention. He has to do whatever it takes because He loves you and he is our manufacturer so he knows our make and model. Sometimes, God will allow situations and circumstances to change us in order to put us back on the right track. Even when God is molding us, it feels like a mixture of both joy and pain and that's because he's mending our brokenness while he's renewing, restoring and reviving us. He's making us all over again! We tend to become blind sighted by being comfortable

245

in loving and giving all of ourselves into those who really aren't in love with us. In marriage or companionship, we can emotionally lose ourselves by being caught in the clouds and being raptured in love because it feels so good to our soul. It makes us feel special! It's an all-time high to be in love, yet we find our hearts being ruptured instead of raptured once we find ourselves when God opens our eyes and brings revelation and clarity. Love doesn't validate your self-worth! Marriage doesn't validate your self-worth. Our self-worth is validated through God and God had to allow the rain to pour in my life in order for the sunshine to come forth. Those broken pieces that became my cycles of life throughout my entire life were scattered internally so that He could put me back together but this time around God had to take away some things to add better things in order to make me renewed and to give me increase and wholeness.

My weakness was the need for true and genuine love. I define true love as a man and a woman who are deeply and intimately in love where both their hearts, mind and soul are connected. This unique love is full of commitment, trust, honesty, loyalty, compassion, respect, honor, consideration, admiration, and plenty of communication where there aren't any secrets or boundaries that have been crossed where each partner can feel their freedom together, be vulnerable with each other without being critically judged and can live in peace with one another even when the storms and waves have a strong current to wipe out what was built up and the rain that pours heavy when there doesn't seem to be any hope due to the thick clouds of distractions or dissatisfaction.

In a marriage, there shouldn't be any secrets or hidden feelings that can damage or defile the trust in a marriage. A marriage that God has put together isn't made for a third party to join in on either side. This love should be pure loyalty and commitment and a love that can stand through the raging storms and the seduction of temptations because it was built on a strong foundation. This type of love between a man and a woman can still stand the test of times. This is a type of love that will always be admired and desired by a virtuous woman of God. The great news is God is faithful to give you what you need when you are doing all that you can do to stand in faith.

We have to be true to ourselves by asking ourselves that one question. What do we really need for our soul? Do we settle to stay in the mindset of brokenness because we need love so much, the false concept of love, that interferes with our emotional intelligence? When I began my true relationship with God, I began to develop a deeper love for God and when you love God, you will have self-love and a true identity that comes natural because God helps you to discover more about yourself and because God is a God of restoration and of abundance, He gives you more than you need. He gives you a new identity of self. He gives you confidence of who you are and where you are going. This is how I became confident in my calling. I no longer cared about what the people would say. I no longer cared about not being accepted, I was already familiar with that anyway but I became stronger because I wasn't trying to please people. My main focus was pleasing God. I no longer put myself on the back burner. I could finally experience a love that was healthy and a "Forever" Love. It's not the love from a human that has the possibility of fading away or that false concept of love that contaminates the soul and diminishes our peace. It's that agape love which is the highest form of love. Why would we want to settle for something that isn't real? Do we continue to deplete our souls for the sake of chasing someone's heart who doesn't have our best interest? Do we even make our hearts weary and drain ourselves mentally for someone whose eyes are set astray beyond our presence? Or do we set our focus and affection on God by loving ourselves, operating on our gifts that will one day make room for us, allow God to give us joy beyond what happiness couldn't give us. In contrast, do we allow God to be our main priority where our thirst for love is fulfilled and our hearts, minds and souls is healed and restored where we have the wholeness to serve others who are dealing with the same trials, circumstances and cycles that we've struggled with all of our lives. We have to ask ourselves this question for the sake of knowing who we are and how important and valuable we are. When no one can love you, God loves you! When that significant one can't see your worth, God already knew your worth. We ask ourselves this one question in order for us to take off the blinders and dig deep into our spirit to find clarity of our short and long term benefits. These aren't benefits of what the world can offer us but these are the benefits that will strengthen our soul and give us a joy that no one can replace. The benefit of purpose that we must consider is our ultimate goal on how we are created to impact the lives of others. God's plan is to prosper us and to give us a better future. God will never leave us or forsake us! He is our provider when we don't know how we can make it emotionally, mentally or financially. He is our protector when we don't feel secured. He is our healer when our hearts are broken. He is our guider when we don't know which way to go or what choice to make. God will lead us to our provision and this is why he has to expose the truth in order to set us free. Even when the truth hurts, the pain is necessary for the power of breakthrough and for the anointing which gives us our victory!

CHOOSE TO EXPERIENCE A LOVE LIKE NO OTHER

God is asking that simple question! He's saying, "Choose you this day?" What is it going to be? The love of the world or the love of God? He wouldn't ask this question if He didn't really want you to be a part of His love and all that He has for you. We have destiny and purpose in our lives that must come to us and through us. We have to let go of the comfortability of what we consider normal because what feels normal to us is not the normal when we don't have self-love. We have to accept the uncomfortable and get out of the crossfire of living in pain, the heartbreaks, the disappointments and the cycles that depletes our peace. If we want things to change in our lives, we have to make the decision by getting out of our comfort zone, even when it feels scary and tormenting. It is the trick of the enemy as always when fear sets in. Getting out of the comfort zone is the zone where God is taking us. It can feel uncomfortable what's in front of us yet we have a peace that gives us comfort that all things are possible. Sometimes God has to separate us from people in order for us to operate effectively in our assignment. God will also remove people from our lives in order for us to move forward in our purpose and in our peace. Where God is taking us, they or that one significant love you have held on to, can't go with you! I had to choose God over everything! Without God, we are nothing! I had to choose what was best for my mind, heart, soul and spirit. I chose self-love! I chose God! This is where self-love begins and it was self-love that I needed in order to heal. When God removes himself from a situation, all the goodness goes with him. You can't have the good without God. In the same aspect, when God's love abides in you, all the goodness remains in you and you can see the change within you. When you love God, it becomes natural to love yourself!

When your relationships or marriages are struggling, having a relationship with God is what gives you the strength to navigate through the storm. When God is in your business, he knows just what you need because he also knows what your mate needs. When you have discovered a relationship with God, you are no longer feeling like the victim and you won't live a life of sadness where depression tries to squeeze its way back in, God is right there holding and sustaining you because he has the master plan and he holds our hands while we are striving in our faith.

There is not anything less or anything greater you could do to have the love of Jesus. His love is not earned by our works, nor do we have to beg for it. His love is intentional! He loves us when we don't love ourselves! I had to learn that for myself. In our sins, He loves us! When we think He's not with us even in our roughest and toughest moments, He was and is always with us. No one could love us the way our Lord and Savior loves us! His love for us will never fade or end because It's an everlasting love!

As this chapter reflects on relationships in the natural and discovering a relationship with God in spirit, we can clearly examine the similarities and the differences of how God's love is the highest love of any relationship we can ever have. We can understand the similarities of love and what's required to sustain a healthy relationship in how we give and receive love and God's love language is received well when we communicate with him in our prayers and when we talk with him by reading his word (the bible) and those moments of listening to that still small voice and through people who are anointed by God to prophesy to us. This was my personal relationship with God that has sustained my walk of faith after the healing, deliverance and restoration took over my life. Knowing and trusting God has kept me covered and wrapped in his arms. It's a reassurance that I no longer have to be afraid. I know longer have to suffer from anxieties, insecurities, the feeling of not being loved and knowing my self-worth. The choice is yours. What is it going to be? The love of the world or the love of God?

My desire is for all to experience who God is and get to know him on a personal basis. You will never be the same. Your breakthrough and deliverance for a victorious win is right in the arms of God! So, what does peace with God do for us during uncertain times? It grants us hope. Discovering a relationship with God is hope that the life we live on earth is just the beginning of our forever life with God. When we've taken our final breath in our temporary body on this earth, we are ushered into eternity. This life in our forever home is eternal and abundant. But, they are both just a continuation of what was begun on earth. This is why God has begun a new thing in us. "..And I am certain that God, who began the good work within you, will continue his work until it is finally finished on the day when Christ Jesus returns." Philippians 1:6

Section 3

Living in the Presence of My Better Days

CHAPTER 7 - PAIN TO PURPOSE

AWAKENED FROM A DREAM THAT CHANGED MY LIFE

One Friday morning I awakened from a dream that felt like a vision. I had never experienced a dream so precise, so detailed and to the point of being able to remember conversations. This dream was definitely a message from God. As I arose from the bed, I had to take a moment to sit and to meditate on what just happened. I was literally in tears because I was very convinced that I had just experienced a vision. In the dream, there was a meeting at a home where I once resided and at that home was my mother and my two uncles. It was like we were there waiting for a meeting. However, my grandmother who has been deceased for nearly over 18 years now got on a conference call to speak with all of us. I remember sitting in front of a window where my back faced the window and I could hear my grandmother's voice so clear as her southern accent with a strong presence in her voice brought comfort to my heart. I was thinking to myself how much I had missed her just by listening to her voice again. I can remember being so excited to hear her voice. I had desired to ask her things but her tone and firmness wouldn't allow me to. She seemed very authoritative with instructions. Her message was to the point and not casual talk at all. It was like she made it brief and to the point with very clear instructions. She first talked to my mother and when she began talking to her, all I could hear was muffled sounds. I was not able to understand or comprehend the conversation and it was like I wasn't supposed to know what they were saying. Then she started to speak with one of my uncles and it was like she was giving him clear instructions but once again, their voices were muffled and I was not able to hear what they were saying, then she spoke with my other uncle, it was the same situation. I couldn't hear a word but I knew that they were talking. By this time, she said my name, "ANGEL" and she placed emphasis on the last syllable of my name. When she was living, the only time she would call my name and put emphasis on that last syllable was when she demanded my attention or when I better listen or obey what she requested from me. This time, I could hear her message very loud and clear. She said to me, "ANGEL, Did you do what I told you to do?" I replied, "No ma'am" and she didn't allow me to express any excuses. Then she implied that I need you to complete this assignment. I need you to creatively educate the next generations about their family history and I need you to share photos of who they are and where they come from." I replied back, "Yes ma'am!" She then spoke to all of us in the room that someone was coming in a few minutes to the house. She said to look for them. So, I immediately turned around to look in the window. It was dark outside. I turned back and then I heard the doorbell. As soon as my mother and uncles were approaching the door, they opened the door and I immediately woke up from the dream. I never got to see who was at the door! On this Friday morning, I really couldn't get myself together. I felt nervous yet I felt so much joy and peace but there was something that felt urgent in my spirit. It felt like I was on a time clock and I felt like I had to rapidly complete this assignment because my spirit was confirming that this was not a dream. I went to work and I shared my dream with my coworker and she was very inspired by what I had dreamed. Weeks later something happened! Was this the manifestation of what I had dreamed? Two weeks had passed to be exact and on a weekend, I believe this was a Saturday afternoon. My relative called me to tell me that she was coming to deliver something to me. It was a rainy day and a very windy day too. The dark clouds from the rain immediately changed the day to night. As I opened the door, I received a huge bag with all types of great information, family history, photos and newspaper articles neatly stored in the bag. I was in complete shock! The message from my relative was that she felt strongly led to give it to me and that she was coming to my house to make sure that I received it but would later need it back. She wanted me to take the information and to create something with it. I immediately knew that this had to be a message from God because the dream had warned me that someone was coming and to expect them to arrive at my door but the dream never revealed who that person was. It felt like the dream prepared me for what was to come. In addition, my grandmother gave me an instruction. This felt more like an assignment with authority and with a deadline where it had to be completed soon. I felt an urgency and it was spiritual! Right after the dream, I can remember praying to God and asking God to please show me what this dream meant. I am not a dreamer so I normally don't remember what I may have dreamed and I have never dreamed of my grandmother. This was the first time I ever experienced dreaming about her which made my heart glad to hear her voice again. It's not ironic nor is it by coincidence that the relative who came knocking on my door felt led to deliver this large package to me. It was like reality became the conclusion of a dream but it really felt like a vision. I couldn't understand the instructions and why I had to do what I was assigned to do but with all the resources and support from most family members who cooperated with me, I was delighted to complete this assignment.

I had no idea what I was getting myself into and I had no idea of all the hard work and time it would take for me to complete this assignment or where this would take me in the future but once the project was complete and finalized, it became a spiritual and divine awakening and it gave me an inner boost to prepare myself for the next assignment. I was no longer concerned about the "Why" but I was more concerned about the "Next". This experience changed my perspective of how God speaks to us and sometimes a dream or a vision is all you need even when you can't understand the assignment. God also showed me how he would supply the things I needed to complete the assignment. When I think of the goodness of God, it brings me so much joy because God will test our faith and our obedience even when we don't fully understand the "Why" in the assignment. We just have to trust as to where the assignment will take us. I must share how God even blessed me right before starting the assignment, my old computer went completely dead. It literally crashed. I wondered how I was going to start on a project without a working computer. A family member came through and unexpectedly blessed me with a monetary gift towards helping me purchase a computer and although the monetary gift wasn't enough to purchase a brand new computer, God blessed me to purchase a refurbished Macbook computer that would allow me to fulfill the task. It took a lot of work and countless hours. It took a lot of prayer and a lot of patience but it was all worth it because stepping out on faith and to witness the hand of God intervene on my behalf was confirmation to show me that God has a plan for my life and even more than I can see. God doesn't give us the big picture at once because it may frighten us, so he works with us in parts and walks us through the journey. This assignment wasn't connected to pain but it allowed me to feel so much joy and it kept my mind focused and full of anticipation. It taught me the importance of family, my biological maternal history, family culture, my genealogy and life itself and how precious and short our lives are and to enjoy the gift of creativity to step out beyond my comfort zone and to make the best of our lives. More importantly, to create an inheritance for our next generations. What inspired me the most was how my obedience to complete the assignment paved the way for the next assignment. This was the journey toward my divine purpose! I was never the same since I had experienced that dream. My life had changed for the better. This opened doors for me in more ways than I could imagine.

During this time in July of 2018, I completed the family project for an upcoming family reunion which was only two weeks away. I had to fulfill the assignment that came to me in the dream that felt like a vision. The time finally came to complete the final touches of the film that I created for the family. This was very special to me and I learned so much about the history of my family. I often wondered why God led me in this direction to dig and investigate very interesting facts and shocking revelations about the history of my family on my maternal side. There was so much to learn and the more I gathered information, the more I became confident with my African American heritage and the cultural blend of other races that makes me who I am. My identity of where I came from gave me a sense of courage and strength, the more I discovered where my talents, creativities, ambitions, entrepreneurship spirit and skills originated, the more I became motivated to strive the more in my gifts and purpose. This project not only inspired me but it gave me a sense of strength, courage and the confidence needed to step out of my comfort zone, to take a leap of faith, and to take the small steps to present this project to my extended family members and meet many family members I've never got to meet during the journey. I had no clue of how extremely large my family was and how many generations of families are spread across the United States. I lost count as I would try to number them from 6 generations that came from 13 siblings who were birthed from my great-great grandparents who were from Oktibbeha Mississippi. It would be impossible to calculate the magnitude of how huge the family expanded over many decades until this present time. I may not have known these family members but it was that special feeling to know I was a part of a great lineage of great historians, educators, business entrepreneurs and skilled professionals. I had the opportunity to learn so much from their memorable moments to the inspiring history of my ancestors going all the way back to the early 1800's.

At the family reunion in July 2018, many family members who were in attendance gathered together and were touched by the movie video I presented that night. Since the family reunion was located at an open park, strangers started walking by to watch the movie and felt intrigued as they watched with such amusement and interest, which was a compilation of great music, photos where many familiar faces of the past, living and deceased, known and unknown were honored and remembered. It was touching and brought tears of joy and pain to many of the family members present on that day. A blend of music from the classic gospel to the classic R&B and soul music filled the atmosphere with inspiration and the feeling of love and family unity as many sat and wept by the presentation that became emotional for the mature generations who could recall those moments. It was educational and inspiring for our younger generations present. I was so exhausted that evening from all the hard work of trying to stage it together. With the help of a few family members, we were able to make it happen. After the reunion and before I fell asleep that night, my soul was fulfilled because I knew that my grandmother would have been proud of me. I knew that there had to be a purpose for all the diligent and relentless work I had put into this presentation. More importantly, I obeyed what I was told to do in the dream and I couldn't take that assignment lightly! I'm still in awe of it all. I am very much aware that God will call us to do a specific task but it's better to be obedient and do what he tells you to do regardless of the fact because obedience is always better than sacrifice. There is one thing for sure in this life is the legacy we leave on earth is building treasures in heaven. This is our purpose for the kingdom of heaven. "A good person leaves an inheritance for their children's children, but a sinner's wealth is stored up for the righteous." Proverbs 13:22 KJV

Nevertheless, we must keep in mind and remember after our lives on earth ends, people will remember us by our works on earth, our legacy and our expressed vision. They are not going to talk about how much money we left in the bank or what type of cars we drove on the day of our memorial, but they are going to talk about the life we lived and what we did with our lives here on earth. Our legacy is what we leave behind for those to inherit and if we know quickly how people forget the dead, we will stop living to impress people with money, clothes, houses and cars and start living to inspire people. The mindset and purpose is to leave a legacy not a liability.

The following year I had enough courage to do the same thing, I was led to create a family memorial presentation for another family reunion but this time it was on my mother's father's side of the family. This too was an exciting opportunity and although I didn't dream about doing this again, I felt led to complete this project and the presentation became phenomenal. I was pleased that I could be a part of bringing great and memorable history to the family and to the youth of generations. It was indeed hard work but all the hard work would soon pay off at the end when it was time to present the movie to family in July of 2019. In the same manner, I was able to tell the story of my great grandparents and all of their nine children and shared momentous family memories of photos and the biography of my great grandparents which touched the hearts of many as well as 6 generations of family members. I created DVD's for the family to have as keepsakes and to share with their children and to our future generations. This family reunion was indeed another success! Success through God's eyes is different from the world's point of view. Through God's eyes, you, being faithful to your God-ordained purpose, desperate adversities, struggles, issues, or combat is one of the things that could be counted as a success. Some are called to serve in the limelight, while others are called to service in the shadows.

"You can't really know where you are going until you know where you have been. ~Maya Angelou ~

ALL THINGS ARE WORKING TOGETHER FOR OUR GOOD

As I sit and think about all the wonderful things God had done for me and collectively think about all the pain that I endured for many years and in areas where God is yet molding me, I become more and more convinced that this life I live seems more like finding the pieces to a jigsaw puzzle without knowing what the outcome will look like in the end once the jigsaw puzzle is finished. Every piece of my life mattered and it was for my good. This is why I know for a fact that everything that happened to me whether positive or negative or whether in the natural or in spirit was for my better good. In this season of my life, I think most about how God was trying to grab my attention from so many areas of my life and how the closer I became aware of his presence was the more he began to show me his true love and the reflection of who I am and why I exist. What was my true purpose in this life? Why was I born? There had to be a reason for me to be here and to still live and to tell my story. As I look over my life and as I examine all the trials and circumstances, I must say that God has blessed me to make it this far. I must say that my life in this season closely expresses the condition of my heart, soul and spirit.

In the book of Philippians 3:12-14, it states, "I admit that I haven't yet acquired the absolute fullness that I'm pursuing, but I run with passion into his abundance so that I may reach the purpose that Jesus Christ has called me to fulfill and wants me to discover. I don't depend on my own strength to accomplish this; however I do have one compelling focus: I forget all of the past as I fasten my heart to the future instead. I run straight for the divine invitation of reaching the heavenly goal and gaining the victory-prize through the anointing of Jesus."

I must say that the relationship with God has given me the confidence to run this race with peace, ambition and in obedience. Having a relationship with God has allowed me to experience his love, peace and joy on a daily basis when I am yet feeling the weight of the world and when I yet struggle in areas that I still need God to help me because it nurtures my heart to know that although I hold the gift to help others, God is yet still helping me. My heart is pure and humble to accept that I am not perfect, yet I have grown and matured in the spirit to grow higher because I will never know it all but I am in the matured state of mind to know that pain comes with the power to become stronger! I am becoming so much better and so much wiser! This is why all things work together for the good of those who love God and who are called according to his purpose. Romans 8:28 KJV

I believe that God gave me that dream in February 2018 to prepare for my season, a season of growth and divine alignment. It was the choice I had to make whether I would obey and step out in faith or to sit back and allow this blessing to walk on by but I chose to step out this time. I chose to ignore all of the naysayers. I chose to ignore rejection this time. I chose to walk differently! I chose to not ask questions and just do the work and find out the "why" later. I began to focus on the how! How can I help someone else through this journey of life feel the love of God and to walk in their healing and in their purpose? This is the "why" in why God had to place the desire in me. In that season when I had that dream, I saw it in the natural. I placed more emphasis on my natural identity of who and where I came from but as God opened my eyes months later, I became more aware that the dream was a spiritual awakening. I had to know who I was in Christ and I had to know my spiritual calling. My assignment here on earth. This was spiritual!

When we clearly understand who we are and why we exist, we must think about who created us. Jesus came for a purpose which means that we were created on purpose for a purpose! We have to know the characteristics of our creator, our Father in heaven.

We have to know who our creator is. We don't have his thought patterns and He clearly doesn't think like we do, but in due season, God makes everything perfect. This is why God works in seasons. Remember God isn't finished with you yet! He's working a new thing in you and through you and in due season your harvest is coming. This is what I kept feeling during the time I was working on the assignment to complete the work. I had to realize that it really wasn't my grandmother calling me to give me instruction for the assignment but symbolically it was God calling me to a higher assignment. As I stated before, I really believe I had experienced a vision from God. I had to answer, accept and walk in faith. What do I have to lose by allowing God to move in my life? God was calling my name. I didn't literally think that it was my grandmother speaking to me as the dream made it so very clear but from a spiritual perspective, I knew that God was delivering a message to me. A message of unity, a message of love, a message of hope and a message of knowing who I am and not just from my earthly heritage, yet God allowed me to understand who I was from a heavenly realm, a spiritual inheritance! It became vivid after I had completed the assignment which was from an earthly presentation in the eyes of my family to inspire and to educate them but God gave me more than what I could give the family, he gave me spiritual awareness! He allowed me to see more of how my passion was connected to my pain and how the assignment was therapeutic for me. He allowed me to see how my pain had to birth my purpose. The pain that I had felt for so many years felt like I was dying in silence and no one knew the type of pain I carried for many years. It didn't diminish my intelligence and it can't weaken or remove my gifts but it affected my heart, mind, soul and spirit and it made me question many things in my life. This is why God reminds us to not be weary in well-doing but in due season we will reap if we faint not meaning, don't give up on those desires! Don't give up on those hopes and dreams! Don't give up on your faith and what was planted inside you to persevere! What God has for you, is for you! God is opening doors for you that no man can shut and he is also closing doors that no man can open but you have to love God, serve God and follow his commands and seek him on a daily basis to receive the fullness of what he desires for you! You must be humble and be obedient to God in order to receive his blessings and favor. In John 15:17, "So this is my parting command: Love one another deeply!"

HOW MY PAIN WAS PURPOSED FOR GOD'S GLORY

In July 2018, As I sat in my car on my lunch break to take some much needed time away from the busy 8 hour job that

263

felt mentally draining and overwhelming from time to time, I would often tune in to YouTube to listen to someone speak words of inspiration to encourage and to bless my soul. During this time in my life, I was seeking God and yet dealing with daily challenges to keep my faith strengthened. However, I was feeling different in my spirit ever since I had that dream and I knew that something was happening to me. I knew that healing and deliverance was taking an effect on me and it was that one day I will never forget, I got caught up on this particular video and I couldn't stop watching it. During this time it didn't really matter what time it was,I wasn't concerned with how many more minutes I had left on my lunch break, I had to listen to what this young lady was sharing in her testimony. She was sharing her story. This young lady started talking about how God had blessed her and her husband after they endured a financial setback and she expressed in detail how she got fired from her job while thinking this would be the day that she would get her raise. Her entire testimony caught my attention as if I was hypnotized by the words that were coming out of her mouth. I had never heard someone be so transparent and opened about their story. Her story was appealing. It was relatable! She was raw and unapologetically the truth. I immediately was taken away by her testimony and at this point I had to finish the entire video. She shared how God blessed her because she had no other choice but to trust him, I had to find out who she was and find out more about her. So, I became more and more interested in all other videos she posted on YouTube. After watching countless hours of Dr. Shamieka Dean's Youtube channel, my spirit felt connected and it was that moment when she spoke on using our gifts for the glory of God and when God speaks to us. This particular live stream, immediately gave me the chills. Something inside of me rose up. It was like envisioning me as a dying flower that needed a little water and sun to resuscitate me. It was like my soul needed some CPR. Her messages clicked with my spirit and I was able to understand and receive her messages on a level of spiritual maturity as well as her natural ability to trust God in the midst of her trials. It was the perfect timing. I needed to hear this! My dream would now make even more sense as I became more and more interested in why the dream was necessary for the assignment God called me to do. I believe God allowed me to discover her in this season because he was preparing me. My heart was being conditioned. The more I listened to what Dr. Shamieka Dean had to go through to get where she is today, the more I felt connected. She talked about the pain of what she suffered throughout her life and although I hadn't experienced all that she had suffered through, I could still relate to the pain she endured, from toxic relationships, not having her father in her life and feeling broken, rejected and disgusted. As I listened to her videos and read one of her books she wrote and about her life, I began to reflect on a few years back. In 2017, I was still battling with my commitment to God. I would occasionally smoke marijuana (weed) to get a relief of everyday stress and sometimes pop a bottle of wine and relax my weary mind and although once those counterfeit soothers would soon fade away, I would find myself once again struggling to gain peace and joy in my soul yet I knew how to pray in the midst of wavering faith. My faith would waver in doubt when God didn't answer my prayers on my time. I would think about the meaning of faith and that all I needed was just a little faith to get my prayers answered. I just needed a little faith to get God to move on my behalf. Well, I would tend to lose my faith because I had this time-watch in my mind when God would move and these prayers should be answered by a certain time-frame.

I had to learn the hard way that it would never be on my time watch. God moves on his time watch only! I couldn't forget

265

how God was still good to me for allowing me to get through each passing day and I could remember how the presence of God would consume me but I didn't take the time to get to know God for myself. I would only pray to God when I needed him to take away that moment of pain and stress that seemed to overwhelm me and consume me, yet God was still merciful and gracious enough to answer my prayers at the right time. I would often feel a sense of guilt because it was like only calling your father when you needed money or help. It just didn't seem fair to do God this way. Sometimes, we tend to put God in this box as if we only talk to him when we need him and when things are going well, we don't think about him and then we feel that God is angry with us if we hadn't talked with him in a while. We tend to feel condemnation as if we aren't good enough to meet God's standards. As for me, I've always been pretty hard on myself like many people can relate to. I didn't feel like I could meet God's standards because salvation always seemed too strict and boring. I felt like being saved was no fun and I would have to stop everything. It was hard for me to try to live this perfect life before God because I'm just not perfect and that was why I couldn't live this life called salvation. I was afraid to be in and out of church and not consistent because I was tired of letting God down. I felt that I just couldn't keep grieving his spirit. I was always taught that God doesn't strive with all men, meaning that he won't keep pleading with you forever to open your heart to him. Either I was going to serve God with all of my heart or I was not! It was simple at that! God had to show me how important it was to have a relationship with him. This was something that took some time for me to understand, in fact it took most of my life to truly understand what that really meant. Being in relationships and friendships seemed a bit difficult for me and although being in a marriage requires a strong relationship, I still suffered through insecurities and trust issues. I had to protect

266

myself from inner pain and I kept walls up to guard my heart because I was too afraid to allow people to hurt or offend me again. I didn't keep friends for long because I couldn't trust them, although I was a very friendly person. I just found it very difficult to trust people, in general. A wounded woman becomes afraid to speak her truth, she lacks self worth, she tolerates toxic people, she seeks external validation, she's a people-pleaser, she apologizes for who she is, and she has negative self-talk but an "Awakened Woman" honors her truth, knows her worth, sets loving boundaries, feels validated from within, inspires others to shine, lives unapologetically and speaks gently to herself. She is also not afraid to collaborate and build relationships and friendships because she can trust God to lead and to guide her in the right direction. She allow God to give her discernment on who to trust and who not to trust. She doesn't have to compare her gifts and identity with others because she knows that she is fearfully and wonderfully made. She doesn't have to compete with anyone else because she knows that the gift God has given her is only for her. In fact, she is encouraged when she sees others move actively in their gifts! She is a women of wisdom and compassion and encourages and becomes a support system to others by supporting them in their gifts!

An awakened woman has been healed from the spirit of offense and doesn't have to build walls around herself because she won't allow others to burden her spirit but she can look beyond the faults and failures of others and see their pain and their need for healing. She doesn't become their victim but they become her victor. She doesn't exaggerate on their messiness but she comes to bring them a message in the midst of their mess. This awakened woman was me. I had to learn to accept the pain for growth and that pain teaches you, that pain matures you and that pain reveals reality. Most of my pain was formed from the lack of love as I explained throughout this book. My pain was necessary for my calling, my identity, my purpose. My pain and affliction reminds me of the book of Psalm 119:71, "It is good for me that I have been afflicted; that I might learn thy statues." If it hadn't been for pain, I wouldn't have the experience or the passion to help someone else seek healing from their troubled soul. God took me on the journey to appreciate all that I had suffered would become the test that victoriously became my testimony. When I think about how the lack of love brought pain in my life as early as a little girl in need of her father's love to the lack of desiring to be loved as a young women through toxic relationships of men cheating and lying to you and telling you how much they love you when their behavior speaks the opposite, it's for God's glory because it taught me what ministry looks like!

My pain taught me that a man's eyes can never be satisfied when he is possessed by the spirit of lust and that he becomes more infatuated by it when he entertains lust or is intrigued by the entertainment of lust. Lust is a spirit and he becomes spiritually paralyzed and caught in the web of his own sins even when he knows he is supposed to do what is right. The pain of disloyalties taught me how it wasn't my fought that I endured brokenness from those past relationships, it was not just me that needed healing but these young men I dated needed healing whether they would admit to it or not. This goes for both men and women. Many young women grow up believing that a man is in love with them but he is only feeling lust for them. This intensifies the woman's emotions when it intensifies his organ. Yet, I paid the price like many others learning how love hurts, especially when you don't receive it the way you expect to receive it and how you cannot place a value or measure your worth based on how people you love so much will mistreat or disrespect you. You cannot make someone you love feel bad take revenge towards them because they don't love you! You have to know your worth and let them go. When love is no longer served at the table, it's time to leave and gracefully walk away! Sometimes God has to create the exit plan to help you walk away when that person no longer love you. It's not your fought if he stopped loving you but it's your fought if you chose to stay. You have to have the identity in Christ to know that you are created in the image of God and called for a purpose. That man that couldn't love you may have been a lesson or an assignment but he's not your purpose. You're not a rug that lies on the floor only to be walked on, washed up and thrown away once you're worn out! You're so much better, if you could only see how important and valuable you are, you would have the power and strength to walk away from the poison and walk courageously into your purpose and destiny!

The journey of life felt like one of the most unpredictable roller coaster rides because when one moment you're going up and it feels great and then within seconds your heart is plummeting down and spiraling going through loops, jerks, spins and drops all at the same time. My pain had to prepare me and it taught me when someone mistreats you or criticizes you, it's none of your business because the problem inside of them is the weight that they are carrying! However, when you make their problem about you, you are now carrying their weight, and not only are you carrying yours, you're carrying double weight. Our main goal in life is to be accepted and I truly understand because we are humans with emotions and feelings. We want to feel accepted and this is natural but when we feel rejection, it triggers negative thoughts and it causes something to die in our life. It affects our: self-esteem, optimism, faith, humanity, trust, compassion, internalized feelings and causes us to fell bitterness, frustrated, disappointment and isolation. Once again, this was my pain that drove me to focus on pleasing God and not people. I knew my pain and what I went through had to happen. I had to endure the affliction throughout the years and my biggest breakthrough came once I accepted the truth about intimate love, that there will never be a man on earth that can love me the way Jesus loves me. This is the agape love. This is the highest love and it's everlasting! Jesus' love for us will never die! His love is not based on conditions. The rejection I suffered growing up created the need for acceptance but it taught me a great lesson about myself. I learned that although I was rejected for being different, I couldn't fit in because I wasn't a follower! It taught me that I am a leader! The rejection I experienced was God's protection! They couldn't accept me because they were not assigned to me.

As I wake up every morning to give God all of my praise, I can't help to thank Him for his grace and mercy and how he has healed me and yet healing and making me whole from my past. He had delivered me and allowed me to see how much I have grown in him and how I came a very long way in faith. He has allowed me to know that he has so much in store for my life. He has ultimately allowed me to find my purpose in life and how my pain from my past is what gives me purpose today to overcome all the trials, troubles, opposition and sorrows this life brings. When Jesus lives inside us, his Holy Spirit by supernaturally enlightens power within us to become more than a conqueror! We became game-changers and kingdom builders because he was and still is our promise keeper until the very end! We become the better version of ourselves! We become victorious! My prayer to the Holy Spirit, "Help me to forget the pain associated with the past and as I visit my past from now on let it be for only moments of remembering how you broke the chains from my life, removed the weight from my soul and brought me out of bondage. Lord Jesus, allow the pain I've endured remind me how you healed and delivered me to give others hope! Thank You Holy Spirit! Thank You Jesus! To God Be The Glory!

EVERYONE IS GIVEN A GIFT FROM GOD

"Every good gift and every perfect gift is from above, and comes down from the Father of lights, with whom there is no variation or shadow of turning." James 1:17 KJV

My greatest fulfillment was the season where God uncovered my purpose and allowed me to discover what he had birthed inside of me. In order for me to uncover my purpose, he had to heal the wounds inside, deliver my soul, and he gave me revelation to gain a spiritual perspective of my life and the lives of others. It was like being that single beautiful flower in the middle of the field, surrounded and overshadowed by the weeds and the shrubs, to grow and to stand beyond and over all that surrounded me to hide me and to prevent me from allowing the sun to shine on me. God's love had to shine on me. God had to cleanse my heart to make it pure in order to align me into his perfect will for me. So in August of 2018, God led me to take an online course, It was a master class to "Uncover Your Purpose" and it was created and taught by Dr. Shamieka Dean. This was the season where I took several courses where it paved the way for a new start in my life. I went into deep prayer and I asked God, "What is my purpose in this life?" I knew my gifts and talents and I also knew that they were a part of my purpose. In fact, our gifts and talents are the tools that God gives us to work in our purpose. It's those pieces of the puzzle that will soon make the complete and finished work of our calling. When I thought about my gifts and the talents that God blessed me with, I had to think back to the days of my youth and how I would write in my diary at the age of ten years old. I would write about how a particular day had impacted my life, whether I was feeling

271

sad, happy, frightened or excited. I enjoyed journaling to release my feelings at a very young age. I also used to write fictional stories, poetry, music lyrics and I enjoyed writing essays for homework assignments for school and college. I thought about how writing became easy for me and how I would receive compliments from teachers and college professors. In addition, I always enjoyed singing and I used to rap a few lines, here and there during my high school years. It was those early years as a child where my great-grandmother would call me up to sing at her church. The song that she would have me sing as a solo was "I'm Looking For a Miracle" written and sung by the The famous gospel artist group, "The Clark Sisters". I can remember being extremely nervous when she would call me up to sing one of her favorite songs because I never liked being in front of crowds or any large audience. My introvert personality showed outwardly and I only liked being around close family members. I didn't like to be on the front-lines of anything. I was always comfortable behind the scenes. I felt that was where I performed my best but yet, my great-grandmother saw differently and a few relatives knew how I was extremely nervous, they insisted that I sing anyway. So they continued to push me to sing in the midst of my nervousness. I did it in obedience and I had to ignore how uncomfortable this made me feel but in the end I felt glad that I did it!

Now, as I fast forward to those moments in my early thirties, where I enjoyed singing in the choir and when it was suggested that I sing a lead song, I would decline the request every time because once again, that feeling of nervousness and being uncomfortable would always get in the way just like it was, being that nervous little girl. However, there were those moments where I stepped out in faith through my deepest fear and I would sing from the bottom of my heart. My voice would tremble but I noticed how God's anointing would take over me once I put my heart into the song. I also think about the gift of graphics design and how God allowed me to utilize my skills in designing printed material such as: flyers, business cards, event programs, book covers and many other stationery materials. I also designed t-shirts and I created photo portrait collages. Someone could explain to me what they would want and I could immediately create a picture in my mind on how the finished work would appear. I knew that it was a gift from God and I utilized this gift to help many clients and customers for over 25 years as a part-time hobby while I worked a full-time job. As I reflect back on those years of being a young single lady in my late teens and attending church with my mom and sibling where I grew up in, I now often wonder where I would have been now, if I could have created a children's ministry of my own. I believe I could have made a great impact on the lives of many children for the sake of Christ if I would've committed myself and submitted to God in the way that He desired for me. I knew that God desired for me to work with children at that time and season of my life. I could remember as a teenager reading to children during Sunday School hour at church and I would read about parables in the bible. I would paraphrase the stories by acting several roles for the children to understand. I also remember teaching the youth about God through games and activities that I created. I could remember being passionate about it and couldn't wait for Sunday mornings to come and then many years later as a wife and a mother, I would find myself doing the very same thing and that was working with the youth again at a different church I attended. I worked with the younger children from ages two through twelve years old. I would find all different kinds of activities and ways for them to learn and for them to discover God's love in an epic and radical way. Most of all, I enjoyed being creative and it brought so much excitement and joy. What stands out the most in my mind was this particular song I would teach them. The song was actually a scripture in the bible. I learned this song as a child and the words and melody will always stick with me. In fact, the melody of the song was created by my late cousin who passed away in her early 20's when I was only 10 years old. She taught me and a few other children in our youth group many different songs. I carried this song in my heart for many years and I shared this song with generations of children. It's called, "Let us Love One Another". It goes like this. "Beloved, let us Love One Another, for love is of God and everyone who loves is born of God and knoweth God, he that knoweth not, knoweth not God for God is Love. So, Beloved, let us Love One Another - 4th John 4:7 and 8. The melody makes you think of a fun jingle. It's really catchy!I That is the reason why I remembered this song all those years. I really wish you could hear the melody of this song because it's the most precious song I've ever heard and I've never heard it sung in that way ever since. I will always remember my late cousin, Donna Williams who created the melody to a bible scripture that stuck in my heart all those years since I was younger than ten years old. The melody of the song is the scripture itself that speaks on the most powerful fruits of the Spirit of God and that is love! That's what makes it beautiful and special!

Many years flew by and that season to work with the children ended. Things changed and life happened. Yet, I felt that I let God down but He never changed His love for me. I was yet broken in my heart but in those days of working with the children, they brought me so much joy inside. Other things of life got in the way which prevented me from continuing in that area of ministry. I lost so much precious time over the years when I stopped attending church but God still never stopped loving me and His grace and mercy was always with me. As I reflect back to those days, no matter how far I drifted away from God, I knew that there was a calling on my life as there were many other areas I was gifted in. Now as we fast forward to this present day, God has given me the pathway of piecing together the hobbies I enjoy the most along with all the gifts and talents to unlock my purpose. Once I started to develop a relationship with God and continued to become familiar with his voice as he was calling me and placing desires in my heart, in areas that seemed unfamiliar to me, I began to understand that this was simply not about me. I am just a willing and enabling vessel and ready to work. God placed the desire in my heart to reach after souls and to align my heart posture so that God could use me for His will. This means, no matter how uncomfortable it may feel to step out in the front lines or no matter why the goal of the assignment doesn't make any logical sense, I still must obey what God is calling me to do. I had to learn that the assignment for our seasons in life will always seem bigger than us. That is, because we're looking at the assignment in the natural and not in the spiritual light. It won't make sense because for one thing, it's simply not about us. This is where I had to continue to stop and repeat to learn this because I made everything about myself. Sometimes God will make us repeat our tests until we finally get it. Sometimes God allows us to make mistakes in order to remember the promise once he opens our eyes to revelation. The gifts and talents that God blesses us with will always be unique and special with a divine anointing. Just when you feel that your ideas, techniques and strategies that God gives you will be copied by someone else and your fear is not to share what God had done for you and through you because there are so many people out there that you will steal your ideas and receive credit for them. It's okay! Once again, it is the enemy working to prevent you from using what is so precious for you because it is a special gift operating in the supernatural. You must continue to share God's gifts and not feel intimidated by others. They may copy what you do but they can't copy the anointing to do it better than you. I used to believe that talents and gifts were more for hobbies and passover time to allow us to reinvent and to regroup ourselves as an enjoyable pleasure but God gave me revelation that your gifts will make room for you, meaning our gifts and talents becomes our source of income while they also become our purpose in life, whether it's our career path or our entrepreneurship in business, it is His purpose to bring us spiritual and financial prosperity and freedom. If you have breath in your lungs and the blood is still warm in your veins, God has given you work to do. So what are you going to do? What is the work that God called you to? What is your assignment in this season of your life? What are your talents and gifts and what are they for? Take a moment to think about that even if you have to think back to the days of your youth. Sometimes, it's the simple things of life that helps us uncover our purpose by connecting them to our gifts, talents and our passions.

In Jeremiah 1:5, it states, "Before I formed you in the womb I knew you. Before you were born I set you apart; I appointed you as a prophet to the nations."

When I think about how God often uses people with the worst past to create the best futures, I tend to think about Apostle Paul in the bible. He was a very intelligent man and before he became an advocate for Christ, he persecuted and murdered Christians. We would consider looking at Paul's past as being horrible. God transformed Paul's life for the better by allowing Paul to be converted and born-again as a believer and follower of Christ. Even in the midst of Apostle Paul's struggle, we should be reminded how our past is not our present. We too, have been changed because in Christ we are made new. Even in the midst of Paul's struggle of being a prisoner, he never gave up on his purpose. In fact, he persevered the more. Paul persisted through his purpose while

276

being chained up as a prisoner. He prayed for the sick and he never stopped leading for the cause of Christ. Setbacks in life often become our set up for our breakthrough for victory. Its a preparation for our greatest comeback! It's finding our purpose and destiny through our higher calling. No matter the struggle or opposition, Apostle Paul had to go through the struggle and affliction, he went through it for the sake of the calling on his life. He knew that his purpose wasn't about him. It was bigger than him. Paul had the vision and it was lit! Paul didn't allow discouragement or stress to overcome him due to his condition to stop him from igniting the purpose and the vision within him. In Zechariah 4:6, "Not by might, nor by power, but by the Spirit, says the Lord Almighty." Our purpose is far much greater than our struggles and when we operate in our purpose, God will bless us through obedience and faith because we serve an Almighty God as we use our talents and gifts to help us do the ultimate calling for God's kingdom and that is to spread the Gospel of Christ everywhere we go.

WHAT ARE YOU PASSIONATE ABOUT?

Passion, skills and talents will give you the tools to live out your calling and your relationship with God. It will keep you on your destiny track. Always remember, your alignments determine your assignments! Ask yourself, what makes you passionate? What makes you cry? What makes you emotional? What grieves your spirit? What was or still is your pain? This is all connected to your assignment. When I took the course, "Uncover Your Purpose". I learned how our pain and our passion is how we can find our purpose. This is why we have to find it because it's always been there. It's always been inside of us. The passion in us is the fire that drives us! Our passion is the fuel for the engine! The fuel is our fire and that fire burns on the inside, just like pain burns on the inside.

It gives us the passion to not give up because it becomes very meaningful to us! God wants us to navigate through the journey and pathways to find it. He wants us to do the work. The work in us is how we exercise our faith to grow in our purpose and I had to really think that through. I actually had to sit back and be silent for a while in prayer to focus on my pain. I really didn't want to think about my pain but I had to, in order to connect those missing pieces to the unfinished puzzle. My pain became my passion as God took me into deep revelation through prayer and fasting. I thought about how painful it was to have been a little girl who desired to have her father in her life, to spend time with her, to protect her, to love her as his own, and to guide her and teach her about life in this cold and dark world. I think about how I just needed my father's affirmation of love and God allowed me to expand that thought. It was like he spoke to me and said "What about the other little girls who are fatherless? And what about the women who are still bitter, insecure and are still suffering from being a fatherless daughter?" I thought about it for a while and the thought wouldn't leave. It started to grieve me! It became my burden and it became my pain for them. For, I know what it feels like to suffer for so many years. I can empathize that type of pain as a woman. I know that it affects a man when he is a product of being a fatherless son. My heart goes out to all men who were fatherless but I don't know what it feels like to be a man, so I must focus on how this affects women in general. This pain and this burden I feel became my passion. My passion was to share God's power of healing the heart, mind and soul and to allow God to transform those who have lost hope or those who have desensitized their pain by normalizing their dysfunction and their bleeding wounds with anger, insecurities, low-self esteem, bitterness and unforgiveness. Once I received the revelation of my true passion, I became awakened! I started to seek God for more revelation on how to connect this passion with my gifts and talents. I also became enlightened and excited because God's presence would fill me up with his glory for desires that I had never desired. These were desires in areas that I would have never thought about. There is no way I would have a desire for something that seemed imaginable and so intimidating. It had to be of God and God once again reminded me that my purpose isn't about me but it's to become open to the Holy Spirit and to be used to serve others. Once this revelation marinated in my spirit, I noticed a change in my spirituality! I noticed how I was healing, growing and seeing things differently. Things around me started to change and I was finally getting a breakthrough. That breakthrough was unspeakable joy! That breakthrough was the peace that passeth all understanding. That breakthrough was the ability to love others, even those who were mean towards me or hated me. That breakthrough was what I needed in order for my faith in God to be made whole. I could see myself again, as that beautiful flower in the field growing with thicker roots and not withering from the environment around me. So, the sun that was shining on me, allowed me to stand out before the weeds and shrubs and tall grass. I was no longer the same although I had a long way to go but I surely had no interest in turning back at this point of my life. On social media, I immediately felt led to create a business page to advocate inspiration and social change for our fathers to love their daughters, even if that means the children are no longer with their mothers. I also honor fathers who are in their children's lives and my message would advocate to stop using kids as hostages, bargain tools and bait that would prevent them from being in the presence of their fathers or vice versa. In addition, I would also advocate to stay balanced as a parent. Our children are observing every move we make and our reaction teaches them how to respond. They learn by example so our actions will speak louder than our words. In one post, I remember sharing that if you, as a parent isn't balanced, the child becomes temperamental, selfish and entitled. My goal to advocate my page was for the sake of reconciling fathers and daughters. I shared photos of many fathers (young and matured) spending time with their daughters and I would write inspiring and motivating captions to promote unity and bonding time. The page immediately attracted the attention of many viewers and followers and from time to time, I would receive feedback on how it was a beautiful thing and how it brought encouragement. I named the page @daddiesanddaughters on Instagram. You may check that page out if you'd like. From a spiritual aspect when I think about reconciliation of fathers and daughters, I think about the reconciliation to our heavenly father. We are reconciled through the sacrificial blood of Jesus. Jesus died for our sins so that we can be reconciled with Christ. This became my spiritual awakening and the fruits of this assignment are love, joy, peace, gentleness, goodness, patience, faith, and self control. These are the characteristics that are needed for the sake of reconciling our fathers with their daughters. So, my passion is for God to heal our children from broken hearts and for them to not carry their brokenness into their adulthood lives. My assignment is not only to spread the love of Christ to all who are willing to accept Jesus into their hearts but to also allow the broken women to receive the power of healing and wholeness and to also find her purpose in life just like I did. My assignment is to encourage fathers to become active in their children's lives! It is my true passion that God has allowed me to feel this great burden in our society. I feel in my spirit that there is more to come, yet I don't know where God leads me next but I am surely in preparation with joy in my heart for the journey ahead as the glory of my life was birthed from the story of my life. It's the pathway of my life to trust where God leads me.

WHAT DOES A FULFILLED SOUL FEEL LIKE?

A fulfilled soul feels like overflowing joy. It's that kind of joy you feel on a typical day when your mood or response to a negative comment or outcome didn't go your way, yet there's a joy that remains and a peace that keeps you calm.

Sometimes it can feel like we're living our lives just to get to the next day. Living paycheck to paycheck doesn't feel like purpose. It feels more like existing. When you go to work, it starts to feel as though everyday is the same. The only motivation you can feel is waiting for Fridays to come just to enjoy a few days to start all over again. The motivation tends to fade away once you realize your paycheck is spent even before you receive the deposit into your bank account. On the other hand, people tend to idolize things for fulfillment. These things can be our loved ones, family, friends, our houses, cars, clothes, jewelry, jobs, businesses, a loaded bank account and material things. The purpose of man is greater than materialism, more than money, more than power and the things of this life that entertain us in the natural but at the end of the day it does not fulfill the soul. Have you ever heard of people who shop for therapy? People who think that shopping is a therapy may see it as a strategy for healing. Anything you have to keep doing over and over again is not therapy, it's a decision and compulsive shopping, when it's done for the sake of only bringing you fulfillment, it only becomes an expensive habit. There's nothing wrong with shopping, as long as it's not your source of therapy for healing. Shopping isn't therapeutic because you're going to keep shopping and shopping and shopping. You'll have a closet full of clothes with tags on them and no where to go. You might be solving a problem in one area but in the midst of it you're gaining another problem. As we see how people think they can heal themselves by finding things or people to fulfill the void in their soul, just think about what you picked and reflect what your life has chosen. Are the things of this life given to you to fill that void non perishable? Everything in this life won't live forever. As humans, we won't live forever. So think about what you prioritize or idolize to fulfill your soul. For me, my soul became fulfilled once I received revelation, wisdom and knowledge on my purpose in life. It was more than just existing on earth and counting the days of the week as they pass us by, but it was life and when you find that purpose to live beyond being just a citizen of a country, a human being, a black woman, a wife and and a mother, you become fulfilled to know that there is more to life than just existing. When you find your ultimate purpose on earth, your heart is in alignment with God and you are in submission to God's will. This is a fulfillment that is unspeakable. My better days came once I discovered my ultimate purpose and not just discovering them but operating in them. I noticed how happy I became inside. I wasn't dealing with depression and stress as this was my normal daily experience. Those days were tormenting to live through because although I was blessed and grateful for my family, job and well-being, I wasn't healed and set free on the inside. I needed freedom in my spirit and I was able to dream again and I started to speak positive words to myself and to people around me. I have always enjoyed encouraging anyone around me, even if it were a stranger. I just always had it in me to bring words of encouragement and words of inspiration, no matter your age or who you were. God allowed me to dream again and therefore I started to speak those things that I desired into existence! I spoke words of affirmation to myself and to my family. I noticed how my life started to change. It's impossible to chase a dream that ONE cannot possibly dream. You must see the dream in your heart in order to speak it out of your mouth.

As I reflect on my days of being a single woman and desiring marriage, I really believed that marriage was the anecdote for my healing and deliverance for the sake of love. I really never focused or thought about my purpose back then because I was so deeply focused on being in love and feeling loved. I felt that marriage would allow my soul to become fulfilled because it would replace the void in my life but I didn't know any better. I witnessed great and long lasting marriages in my family although there were many divorces as well. After 20 years of being married, I had to learn that marriage does not fulfill your soul, you must have a fulfilled soul before you enter into a marriage. You must have inner healing before carrying baggage into a marriage. Marriage is designed to enhance the greatness in you. As I said earlier in this book, marriage becomes an accessory and not a necessity for your life. You must know who you are and not hide your identity under the identity of your spouse. Your spouse has a purpose and so do you. If you don't know your purpose, you don't know your mate because you will only rely on the chemistry and the compatibility but not the spiritual compatibility of God's will to join in a marriage. God made us for a purpose, not for a mate. Marriage is not a requirement nor does it bring total fulfillment, only your purpose brings fulfillment. Fulfillment comes when you express the vision in your heart. If you don't fulfill your purpose, you will never be fulfilled. You must decide your assignment and discover it. Even through the ups and downs of my marriage and when there are moments when opposition and disagreements create problems and sometimes those moments become intense, it was those moments where I felt hopeless and doubted that God would bring healing and deliverance to my marriage. Yet, God has to teach us that through opposition, pain and struggle, that's where we find our power. That's what keeps us on our knees in prayer and supplication to God to persevere in faith because as we operate in our purpose, our first ministry is our family and this is why my husband is my first ministry. What we go through as a couple has to happen for the sake of winning my husband's heart to Jesus but my actions and character must align and model Jesus in order to reflect and to influence the love of Christ into his heart and to help women who are single and seeking marriage and to those who are in their early years of marriage or desiring marriage.

As our ultimate goal is to spread the gospel of Christ into the hearts of souls, our true deliverance within ourselves is the act of service. This becomes an act of love. Serving others is the selfless behavior that God wants us all to have as His children. Serving others is the ultimate example of Jesus. When Jesus died on the cross for our sins, he paid the price as a sign of humility and love that we ourselves represent as being united in Christ.

Being selfless over selfish is our service towards being loving and kind to others. In the (KJV), "For even the Son of Man came not to be served but to serve others and to give his life as a ransom for many." Matthews 20:28. This is the true representation of our Lord and Savior. When we have a true relationship that is intimate with God, His spirit inside of us changes us and gives us new desires and new hopes. These are desires that we may have never desired to have and this is how change and growth develops within us. It's the glory of God that lives in us when we start to submit totally to Him. It's a full surrender.

Loving God represents how love and kindness is shown towards others, even difficult people who are hard to be around or to live with. They can be family members and others who we work with or employees who work for us in a business relationship. Most importantly, helping and being kind to those who can't pay it back is a strength from God to allow us to love beyond our own strength. Those who are less fortunate than we are and/or just need a helping hand is where we can begin to show our love to God through serving others in need. Sometimes our time can be just as invaluable as

284

giving money. Spending time with people who are lonely and in need of encouragement or just to know that they are worth our time would mean a lot to them. It's those little things in life that go a long way in a person's heart. Taking the time to intentionally serve others refreshes our heart with grace and love. In the KJV, it states, "God has shown you His grace in many different ways. So be good servants and use whatever gifts he has given you in a way that will best serve each other. 1st Peter 4:10

Do nothing out of selfish ambition or vain conceit. Rather, in humility, value others above yourselves, not looking to your own interests but each of you to the interests of the others." Philippians 2:3-4 TPT

This is what it's like to have a fulfilled soul. It starts once you realize that purpose lives inside of you! It's time we start feeding our spirit man more than we feed our natural man which is our flesh, what our body desires. Whatever you feed the most will reign, rule, and dominate over your life the most! Feed your body the fruits of love, joy, peace, long-suffering (patience) gentleness, goodness, faith, meekness, and temperance. The fruits of the Spirit are found in Galatians 5:22-23 Moreover, whatever you give more time to will grow, strengthen and reign, rule and dominate. What do you give most of your time to in your daily life? Whatever that is, it will reign, rule and dominate your life. It's simple as that! Your struggles, your challenges, your sorrows, your worries and warfare of life must be extinguished when you feed it the word of truth which is the living Word, the bible. The words of the bible are powerful and it is our sword of protection. Always remember that no matter what tests you're dealing with or when temptations may come, your struggles are there for a reason because God has planted something inside of all of us. When we move our purpose into action, it brings our soul total fulfillment and for that reason, we must triumph and keep joy in our hearts to know that we are becoming better every passing day. Each moment of our lives, we are growing higher in love for Jesus. Let's start this day with a day of thanksgiving to God. Our lives are in his hands and God's love for us is everlasting. With that in mind, this helps us to know that when we serve God from the bottom of our hearts with our gifts, talents, purpose and passion, it all comes together in one great puzzle. When we receive clarity and God reveals to us the picture of the puzzle, we not only gain a fulfilled soul here on earth but we are yet fulfilled in our spirits to know that our reward is waiting for us in our permanent home of heaven's glorious gates which is the kingdom of God.

THE COST OF DELIVERANCE IS PAIN

The cost of deliverance is pain. It comes with a cost! How would I have tears if I've never cried? How could I ever have peace if I've never experienced worry, stress, fear and tormenting moments? "I leave the gift of peace with you—my peace. Not the kind of fragile peace given by the world, but my perfect peace. Don't yield to fear or be troubled in your hearts, instead, be courageous!" John 14:27 TPT

How would I ever know the value of trusting someone if I've never been betrayed? How would I ever know what it feels to carry heavy weight or baggage in my soul if I had never carried the burden of brokenness? How would I ever know what it feels like to be healed if I've never been sick or terminally ill? How would a cheating or ungrateful spouse know a good thing unless his companion is gone? The cost of deliverance was the pain I had to suffer to remind me that if I've ever felt mistrust, rejected, betrayal, lied to, experienced

286

the pain of infidelity or horribly disappointment, I have no choice because I will make it regardless. If I made it last time and the time after that, I will make it again. If I survive the trauma of my pain, I can live again and I will make it through my trials and troubles. The cost of deliverance allowed me to know that my pain was on purpose to share the struggles of my past with others, to give them the hope to know that their pain is not by accident or mistake but the pain and the struggle is necessary for ministry. It's necessary for my strength, it's necessary for my faith and trust in God, it's necessary for the journey which is the process of my sanctification, it's necessary for the assignment to prepare me for where God is taking me. If God can take me through it, He will get me out of it. I just have to wait patiently on him, trust the path he is taking me, trust to know that the pain isn't forever because joy comes in the morning. It will soon be over and next time I will have tougher skin to overcome the next challenge because God had already made me an overcomer! Just understand this.......What the enemy meant for evil, God meant it for good! In this life if there's no pain, there's no gain. Just like it's not fun to go to a job that is laborious, tiring, listening to a mean and irrational boss who only cares about the profits and not the workers, yet you continue to work that job. It's a struggle to go there everyday for 8 hours in a day. Sometimes, it can feel like imprisonment but you wouldn't work there unless you had to, right? Well, the gain is the paycheck that pays the bills, puts food on the table and a place to live. You have to work in order to eat. In this life you will have to go through something in order to gain something. In this life you will have to experience circumstances in order to gain knowledge. Personally, the cost of my deliverance meant that God had to break my heart in order to save my soul.

CHAPTER 8 ARISE: I AM Who God Says I AM

A SPIRITUAL AND MENTAL PERSPECTIVE OF SELF DEVELOPMENT

On the last Sunday evening of 2018, as my youngest daughter nervously prepared to take the big step for her baptism, we were excited and filled with anticipation as the time was getting near. It was great seeing the support of family members coming to witness her major experience. This Sunday evening, the snow flurries soon turned into a snow storm but thankfully we made it to church safely. We walked in the one room of the church where the ministers gathered around us to explain the meaning of getting baptized. I was just as excited as my daughter as she kept a smile on her face the entire time and remained very quiet. I could tell she was trying to stay calm. This was her first time ever getting baptized and she really didn't know what to expect but she had made the decision to get baptized months prior to this day. In fact, she inquired about getting baptized early that summer and as soon as the opportunity came, I will never forget that Sunday morning when she looked at me right into my eyes and said, "Momma I want to be baptized!" and I knew she really meant it. After she and a handful of other members were dressed and prepared for the baptism, we walked to the front of the sanctuary and as I walked with her down the stairs to the pool, there was a feeling that came over me. I knew it was the presence of the Lord. I felt it strongly. My heart was receptive and pure and I was full of joy. When it was my daughter's turn to walk into the pool, I stood afar and I had the perfect view of her with my camera in my hand, videoing her and hoping I wouldn't drop my Iphone because I was trembling with joy. They soon emerged her into the water before they prayed over her. At that moment, it was a slow motion effect that came over me and I could feel something jump inside of me. I brushed it off because I thought, "well that's just the typical me being excited for my baby girl. As she was dripping wet walking up the stairs to greet me with a towel wrapped around her body, I asked her how she felt, and she just kept laughing. I said, "Alaynna why are you laughing?" she said, "Mom I just can't stop laughing because I'm so happy and I can't explain it." Right then, I knew God had touched her. She was only twelve years old at this time and she really couldn't put in words the spiritual transformation that was taking place inside of her. Later, my daughter and everyone who were baptized got dressed and we had to meet in a room where the ministers met us there. They congratulated everyone and gave them all their certificates. They immediately noticed something different about Alaynna so they asked her, "How do you feel young lady?" She replied, "I feel good." We all took our seats and at this moment I was wondering how my family members were doing because I couldn't see them during the baptism but they were able to see us in the balcony of the sanctuary. As we sat patiently in our seats, I was thinking that they would pray over us and send us on our way but that wasn't it. One of the ministers asked all of the members including my daughter who wasn't a member yet, if they would like to receive the holy spirit. My daughter whispered in my ear and asked, "What is that?" Before I could answer, they explained to her that receiving the holy spirit is a gift from God to speak in a heavenly language but you must first repent of your sins and confess them to God and turn away from those sins. It's humbly surrendering to God with a pure heart. We all stood up and started praying and at this time I had desired to receive the holy spirit. I knew the presence of God was always on me but the shock that came immediately was when I began speaking a different language as I was praying. Immediately, I began to flow in the Spirit. It was the supernatural. This was supposed to have been the day for my daughter to receive her blessing from God, yet I got a gift that I hadn't expected. God gave me the gift to speak in a heavenly language. This was an utterance that is unknown to man but is only spoken to God. It was a night I will always remember. The ministers were rejoicing full of praise because not only did I receive the gift, so did my daughter and others. This would explain the leap that I felt inside of me and brushed it off thinking I was just in pure happiness. I believe that my spirit was receptive to the anointing of God and I've been speaking in the heavenly language in my prayers ever since that day.

In the development of who I am becoming, I discovered how my spiritual growth opened a new elevation for the gift of prophetic activation through prayer and fasting. I couldn't quench the Spirit of God. It was bigger than me and this time I had to allow God to use me as a vessel. That's all that I am but so much more. I was changing and blossoming into that new and beautiful flower and the thorns that grew with me were not the thorns of my past, they were the thorns of my protection to cover me from the warfare that would rise against me. As I was and currently being groomed by God, he allowed me to self examine myself. It was like taking a scanner to detect all that needed to be fine-tuned. This allowed me to humble myself and to examine my character, my identity and my persona of who I was by the fruits of his Spirit. This was self-examination for a purpose and that meant that there was going to be plenty of work to do. As I reflect on self development mentally, emotionally and spiritually it's the work that prepares you to become your best, doing your best, and bringing to life all that has been dead and dormant. It brings you to the next dimension. It was time for me to rise from a spiritual sleep into a spiritual awakening. This was my time. This is my season and this is my purpose for destiny!

THE CONFIDENCE, COURAGE AND FREEDOM TO TELL MY STORY

During the late summer of 2018, I felt the urgency in my spirit to use my gifts in writing and to write a book about my life. I was a bit hesitant when I felt that urgency and I pushed it away because I thought to myself, who would want to hear my story? How could my story help anyone? I was so private with my life and I had no plans on telling people what I went through, how I went through the problems of my life and when it all happened. I was afraid, yet I felt the calling to do it. The more I ignored this feeling, the stronger it became. It felt like I couldn't get peace unless I took that step to start and gave it a try. After taking an online course, my soul became filled because this was that moment when I started using my gift in writing for the glory of God. Even throughout taking the mentorship course to write my book, one particular session immediately gave me the chills because the instructor was ministering to me as I started to pour my heart out in tears. I never meant for this to happen in front of a group of other inspired writers in the session, but I had to allow God to intervene in this particular session. It was the breaking point of my breakthrough that I really needed. It took me back to the first time I got to discover the anointed women of God on Youtube, her testimony about the story of how God transformed her life became her transparency for me and how I could relate to her in so many different ways. Her story inspired me the most because it was her purpose that she discovered in order to see growth and prosperity into her life. It was as though she was talking to me when she shared her story. How did she absolutely know that I was pondering this in my heart? I too had desired to discover my purpose from God and to gain prosperity in my life. I desired change! It was so ironic because it's not like I called her up and told her how I'd been feeling but it had to be God. God used her to announce her new course, "Uncover My Purpose". Once I took the course, it wasn't hard to discover what my assignment was, every test in her course I took was confirmation that I had to do what I was birthed into this world to do. This was an assignment that had to be done whether I was intimidated, nervous or uncomfortable, God had to heal me in areas that I thought were healed. Since I had struggled with rejection for many years, it affected my confidence and courage to pursue this endeavor. I was also in fear of the criticism I would receive. By this time, I knew deep in my heart that I had passed the test of forgiveness by forgiving my father, yet there were other struggles inside that needed healing as well. I had to take the risk. I had to give God a chance for me to see how real he is in my life. Not only was I walking in faith but I had to take a leap of faith because something deep down inside was leaping. After taking the course, it paved the way for me. It was groundbreaking as if a new business had started where I was there cutting the ribbon. The course allowed me to uncover all that was buried inside under all that debris of baggage. I couldn't become the better person that God intended me to be because my pain had weighed heavy on those gifts and talents. Those shackles and chains had to be broken from my life in order for my breakthrough and deliverance to come. It had to happen because my assignment was being birthed inside me. Later, I took another course. This time it was a mentorship course to write with a strategic plan and under God's anointing. This had to be God because God blessed me to receive the blessing by being selectively chosen to win this course paid in full. Now, there were absolutely no excuses this time. There were a total of 4 weekly sessions during this course and the sessions were virtually in a classroom setting where each of the students were seen and we had the chance to interact with our experiences and discoveries as we completed assignments on a weekly basis. I learned so much in this course and I immediately went to work once I had completed it. During my writing journey, I would pray early in the mornings to ask God to lead me to write and to allow the words to flow from my spirit. With every morning feeling refreshed, renewed and continuing to partnership with the Holy Spirit by allowing the anointing to pour out through me where limitations were gone, I made up my mind that I would no longer write with hesitation, fear or in areas that are bleeding because I'm writing my experiences to therapeutically heal areas that are needed. I had to write from a healed area so that the message could become a source for inner healing for others. I felt like I had been in labor while having to experience moments of my past that I did not want to face. This was a labor, yet nurturing under God's protection and yet an obedience that gave me insurmountable peace and joy. Some days felt very challenging to write while other days felt I was smooth sailing like an easy Sunday morning.

MY STORY IS FOR THE VICTORY OF GOD'S GLORY

God must get the glory for my courage to tell my story. The word even says in the book of Revelation 12:11-13, "They conquered him completely through the blood of the Lamb and the powerful word of his testimony......" I felt encouraged one Sunday morning that to my surprise, had the opportunity to meet gospel artist Richard Smallwood at a book signing after church. I was delighted and felt empowered on how he too decided to write a book about his life and how he struggled with depression. When I met him I shared with him my own journey of writing my book to share my personal struggles with depression as well. He smiled at me and gave me a word of encouragement. It was very enlightening to meet him as I have always been a fan of his music, especially one of my favorite songs, "Total Praise".

In the fall of 2018, I obeyed the assignment to start my Youtube channel. This was my biggest test and challenge. I ignored this calling for many months and I struggled with this. My comfort zone was always to ensure that everything operated well behind the scenes. Never had I imagined being in the focus point. I thought maybe this must be God speaking to me but I wanted to be sure of it. I kept ignoring those feelings I would feel. I just thought that God couldn't be telling me to do something that I wasn't comfortable with. This has to be something that just popped up in my head. There's just no way I could do this. I fought this with every fiber inside of me. Every time I thought about it, butterflies would fill my belly. I just didn't have the courage to do this do this. So, I started practicing by recording myself in front of my video phone camera. When I looked at the video, I immediately erased it. I have always been a very critical person when it came to myself. My videos just weren't good enough, plus what would I say on these videos? What could I possibly talk about? Many times I would go to God in prayer and ask him if it was His will that I speak on social media. I wouldn't get an answer right away but later I would receive confirmation in various ways whether it was from a preacher sermon, whether it was from someone suggesting me to do it or whether I would feel it in my spirit, I would hear about it every single day. I felt that urgent feeling again and one day I made that step to just do it! God had to show me that it wasn't about me. He reminded me of what I would say during my prayers. I would pray to God and ask him to use me as a willing vessel. I soon realized that he had to do the work through me but I also had be obedient and available to do the work. I had to be the mouthpiece. More importantly, I had to be obedient and therefore it wasn't about me, once again it was about advancing the kingdom of God. It's about bringing souls to Christ. This is our divine duty! This is our divine assignment. I would often get on the video and speak a word and then I would feel the power of God come over me, this is when I felt stirred up and couldn't stop the video. Afterwards, I would feel bad because the videos would eventually become longer and longer and I began trying to figure out how to make my messages brief. I was trying to shorten the videos and then I realized that I would speak so fast just to make it a 3 to 5 minute video but every time I tried, I'd end up with a 15 to 30 minute video. Then there were times where I wanted to delete the videos because I didn't like the sound of my voice, so I struggled many times with publishing the video to YouTube. After all the struggles of not wanting to share the videos, I had to escape fear and gain confidence to release it to the public. Once I began speaking on videos day after day and sometimes 3 times per week, the fear and hesitation soon left. I currently continue to spread the gospel of Christ and share my story of inspiration on how God healed and delivered me from being an emotional broken woman to becoming a victorious woman with purpose and a vision. God has given me the courage to speak on the platform and the main mission to use my voice to speak words of inspiration and motivation to all who would hear. My words are filled with love and compassion and a mission to lead and win souls to Christ and to speak the gospel of Jesus into the hearts of all and anyone who receives the message. I must admit that I don't edit my videos or perfection because a I want the viewers to see that I am not perfect! What you see is what you get. I am very transparent and down-to-earth because I comfortable being myself. When you view my videos on Youtube, you will know that it's only God because He gives me the strength to become better and I'm getting better as the days pass. "My grace is sufficient for thee: for my strength is made perfect in weakness. Most gladly therefore will I rather glory in my infirmities, that the power of Christ may result upon me." 2nd Corinthians 12:9. KJV

THERE IS POWER IN THE WORDS YOU SPEAK

We must be careful of what we speak because there is power in our words. Your words have power. For example, you might be suffering in poverty. Speak out loud that you won't be in this condition for long! Speak out loud that God has given you the power to gain wealth and prosperity. Speak everyday that you will receive financial relief and financial stability in your life. You have to say it, to see it. The life-changing financial principle is that we should always have contentment. Read - 1 Timothy 6:6-8 KJV

Contentment helps me keep wealth in proper perspective. It reminds me that I didn't bring anything into the world and won't take anything with me when I die. As long as I have my basic needs met, I must be satisfied with that. Our devotion to God is what makes us rich. "Godliness with contentment is a great gain." It's not a prosperity message. It's a responsibility message." Contentment isn't apathy. Content people don't always have the best of everything, but they always make the best of everything. That means they're always thankful for what they have and never complain about what they don't have. However, although I am content and filled with thankfulness, I'm always moving toward achieving goals in life. Contentment isn't about a lack of ambition or intensity, and it definitely has nothing to do with apathy. But it does require keeping our material possessions and even our goals and ambitions in proper perspective. We must keep moving toward God's purpose. Follow God's plan and pursue His mission. God the Father, The Son and The Holy Spirit gives us peace and contentment. 1st Timothy 6:6-8 KJV, states, "But godliness with contentment is great gain, for we brought nothing into the world, and we cannot take anything out of the world. But if we have food and clothing, with these we will be content."

During this new venture in my life, I felt led to create a vision board in October 2018. I created the board and laid out all of my desires and needs in picture form. "And the Lord answered me, and said, "Write the vision, and make it plain unto tables, that he may run that read it." Habakkuk 2:2 KJV

This is exactly what I did and not only did I create a vision board, I influenced my daughters to do the same. So one weekend, we sat on the floor, gathered all our materials with scissors and glue and we began exercising our vision. All of our spiritual and natural desires and needs became our vision. Then I added scriptures to manifest power by speaking everything into existence. Interestingly, two of those items on my vision board came to pass. When we finished with our vision boards, we placed them on our walls in our rooms so that when we wake up every morning to see what our hearts desire, we can speak it into existence. "Where there is no vision, the people perish." Proverbs 29: 18 KJV

Within a week of creating my vision board, I was blessed with a computer and 1-½ years later, I was blessed with a brand new car similar to the picture on my vision board and I could see progression in areas of my life, especially in my finances. I learned a great lesson too and that was to create the vision and make it plain, meaning make your request known to God in detail even if you have to speak the color, design and what make and model. Be detailed with your prayer requests and what you manifest on a daily basis. God is a God that is very keen to specifics. With some of my desires coming to pass, this was truly an elevation of faith and it also surprised my husband and children as well. My daughters immediately became inspired to add more to their vision boards. Every morning you wake up, first thank God for a new day and that he woke you up because the alarm clock didn't wake you up. Next, make your request known to God in your prayers and third, throughout your day continue to speak positive words. Speak to yourself! Remember, there is power in the words you speak. Speak words of affirmation so that they will become your reality. When you think it, you believe it, and when you believe it, you must speak it and when you speak it, you become it! Mark 11:23 states, "For assuredly, I say to you, whoever says to this mountain, 'Be removed and be cast into the sea, 'and does not doubt in his heart, but believes that those things he says will be done, he will have whatever he says."

PURPOSE WILL SHARPEN YOUR IDENTITY

As God allowed me to uncover my purpose, he began molding me and blossoming me into becoming more and allowing me to discover more of who I am in Christ and how unique I am because he made me so beautiful, so strong, so powerful in his image. It wasn't the outer appearance that I was focused on but rather my inner condition. Since I struggled with low self-esteem, confidence and courage for many years, my journey gave me the breakthrough and the healing to revive me and for me to see what he had taken out of me to put inside of me. I never wanted to be an arrogant and boastful person as many people tend to confuse confidence with arrogance but I gradually became confident in myself as I started to grow and operate in my calling. It was those uncomfortable areas of my life I had to break free from in order to work in my calling and likewise when I broke free from low-self esteem, I became confident and gained the courage as I began evolving. The process of evolving is from grace to glory. During the process there were struggles because I hesitated and questioned whether I had the ability and the potential to do certain things, especially the desires that God placed on my heart that were bigger than me. For example, it took healing and deliverance for me to become transparent to tell my story to the world because I felt shame, embarrassment and I felt like who would want to hear my story! Many family members never knew what I struggled through in my past so why would I want to reveal that now? Why should I embarrass myself and feel ostracized and judged by people for what happened to me and why I was such a broken woman but it took being healed, being made whole and forgiving myself to step out in faith. It doesn't matter what people think or say about you. In the beginning it's uncomfortable as we are taking the risk to obey what God has assigned us to do. The Holy Spirit that lives in us will eventually create a new comfortable -- in where we were positioned to be and how we are awakened to who we've always been, we soon realize that this is who we've always been. That is, God knew us before we were in our mother's womb. That is, God knowing our beginning and our end.

When I became an adult, I felt that I had to accept the blame for my broken soul although I knew what created the pain. Having faith and trusting in God, plus not living in fear and anxiety is how I gained the courage to share my story with the world. It was only God that could do that for me because I sincerely didn't have the freedom to talk about my past and my life. I grew up in a family where we didn't discuss our personal struggles and we didn't share them with each other and so everything was kept private. God had to heal me in parts and in areas at times. It took steps and the process is never easy but it's so worth it in the end. "If there aren't struggles, there's no progress" Frederick Douglass

We must know that who we are greater than our present perception. Since we are growing and learning everyday, we will be bigger tomorrow than our present day. As I said earlier in my chapters, I had to challenge my abilities on a daily basis to allow myself to evolve and grow. This is what we must do and that is doing the work. Doing the work is the only way we'll see change for the better. My past is only a reminder of how far I've healed and evolved because I had to learn that my flaws didn't define me. In this new place of becoming the better me, my purpose didn't define me because it's not our identity but Christ has defined me as being beautifully and fearfully made. I learned that not fitting in wasn't a bad thing because God needed me to see the characteristics of leadership in me and that is, that leaders don't fit in! They will never fit in because they are positioned to lead not follow. It gave me a new identity of knowing who I am and why I exist.

In a world where so many people have lost their identity and are confused with knowing who they are, with knowing or unknowingly educated by their roots, they still find themselves unable to know who they are as a person and not knowing their worth. It is imperative that we must find out who we are and why God put us here on earth for a purpose and when we search for a special person to be a part of our life, that special mate, companion or spouse, we really must know who we are before any relationship starts. It's the same as loving yourself before you can love anyone else. Even in relationships with our family and bonding friendships, we need to know who we are in order to build a foundation in ourselves. With all the weight of my pass, the weight of brokenness from stress, fear, rejection, resentment, insecurities and unforgiveness was an identity that was broken in me. I couldn't discover my potential and strengths because I was overshadowed by so much clutter, toxicity and junk. It caused me to become blinded by the goodness that was dormant inside of me. I was so blind where I didn't even realize that I needed to become healed inside. My life reminds me of the scripture in the bible on how the blind man could only see men as trees when Jesus prayed for him. So, when Jesus asked the blind me again, "How do you see men, he was able to see them clearly as men. I believe when we are lost in identity due to being broken from our past, our vision is distorted and blurred and we can perceive how we see ourselves and the people around us differently compared to how we perceive ourselves and the people around us when our hearts are healed and pure. I can remember before God healed my broken soul, I used to compare myself to others but I would silently evaluate myself based on others success, characteristics and progression of life. This is where we start to feel incompetent when when we compare ourselves to others, we start to view everyone around us as superior to us and this is why renewing our minds is so important to knowing ourselves. When we start to compare ourselves with others, we lose the courage and confidence of our own identity and we can't operate in the purpose that God has called us to do because we'll mimic someone else and we will not be able to perform under the anointing properly. What God has for us is for us and what God has for someone else is not for us. All of our strength, confidence and courage comes from the Lord. "I can do all things through Christ which strengthens me" Philippians 4:13

When Christ has given you the strength it's going to be beyond our natural strengths so therefore we must not allow people to break down our confidence by valuing their opinions over our beliefs of who we are when we believe in ourselves. This gave me revelation and wisdom to not always share your vision, hopes and dreams with everyone because they will not always have the ability to see your vision and your dreams like you see them. They may criticize you because they simply won't understand it! One of my biggest faults was valuing others opinions over mine. I had to start believing in myself. Confidence has no competition when it comes to self-identity through Christ. At this present time, there are 7.5 billion people in the world and you let the opinion of 1 or 2 people make you think you're not enough. You are worth more than you can imagine. Each day, I had to make it a part of my affirmation that my confidence and courage is strengthening." Little children, you are from God and have overcome them, for He who is in you is greater than he who is in the world." 1 John 4:4 KJV

Knowing who lives inside of me is my self-Identity. My self-identity is is a knowing of what God thinks of me and who God is to me. God has to send somebody into your life that speaks something different to get you to dream something different. That's where it started for me. It took someone to help me see the light inside of me for me to realize that I am more than what I've always thought I was. The light that shines in me, shines brighter than it ever has! It took encounters with Christ to realistically accept all the goodness and greatness. God's love inside of me gave me a reason to believe! My belief system became my reality. The reality is we are something different than what we presently see right now. 1 John 4:4, states "You are of God, little children and have overcome them, because He who is in you is greater than he who is in the world."

I'm just not anybody. I am a queen. Queens are queens long before they realize it. Someone needs to tell you who you really are. Adjust your crown and sit on your throne. You are not a grasshopper, if you are a man, you're a King! If you are a woman, you're a Queen! This is how God sees you! Ladies, no matter what decision you have made, you're still a queen because God has crowned you. I had to realize that I am a queen. You will gain confidence in your discomfort and that is okay because that is how you grow and learn. This is how I had to grow, it was the pain that created the pressure. Without pressure how will you know your strengths? That was my process and it still is a process for me as I continue to live by faith. By gaining the confidence and courage to operate in my purpose, I received the benefits of God's wisdom and knowledge. Most of my prayers are to receive the benefits of wisdom and knowledge. When God lives on the inside of us, we receive his promises. When we walk in obedience, we please God, we walk in the will of God, we walk in the gifts, talents and purpose of God. Developing a relationship with God and being a joint heir of Christ, I had to first submit to God by asking Him for wisdom and knowledge. This was not the wisdom and knowledge of what professors and scholars gain but heavenly wisdom and knowledges gained from God, an anointing that can't be compared to nature. When Christ's spirit lives in our hearts, there's a faith of knowing that God will give us the wisdom to walk in wisdom, to make the best choices and to use our time with our family and in our purpose wisely, yet we must give God the first fruits of our day before we give our time to the concerns of our life. God wants to give us wisdom in the midst of our battles. "Wisdom brings joy and the joy of the Lord is our strength. If any of you lacks wisdom, let him ask God, who gives to all liberally and without reproach (expressed disapproval of rebuke), and will be given to him." James 1:5 KJV

Don't count it strange when God sends a messenger to you to give you a message of life, healing, purpose, guidance and courage. At some point, God has to send someone into your life to speak to the real "you" that is buried beneath the years and decades of miseducation, a preconditioned mindset, and/or a broken spirit. They must say to you, "ARISE" take up your bed and walk. ARISE and Live! God is fighting for you, but you also need to do your part in nature. Your part is the responsibility of making that decision to follow Christ and fight the good fight of faith. 1st Timothy 6:12, NIV: "Fight the good fight of the faith. Take hold of the eternal life to which you were called when you made your good confession the presence of many witnesses." Fight to wake up. Fight to get out of bed. Fight to face the day ahead. Fight to show up to work. Fight to be present with your family. Fight to love your spouse. Fight to focus on your relationship with Christ. Fight to get to church. Fight to be fully alive. Fight the spiritual warfare of lies, deception and unbelief. Following Jesus doesn't mean you won't have problems in your life. In John 16:33," I have told you these things so that you might have peace. In this world you will have trouble. But take heart! I have overcome the world." No matter what troubles or circumstances you are facing, Jesus has overcome the world. Since He lives in you, you are an overcomer! "Greater is He that is in you, than he that is in the world." 1st John 4:4

Enjoying the new "ME" was enjoying the promises that have been given to me. Being a child of God is the security of salvation in Christ, a new life, a new beginning, a new me, a new work that is working through me. Therefore, I have no need to worry about the cares of this life. I don't need to stress, become anxious, become bitter or resentful because the things of this life will not and cannot take away what God has for me and His word is never void. His word is Yes and Amen! As I walk in obedience and walk in God's purpose, He gives me the strength, endurance and dominion to complete the work in me. When you know who you are in Christ, that becomes your power. The chains and the bondage are broken from my mind, my heart and my soul. "Behold, I give you the authority to trample on serpents and scorpions, and over all the power of the enemy, and nothing shall by any means hurt you." Luke 10:19 KJV

When you know your identity in Christ, not only do you know your purpose in Christ but you know how to defeat every fiery dart that is thrown at you because God has given you authority and power? This is why the enemy hates us so much!

"Finally, my brethren, be strong in the Lord and in the power of His might. Put on the whole armor of God, that you may be able to stand against the wiles of the devil." Ephesians 6:10

We are currently living in a War Time Christianity from a Peace Time Christianity. As things in the natural are changing right before our eyes from the country shutting down because of the corona virus which has killed over 400,000 people globally and the tragedies of police brutality which has murdered so many innocent people where a social war has erupted due to the murder of George Floyd and many minorities, especially in the African American communities! This is a civil and social war in our streets and all across the nation where people are protesting, many are rioting and looting and heightened the emotions of hate, division, rage and anger to advocate for social justice and equality. This climax change has affected individuals, families, communities, cities, countries and nations. The wiles of the enemy is pouring salt on the wounds of hearts and it is a plot of social and racial division, hate, evil and total chaos and destruction to sift souls out and to bring evil in. It is a plot of the enemy to kill and slaughter one another. This shift has caused our world from one that we haven't seen or experienced and has affected many of us physically, mentally, emotionally and spiritually. The shift has moved us to fighting for our lives on a daily basis due to the heightened evil in the world around us, to praying on a consistent basis to God as it has personally elevated my faith.

We, as believers and joint heirs of Christ must remember that we are soldiers in the battle! We are on the battlefield for the Lord. We cannot give up! If we give up, we will surrender to the evil forces that are warring against our minds, our bodies, our families, our finances, and the fullness of our destinies! Giving up means to fight in the natural but we don't win when we fight with our hands. We win when we fight supernaturally because this is supernatural warfare! This is what the enemy's attempt and plan is to do and he comes to first attack our minds in order to get inside of our hearts. He adds fuel to every fire and he pours salt on every wound that is bleeding. He will even open up healed wounds. He wants complete havoc and destruction which is his ultimate goal. Before we go into battle of war, We must know what and who we are fighting against. We must go through a spiritual boot-camp that is guided to prepare us through a process to build our spirit. Our prayer life is the process that puts us through training and coaching. Our prayer life is that two-way communication with God. We talk with God and he talks to us. We must learn to hear from the Lord. This is why it is so important to pray without ceasing and fasting our bodies by denying our body from its natural desires, and open our hearts to God by meditating in His word night and day. God is sitting high and looking down at what is taking place in this world! Have confidence and know that trouble don't last always because our joy comes in the morning! The greatest outcomes always comes out if the worst situations when God is present in your life!

Allow God to give us direction as he trains and coaches us through this battle. This battle is essential for the war we are living in. This is why it is so important to know who you are in Christ. Your identity allows you to go into the battlefield with full force and operate in the supernatural. We operate beyond our own self-efforts and abilities. The training prepares us as soldiers physically and mentally so that we can withstand the attacks and strains that come against us. We are in war. This means that we will fight many battles before we gain our victory. Remember, this battle is solely to destroy our minds, our willpower and our emotions. This is why we cannot react or respond based upon our emotions. Yes, we are still humans and we are going to still feel the pain, anger and sorrow that comes with being humans. We are not perfect and that is why God's grace and mercy is in our lives because we fall short of his mercy every single day. This is why praying without ceasing is so important because God won't let us BACK DOWN! Once I received that revelation, I became enlightened with a clear vision and this is how I gained a sense of peace within my soul. I was no longer afraid or frightened but my spirit became burdened by the people who couldn't see with a clear vision and the lack of knowledge. My prayers became intense as I prayed on behalf of our dying world and our people full of pain in their hearts. Not only was my passion to help heal the hearts of women who suffered through the pain of being a fatherless daughter and or being a woman who was scorned by the toxic relationships of her past, but my prayers were that God save my people from themselves because they can't save themselves. They can't heal themselves and they can't make themselves whole. Only God can! My prayers became intensified every passing day because the cares of this life seemed to become evil and more destructive like I've never seen. I've heard ministers say that this evil world is going to hell in a hand basket, and now I truly understand why.

Now that we understand what we are fighting for and who we are fighting against. We need the proper armor when going into battle. In the face of opposition, you need the complete armor. Your armor is worn in parts. It's an assembly! Not a whole piece! It's not a baby onesie battle gear!

In this spiritual warfare, first, you will need to go to your prayer closet and find the pieces in your wardrobe to wear.

This is preparation! Everyday it seems as though I prepare for the next day. This means I get my wardrobe ready for the next day ahead. You will need to find the belt of truth. How can your faith work without the belt of truth. Hearing the word of truth activates your faith. Truth became my revelation and truth became my power to live. The truth unveiled my purpose to live and the truth allowed me to become set free! We must know the truth in order to have the faith! Remember, faith comes by hearing and hearing the Word of God. Romans 10:17 You will also need to grab the breastplate of righteousness. How can your faith work without it? According to Ephesians 6, the breastplate of righteousness is the 2nd piece of armor. This means to obey God's commandments and live in a way that is honorable to Him.

Psalms 106:3 says, "How blessed are those who keep justice, who practice righteousness at all times!" If you don't have a revelation of righteousness which comes from the Lord, the enemy will successfully drag you by your head into the pit of self-condemnation. Every time you make the slightest mistake, the enemy will use that against you because he is known as the Accuser. We're all going to make some mistakes in life of course. Once again we are not perfect. However, that's when the enemy will test your faith, by tempting you at your weakness. He will take that very thing that God healed you from and put it in your face to wiggle it in your eyes, to intimidate you or to see what your next move will be or he will poke you and poke you repeatedly with shame and guilt to make you feel like a failure and a complete failure. He tries to weaken my confidence by other's rejection. It's makes it personal when it's really spiritual! That's where he attacks you, in those personal areas of your life that is kept between you and God. Most importantly, as I've said many times in this book, you must know who you are in the Lord. This is your identity in Christ. When you wear the armor of God, this becomes a part of your identity!

Last, but not least, you must use your weapon which is your sword! Take up the shield of faith! This is your sword of the spirit which is the Word of God. (The Living Word) If you don't wield in faith, it won't work! Your sword is used to extinguish all the flaming arrows of the evil one. These are those flaming arrows of life that come to attack us through people and through circumstances of life. On a daily basis, know that your battle is not through flesh and blood which are PEOPLE but with the spirits that work in the PEOPLE to target you. If you are a born-again believer, you have the AUTHORITY! When you don't know your value and when you don't have identity, you lose your power. The enemy knows this and that is why it's his assignment to not know this!

You have to have the audacity to be a queen in-spite of any kind of hand you have been dealt with. James 4:7 NIV, "Submit yourselves, then to God, Resist the devil, and he will flee from you."

A PURPOSE FULL OF CLARITY AND DIRECTION

As I glanced over at my father sitting next to him on my backyard patio, I was filled with so much comfort, love, joy and peace. My heart was full and we sat back to enjoy a warm breeze with the glimpse of the sun hovering over us. We just sat back, laughed, giggled and joked about the funny things of life, our situations, different experiences and whatever came to our minds. It was a beautiful Saturday afternoon. The aroma from the barbecue grill made it feel like a summer holiday as the music played in the background, the scenes and the sounds of the kids playing and laughing while watching our little puppy play and roll around in the grass reminded me how I was finally in that moment to enjoy a good and relaxing day with family. This time, there was a joy inside me that remained in me. There weren't any feelings of resentment or bitterness. No longer was I smiling to cover up or masquerading any secrets of anxieties, fear, worries or depression but I was now at peace and joy on the inside as well as the outside. It felt like freedom! It felt like purpose! It felt like my journey to destiny and it felt victorious! 2nd Corinthians, NIV, "Now the Lord is the Spirit, and where the Spirit of the Lord is, there is freedom." My purpose of living gave me a new beginning and a new outlook on things. When I think of freedom, I think of salvation. It's liberating to my soul and spirit. I no longer live in my past but in my present. Our present day is a gift to us from God. The things that we take for granted in life such as, waking up in the morning, enjoying our family and loved-ones, being in great health and being able to move around as we please in our everyday life is a freedom but the full clarity and direction of life is living a life of purpose in our inner dwelling.

Galatians 5:1, TPT states, "Let me be clear, the Anointed One has set us free---not partially, but completely and wonderfully free! We must always cherish this truth and stubbornly refuse to go back into the bondage of our past."

I was finally free from my past. The release of all the pain and hurt that had placed me in bondage from my past no longer lived inside of me. The weights of pain had been lifted. The spirit of unforgiveness could no longer live inside of me. It could no longer chain me and imprison my soul. During this time of my life, me and my father's relationship became stronger. He was more like my friend. I no longer expected anything from him. I accepted him for who he was and I didn't criticize him for who or what he was not. Sometimes we tend to get caught up in expecting someone in our life to be a certain way. Those high expectations will cause us to dislike that particular person just because they won't act or do what we expect of them. Sometimes people will only love you based on what you can only do for them. Their love for you comes with a price tag. It's conditional! You will often find that you can't please these people enough and if you don't be careful, you will lose yourself just to hold on to them.

On that beautiful Saturday afternoon as I glanced over at my father and watched him smile, it brought joy to my heart because my relationship with my biological father was different and better. We were in a better place. That beautiful day spending time with my father was a reflection of the present condition of my heart, soul and mind. I was blessed to enjoy a new day and the new version of me and my purpose and passion in my walk in this journey is to always pray for the children of absent fathers. To empathize in their pain and for them to know that they are not a product from the past of their pain. Being that fatherless daughter as a kid, I

learned during this trial to live beyond existence. I learned that I am no longer a living as a victim but as a visionary. We have victory through Christ, our Lord and Savior. He can take us from being crushed to being crowned in our greatest fulfillment of life. When you develop a relationship with God, he will allow you to know who you are, your identity in Christ. Knowing your identity will give you power in your purpose. Your identity gives you power in faith and trusting God. You will gain direction and clarity. You will live a life of fulfillment even when the cares of life come to attack you, you now have clarity to see that it is from a spiritual attack and not from a natural attack and you gain the wisdom and knowledge from God for direction, guidance and instruction. While you're Walking by Faith, Walk in Your Victory!

This journey of life may have had its rough paths and dark valleys but God allowed me to sustain and regain my strength during the journey. This walk of life is never easy. I just needed to see a glimpse of light, just enough to know that it wouldn't be far to sustain my hope and it wouldn't be long if I just hold my peace, endure and hold on to God and never give up! I truly believe that someone's courage, leap of faith, boldness to live, breakthrough and inheritance through God, is connected to the truths and revelations shared in this book! While I have revealed a critical portion of my pursuit of divine release and purpose, I believe that reading this book could very well be your breakthrough towards your healing from your past of being crushed in so many areas of life by allowing God to crown you with his love, grace, mercy and the victory to win. Are you ready to do the work to heal? If so, let go of those bags and leave your past behind you. It's your new season for a better destination! It's time to release the weights that have kept you bound and in hostage from being great and victorious! It's time to speak to yourself that I am who God says I am and I can do what God says I can do. Our lives are in God's hands. He knows our DNA. He knows our blueprint. He has our master plan!

THIS MIGHT BE THE FINALE BUT MY JOURNEY HAS JUST BEGUN

In the late fall of 2019, me and my younger daughter decided to join the church we had been visiting for the last eleven years. I felt that it was time to join and I wanted to ensure that I was making the right choice. I prayed to God and desired to have a spiritual covering over my life and my daughter's life. By this time, my oldest daughter was in her first year of college out of state and her plans were to move away from home and find a church home where she would attend college. My daughters know how important it is to be in church and I am proud to say that I raised them to have a spiritual and personal relationship with God. When they were babies I dedicated them to God and it would be my responsibility to ensure that they are raised in a spiritual upbringing to reverence God and make Christ a part of their life. They will always have God in their hearts no matter what direction in life they take. It is always my prayer that they open their hearts, acknowledge him and allow God to direct their paths. Proverbs 22:6 states, "Train up a child in the way he should go, And when he is old he will not depart from it." NKJV

In the new year of 2020, people posted all over social media and I made a few posts myself that this was the year of 20/20 vision. I remember how I made my post look as though I had laser vision but I made my post to reflect on my spiritual life as the visionary I am. Many across the internet waves were excited for a new year to see the big 2020. It was monumental! It was going to be more than we were ever to expect. I started the new year great and discovered how my faith in God grew more and more. On the 2nd Sunday of the new year in January of 2020, I got baptized for the 2nd time after nearly 20 years of my first baptism. To this day, I still can't explain why I didn't get baptized when my younger daughter got baptized on the last Sunday night of 2018; However, this baptism was special to me because I needed a refill and to feel this new me, a new touch, a better person than I was, over 20 years ago. I felt the power of God consume me and it was the anointing of God that soon began to fill me, to indwell in me. It was an overflow! "Behold, I will do a new thing; now it shall spring forth; do you not perceive it? I am making a way in the wilderness and streams in the wasteland." Isaiah 43:19

Yet, suddenly things started to happen. It was more than that 20/20 vision we were all envisioning, it was news coverage we were watching and it gripped our hearts to hear about the sudden passing of the African American basketball player, Kobe Bryant, his 13 year old daughter and other passengers on the helicopter that crashed in Calabasas, CA. They all passed away on January 26th, 2020 and it shocked the hearts of many. It shocked the nation! Not long after the sad news of Kobe Bryant's passing, another shock wave went through the media. A very deadly and contagious disease started to spread across the globe. We heard about this earlier in the year but it wasn't until March where it began affecting people all around us. It became a pandemic and the fear that saddened the hearts of many families as the infection continued to rise and the death rates rose even higher. In April 2020 during this pandemic, I became inspired and felt led to start life coaching while working a full-time job. I completed the certification in March 2020 and the rest is history.

As the pandemic of this virus brought fear and death to many, it caused the world to shut down and live an abnormal life by staying in our homes where we were restricted to have any Sichuan interactions. The only place you could go was the grocery stores and it became a requirement to wear a mask fir the safety of everyone. The social and economic crisis was a lesson learned during this time as many Americans discovered that they would no longer have jobs to depend on. The unemployment rate left over 25 millions of Americans out of work. In late May, the world became evil as the heart of many tore down businesses, and vandalism of riots and looting swept many streets across the nation for the social injustice and racial inequalities against minorities continued to heighten. Every time I tuned in to the media there was never any good news. There was either chaos and conflict in our government or on the streets. There was and currently is, so much turmoil and chaos and my heart became heavy to watch the nightmare of how a police officer knelt down on a young man's neck while he never resisted but humbly cooperated with police, yet he died due to suffocating because he simply could not breath after being held down to the ground for approximately 8 minutes and 46 seconds, while under police custody. The video went viral all across the globe and as tensions flared and the controversy increased, so did hate, violence, anger, and frustration. In the midst of it all, as I knelt before God with a heavy heart and prayed for our nation, our people, our government and the leaders of our world, God gave me a revelation to see and understand why our purpose in life is meaningful. Why our healing and deliverance in life is so crucial. It's just not my story of being a fatherless daughter who grew up in an environment that brought on supernatural torment and fear to later discover a world of brokenness and discomfort in my well-being, but as a nation, we need healing, deliverance and wholeness. As souls, we need healing, deliverance and wholeness.

In due time, there comes a time where the breaking point is met. There comes a time where something catastrophic events happens when life has to reset, when our soul, mind and spirit has to reset. In this present day, I'm no longer internally in isolation from people, although the world has become isolated with social distancing restrictions but I live a life of solitude with God! For I know that it's all in God's hands, just like I knew my life has always been in God's hands even when it didn't feel or appear to be. This is the time we must wake because we have no other choice but to see our lives in this evil world we live in, from a supernatural perspective This is the time we must "Arise" from our blind and blurry eyes and see that our fight has not been won in the natural. This has always been a spiritual fight for all of us and it's surely has been a fight for me, yet this is the same for us all. Not everyone will agree and that is okay because many are blind to see it from a spiritual view. Many who are blind will only fight in the natural. Our fight is only won and must be done in the spirit of God. God will give us the strength we need in the warfare of life. The battle we see around us shows us that everyday we face battles within ourselves. Isaiah 40:31, states, "They who wait for the Lord shall renew their strength; they shall mount up with wings like eagles; they shall run and not be weary; they shall walk and not faint."

Joy is one of the fruits of the Spirit. Love is the first fruit of the Spirit. Peace is the Third fruit of the spirit. You can't have one without the other. As this world reflects how our personal environments can be challenging where it feels like we are being attacked daily, God gives us a joy in our heart to not be discouraged because the battle has already been won for His glory. There's a difference between joy and happiness. Joy is an attitude of our heart that we must keep in, whatever we go through. Happiness comes in our lives in moments. Moments of promotion, moments of a new business, moments of a new birth or addition to our family, moments of a new relationship or a new marriage, moments of expression of love, or moments of success and achievements. But when our happiness runs out, the Joy of the Lord sustains us! The Lord has overcome our troubles so we have no need to worry about the troubles of our lives. "The Joy of the Lord is my strength." Nehemiah 8:10

Love creates Joy! Let No Man Take Your Joy!!! Joy is the creator of peace! John 16:22 KJV

So, here I am becoming the better version of me which God intended me to be. That better version is who I loved more. Loving myself! God made it my lifestyle and it showed in my daily life. I could see the favor of God on me by the people I would meet throughout my walk of life. Some of my greatest experiences meeting new people, were the reflection of God.

It was like looking at the mirror again to see a reflection of not my past but my present. To look in the mirror now reflects happiness, joy, peace and more importantly love for others. I'm in a better place physically, mentally, emotionally and more and more spiritually. Psalms 139:14 "I will praise thee; for I am fearfully and wonderfully made; marvelous are thy works; and that my soul knoweth right well."

This might be the finale of this book but my journey has just begun. My story of my pain was my choice to die from it or Arise from it. I had to choose whether I was going to work to become better or whether I would choose to settle for less and be comfortable with the mindset of being broken. "A joyful, cheerful heart brings healing to both body and soul. But the one whose heart is crushed struggles with sickness and depression." TPT: Proverbs 17:22

In the beginning, it was the wonder years of my weariness that created and developed the pain in my youth but God still had a plan. As the years passed by, it was the weight of my brokenness that forced me to masquerade the heavy baggage I carried around for years, not wanting the world to see my heavy load of pain but God still had a plan. During those years of baggage, I found myself still living in my past of bondage and I couldn't feel the joy or peace of the present because my past became a part of my life. I couldn't figure out why loving someone wasn't reciprocated in the same manner than I had expected, trying to figure out why relationships wouldn't and couldn't turn into the desired companionship that broke my heart due to false love. I wanted to be loved but God still had a plan. One day God had to take me into his spiritual intensive care unit for a complete and total transition and transformation. During this time of my life, I was going through leaps and bounds on the inside. I was being changed and it didn't feel good as I was being molded and as I was being made over because I had to let go of the past but God still had a plan during the process of letting go. On that road to recovery, God had to speak to me just like he spoke to His creation and life came into existence. There comes a time when God has to speak life back into your soul to start living again and yet God still had a plan! During that moment when I realized that I could be happy again, regain a new mindset, find God during my toughest moments, developed a relationship with God; instead of what I had learned and was taught about God growing up, this time I got to know God for myself and He still had a plan. When God gives you a dream, that dream is the beginning of changing your life. Your dream is vital for your destiny! God places a dream inside of us to give us something to live for, something to look forward to. That dream can help us get through some of the darkest moments and seasons in our lives. When I don't know what to do or how it's all going to turn out, the dream is the light at the end of the tunnel. The dream allowed me to open my eyes and create the vision in my heart. That dream gave me the supernatural ability to submit, to believe and to ARISE from being crushed from pain to being crushed with victory and God still has a plan. That dream allowed me to uncover my purpose and to recreate my identity of knowing who I AM, knowing why I exist and knowing my inheritance which is the power within me. God kept showing me all along throughout the paths of my life that the plan was greater than my pain, the plan was greater than the deficiencies of my life, the plan was greater than my struggles, the plan he created for me was the purpose he hand planted inside of me. All this time, it took most of my life to realize that all the pain I had suffered and endured was predestined for my good. God allowed me to see the beauty in myself. I was as beautiful as a red blossomed rose singled out and alone in an open field. This time I grew into a tall rose and outgrew the tall grass around me that had hidden me. I was no longer hidden but the sun shone on me with opened petals that grew full and healthy. The green stem was filled with thorns and monopolized from the sun because the plants and the weeds that tried to starve me and dehydrate me and cause me to wither could not, because the sharp thorns were there to protect me. The red rose reflects my passion for my purpose in life and that is to use this story to help other men and women. The red rose reflects the true love in me and that is to love myself and not devalue myself and lose myself for the sake of someone else's love. More importantly, there is a love that had to be built in me to love others like Christ loves us all. The deep red reflects my level of commitment. The same commitment most women desire in a true relationship. This is my true commitment to loving God, my family and loving my who I am in Christ to serve others. The red rose signifies the true gratitude, confidence and unconditional love that God has planted in me. The color red reflects the blood of Christ that lives in me and the green stem symbolizes the growth of where God is elevating me. God is still doing a new thing in me and through me. The new me is the new character of a brighter life, it is not based on my opinions or opinions of others. It is based upon truth, my truth is my story for God's glory! My life is living this kind of lifestyle where no matter what my days bring, I won't have to worry, stress, fear, doubt or hesitate because all things will work together for my good because I love God and I am called according to His glory in Christ our Lord and Savior.

MY PRAYER TO YOU

Dear Lord, I place today in your hands, Father. You are the grace, the peace and the protection that I claim over my life. Lead me not into temptation, Lord. Give me the strength and grace to keep my mind and heart pure and guarded against the ungodly things of this life. Captivate my heart and take the reins over my emotions. Allow me to let go of my past and leave it there. Allow me to live in the present moment and take control of my mind. Throughout this day may your presence be so real and so tangible to me that I may not fear anything but walk in complete faith that the God of the heaven sees me. I pray that nothing can separate me from you today. Teach me how to only choose you so that each step that I take will lead me closer to you. I want to walk in your arms, Lord and I want to be aware of you and your powerful presence in everything I do and in everywhere I may go. I speak the protection of the blood of Jesus to surround me and my family. May your pillar of fire be seen where my family and I abide every night. May your glorious fire form a hedge of protection around me in my coming in and going out everywhere I go. Father, I pray for a hedge of protection at my job, my business, every promotion, opportunity or an endeavor in your will. Lord, allow your traveling mercies to follow me and my family at every destination we choose to take. Lord, I ask for your divine protection around me. Father, I pray for the strength to face this day. I don't know what it will bring and I don't know what awaits me Lord but be with me Father. Direct my steps this day into a way that leads me to peace. Strengthen my heart to walk in obedience to your commandments. I ask that you would release grace and mercy from heaven to lead me and guide me. Be my healer! Be my deliverer! Make me whole and fill every void in my life. Break every soul tie and everything that is not like you or from you to break from my life! Be my Jehovah Jireh! Be my way-maker dear Lord! Be my strong tower! Be my Protector and my master! I ask that you would bring me peace of mind and within me, Lord, within my heart. Father, I have faith that you are working all things together for my good. Lord, silence every confusing voice from the enemy because you are God who loves me and even as you are performing that good work in the background, even when I don't see it or don't feel, I know that you are working it out for me in Jesus name. Even as you are working in ways that I cannot see or comprehend and even when it seems too good to be true, I will continue to trust you. Even when I encounter your presence Lord, allow me to answer when you speak to me. Allow me to know that it is you who speaks! I will continue to have faith because your ways supersede mine own. Your ways are higher than my ways and your thoughts are higher than my thoughts. Protect me from any careless or selfish thought or words and actions that don't give you glory. Keep me from being distracted and discouraged by the devil. Keep me from being affected or impacted by any naysayers or negative people. Father, I rejoice in this new day and the light of your presence Lord. May it set my heart on fire. On fire to love you, Jesus. Father, I pray that you open doors for me today. Open doors of opportunity, doors that will lead me to breakthroughs. Father, keep me even from my own carnal works, desires and anything that doesn't give you glory. Help me to walk by faith and not by sight. Help me to walk by your word and not by my feelings or emotions. Lord, I commit myself and my family into your hands in the name of Jesus. I bless your holy name! Amen!

"There is no one else who has the power to save us, for there is only one name to whom God has given authority by which we must experience salvation: the name of Jesus." Acts 4:12 TPT

The process of self development is that everyday I am becoming the better version of who I was yesterday. I'm not who I used to be and I'm not where I would like to be yet it is by faith that my sanctification is the process of how I live my life that is pleasing to God by accepting the fact that although I am not perfect but yet pressing towards the mark of self development and the spiritual awareness of who I am in

Christ! While I'm on this tedious journey to know that Christ walks with me because his spirit of life lives in me. My life is no better than yours and your life isn't any better than mine! In God's eyes, we will always be loved. His love lives everlasting! Love yourself! Love others! Live your life and love Christ who gave his life for you and me! Amen

CHAPTER 9 - YOUR SETBACK WAS YOUR PREPARATION FOR YOUR COMEBACK

HE WALKS WITH ME

It was an early morning in the month of August 2020, I struggled to turn off the alarm and while my body felt weak, it took every muscle inside me to pull my body away from the bed. As I was preparing for work, I was feeling extremely sick but I pushed my way through for work. After day two, the sickness became worst! I didn't have an appetite, no sense of smell and a lingering dry cough made it difficult to swallow, my throat became sore! I immediately started taking all home remedies, from hot green teas, organic honey and lemon juice and I even mixed the honey with chopped fresh garlic, it didn't work! I still felt miserable! By day three, things became worst. In fact, every day got worse. By this time my body started aching and it became difficult to breathe at night. I was literally getting weaker and weaker. My family were feeling sick as well but I was struggling the worst. We decided to take the Covid-19 test because our symptoms were similar to those who were infected by the virus. After receiving a letter in the mail, it was confirmed that we were positive for the virus! I stayed in bed for two weeks feeling week, unable to move my body, my legs and head were aching, I had no energy and I felt lifeless. The worst experience of being infected with Covid-19 was the shortness of breath and the inability to breathe. I felt like weight was on my chest and it felt like I was dying slowly. News got out to family members and friends and it became horrifying because no one could help us in fear that they could possibly become infected. My entire household were ill and we were thankful nearby family members who dropped off home cooked meals at our doorstep to ensure that we had a meal because we were not physically able to do anything. It was impossible for me to walk or stand. This was the worst I've ever felt. I never felt so bad in my life! My husband insisted that I needed hospital care but I refused. I was afraid to be taken to the hospital, in fear that I wouldn't see my family ever again, so I replied very low, "No, I'm not going to the hospital and I'd rather suffer here at home." He kept insisting that I go because I wasn't looking or getting any better and I could see the worried look on his face. As the days seem long and the nights felt hopeless, I had to whisper my prayers to God. I prayed with tears running from my eyes because I was starting to become weak in believing that I would survive. I really didn't know if this would be how my story would end. There had been so many who hadn't survived this deadly virus. So, I asked God as I became weaker in my body where I could barely speak, "Lord Jesus, Would this be the way my life will end?" "Lord, will I survive?" In my spirit, I could hear that still small voice say, "You will live and declare the works of the Lord!" What I was feeling physically surely seemed impossible to believe that I would live but To God Be The Glory! I survived and so did my family. I was very thankful to many who showed their concern and those who prayed for me. I truly thanked those who called me on a regular basis and those who prayed with me. My Apostle (spiritual father), called and prayed a prayer of deliverance over my body for nearly 3 days consecutively and a close relative, who prayed over me and brought our family food and necessities later shared with me what God showed her about my health. He showed her the condition of my internal organs and how they gradually progressed to a healthy appearance. During the phase of my recovery, God showed me many things and many encounters that elevated my faith in Him. It was an experience that only God could work out but it was the God's spirit that transformed me during this process. No one can experience what we suffer alone and no can experience near death encounters where it heightens your spirituality with God! Only you know what you've been through and only you will know what you are truly called and purposed to do in this life! Can no one dictate, criticize, judge or tell you any different! Why? Because you went through it alone with God! God's healing elevated my relationship with him and strengthened my desires to be more like Christ! When I think about how God healed and delivered me emotionally and mentally from my family weary past, I realized more and more how God was with me the entire time. I was never alone! He's very present help in a time of trouble. God's grace and mercies are always sufficient. He was with me before I was in my mother's womb and He's with me now. He was with me during this recent near death experience I felt and I've never been the same since that experience. That experience taught me that God has the final say and when it's my time to go, it's God's will over mine. God knew that I was now in position for the calling on my life. He knew that are assignments that must be complete and since every season has an assignment with God, this was my season for transitioning. God was preparing me in a season for change, even when some didn't and couldn't understand who I was becoming, I chose God's will over other's opinions. Your setbacks may look like you're moving forward but when you're walking in your purpose, the setbacks are preparing you for your greatest comeback!

In 1st Corinthians 2:9, "But as it is written, Eye has seen, nor ear heard, nor have entered into the heart of man The things which God has prepared for those who love Him." NIV

During the journey of my life, I learned that God will only show you your purpose but not the pathway to get there. There was much pain attached to this journey and many times pain is experienced as we continue the journey, whether it's the disappointments from our family, loved-ones or friends, you have to keep walking and soaring and never giving up! God never said that the road would be easy. That's what I discovered during this pathway and what became my savings grace was discovering that Jesus walks with me in those one set of footprints, he carried me through it. I just didn't know it in the beginning of my life, especially as a little girl being traumatized in living environment full of demonic spirits. No matter how traumatized I became from what I endured, God didn't allow any hurt, harm or danger to damage me. It may have felt like I was at my last moments of life but every time the tides and storms of life became difficult, God didn't put more on me than I could bear. He didn't allow me to crack from the spiritual warfare I experienced, in fact he allowed me to become aware of the surroundings and to know that those spirits had boundaries. As frightened as I was being only seven years old to the age of ten, I endured many nights of being tormented and I felt so alone because I didn't think that I could live through it, I was too young to understand what was going on in the house we lived and why was this happening to me? As I matured and reflected on those days of being tormented, I realized if God allowed the Goliath in front of me to reveals its evil, He knew that there was a David inside of me that couldn't be defeated! I just had to know it. He knew that the father wounds I carried to my womanhood had to produce the pain in order to produce a higher assignment for a purpose! He knew that the painful outcome of broken and failed relationships had to break my heart in order to save my soul! He knew that the mental illness of depression forced me to cover up the pain internally to disguise it from others outwardly.

God knew all of this and there's more that He knows that I still don't know because He's an all-knowing God. Why? Because God is omniscient. Why? Because He knew me before He created me. He knows our endings and our beginnings. This was predestined by God. So, we will never have the intelligence of God because we're not God, although we, as believers of Christ and walking in faith inherited the traits of His spirit, which are the nine fruits of His spirit: love, joy, peace, patience, gentleness, goodness, faithfulness, kindness and self-control; we will never inherit who God really is. This is why it's so very important to know who God is in order to understand why we won't understand the assignment, why we won't understand the pain we had to endure and why we must trust and depend on Him even when things just doesn't make any sense to us. Our minds can't and won't comprehend to why we go through and bear pain but the pain becomes a prolific teacher in us. When I think about the pain that you Jesus had to endure while being crucified on the cross, I thought about a man who was a bearer of pain. He suffered at the hands of men. He suffered being an innocent man and He didn't have a fair trial to prove His innocence. I'm talking about a man who who refused to drink vinegar mingled with gall to dull the pain while dying a slow death. He didn't die instantly. He died a slow death! He refused the aid of His sufferings because he chose to go through the pain with a clear mind of His purpose. He knew that it was not His will but God's will be done. God's will is a part of the journey of our lives. Before we can make it to the top, we have to walk up the stairs, the mountains or the unpaved roads on bare feet. In other words, the journey won't be easy! What I learned in this journey of life is that it won't be easy but the journey is necessary is becoming the better you! What I had to learn was the fact that I had to endure the pain of my sufferings. I had to feel it. It's hard to understand why would a loving God cause us to endure pain, well without pain, we wouldn't know what it's like to have feeling! We're going to be happy, joyous and elated some times in our life but it's through pain that teaches us strength, endurance, perseverance, appreciation, wisdom, knowledge, patience and most importantly, our purpose. Many times God has to use adversity to transport us to our purpose. The adversity was a part of the journey when Joseph was thrown in the pit by his very own brothers where he was later transported to imprisonment by King Pharoah. Joseph never complained nor dud he murmur about being enslaved and why he was thrown into prison, yet another innocent man who never had a fair trial but because of his faith and trust in God, he later became King of Egypt. Psalms 110:1, states, "Of David. A psalm. The Lord says to my lord: "Sit at my right hand until I make your enemies a footstool for your feet." NIV

God used the adversity of Joseph's pain, which he felt when his brothers left him for dead. God used the adversity of Joseph's discomfort, which he felt being in an uncomfortable environment of living in prison; to transport him to his purpose! Through Joseph's journey, he used his gifts, talents and his calling as a dreamer during the journey. Joseph's gifts made room for him because he went from the pit to the palace. In life, it's not how we respond to our pitfalls but how we can handle the palace! It's like you have to endure the burden to appreciate the blessing! If God shows you your purpose, be aware that he won't show you the pathway to it but He will walk you through it. What you might see in the beginning may not be what you see on the journey. When I reflect on Moses's journey as a leader and a shepherd, to lead the children of Israel out of Egypt, he went through many adversities because he became frustrated with the disobedience of the Children of Israel. They became impatient and weary throughout the journey which caused Moses to cast the Ten Commandments to the ground. Moses felt the pain of frustration and anger. In the end, God was with Moses and once again, He used adversity to prepare the purpose, which was the breakthrough of preparation for the exit plan from bondage!

As, I have endured so many types of pain like we all have and we all still endure, let's always remember that what we suffered was either self-inflicted due to our poor choices of life or it was for a purpose when we suffer and endure pain in our innocence. Pain is our best teacher because it teaches us to become stronger, wiser and better. Like, the Christian/Gospel artist Marvin Sapp, sings, "Never could have made it" (2007). We become so much better when we don't know how it became possible. Throughout my pain and adversities, God taught me to dismiss and dispatch, meaning dismiss those things and people out of my life who were in conflict with my purpose and destiny, yet continue to love them and pray for them for the sake of guarding my heart. In addition, God also taught me to dispatch people (souls who are lost and seeking improvement and empowerment) into their destination and purpose by using my life story in a transparent way to help others see and believe that there's a possible way, there's hope in Christ Jesus, our Lord and Savior.

WHO IS THE MAN WITH THE MASTER PLAN?

In the late summer of 2020, while recuperating from the sickness of being infected from COVID-19, God changed my plans completely around. I had it all figured out as to where my passions were leading me. God planted seeds in my heart, they were seeds of good desires. I desired to counsel people, I desired to speak messages of encouragement and empowerment on my YouTube channel, most importantly I couldn't help that urgency in my spirit, to minister to many from different walks of life and to share messages about Jesus and the love of Christ. God created desires in me that were bigger and greater than me because these were desires that were uncomfortable for me. Being introverted and comfortable with working behind the scenes, my abilities didn't feel compatible with those new desires.

My plans were to counsel people through life coaching services and write books for the sake of inspiration and building faith in God in the lives of others. It was those desires to leap forward into my purpose. It was those new desires that led me to obeying the calling on my life. When God calls your name, you better answer. Genesis 6:3 states, "And the Lord said, My spirit shall not always strive with man, for that he also is flesh: yet his days shall be an hundred and twenty years." KJV We will not live forever in these natural bodies. This is why now is the time to build up our spirit (inner-man) in Christ! There's a part of God in all of us and it's our spirit. Our spirit and soul will never die.

My plans were good plans and I was compassionate and excited about what I had in mind. It became second nature to pray, encourage others, read my bible and attend church on a regular basis but God wanted more from me. My lifestyle started changing because I desired more and more of God. This was no longer tradition! This was an old lifestyle I gave up that transformed into a new lifestyle but this time the rejection from others were worth it. No longer did I allow the pain of rejection from others make me second guess my decipher! This is my life and you only get one! The rejection from others is and was my separation for the preparation of my elevation. I'm elevating for growth and being redefined for the glory of God! This was part of the master's plan. He gave me beauty for ashes. He led me to minister to many souls who had the mindset as I once did, who felt broken as I was and needed to know my purpose in life, that much higher purpose that is greater and beyond the titles and positions we hold in this natural life. When we come before God on that judgment day to be judged of our works on earth, the titles and positions won't save us! It's what we have done to advance the kingdom of God. Are we ministering to souls and winning them to Christ? Are we feeding the hungry? Are we clothing and helping those who can't help themselves? Are we visiting and praying for the sick? Are we bringing deliverance to soul to be free of bondage? Are we doing the works with a sincere heart and not a boastful one? These are the questions we will be judged by. Most importantly, are we living a life of repentance of our sins? We all have fallen short from the glory of God, so we must repent and confess our sins to God when we have fallen short. We're not perfect people even when we love God and declare the works in this journey. We must examine ourselves and be mindful that we represent God's kingdom. This kingdom on earth is not our home! Philippians 2:12-23 states, "Continue to work out your your salvation with fear and trembling, for it is God who works in you to will and to act in order to fulfill His purpose."

However, God changed my plans! I had it all plan out for the year 2020. My plans were to fulfill my purpose in God while working towards my passion as an Life Coach. I became a certified Life Coach in the Spring of 2020 and it felt exciting because it wouldn't feel like a job but instead; it felt like a joy. Not only would I be that typical and unbiased friend for someone to talk to but my goal was to provide clients with a clear perspective from an secular and spiritual outlook, to help them heal from whatever could be hindering or preventing them from becoming the better version of themselves: whether it's advice in areas of relationships, marriage or finding their purpose, it is my passion to creating goals for the client by helping them become accountable for achieving their goals and motivating them to become consistent with their goals. It's not a cookie-cutter strategy that works for everyone because we all cope differently and we all cope with different problems and struggles. My passion is to wholeheartedly help the client by being a listener and guiding them in the right direction naturally and spiritually. I'm not a licensed therapist or psychologist because I don't diagnose nor do I prescribe medications. However, if someone is in need of psychiatric assistance, I would kindly recommend someone to assist their needs.

In addition, my plans were to continue to use my gifts as a writer and an aspiring best seller's author. With the anointing from God and the gift to write, my plans were to write many books to inspire, motivate and to teach on personal development and spiritual growth under sound doctrine of the gospel of Jesus Christ. Although, these were great plans I had in place, God's plans were beyond what my eyes could see. God's plans were far greater than I could accept because I couldn't achieve these plans alone. God knew that He would have to send me help and He will send people into your life in different seasons to accomplish a new thing in you and through you! When you obey the master's plan, not only is it impactful to your life but He also impacts the lives of others through your obedience. God allowed me to meet new people in different seasons of my life. These were people who poured into my soul and spirit to help me for where God was taking me! God was shifting me in His divine alignment. His alignment was positioning me for something that took me by surprise! Under much prayer, fasting, teachings and preparation, I accepted the master's plan and obeyed the assignment. This was a new birth! God birthed me unto ministry and it happened sooner than I expected.

In the late summer of 2020, I became an ordained Prophetess and Pastor and The Deborah's Anointing International Ministries was formed. In early fall, I enrolled in a seminary program to further my growth in the word of God in theological studies. As this was surely not my plan in the beginning of the year, I remained humbled and embraced the mandate on my life. Some couldn't understand it nor could they accept it. It troubled my spirit fir a little while but I had to go back to God in prayer for strength and it was the spirit of God who confirmed it in my spirit that I must go first to preach the gospel of Jesus Christ. I had to obey the calling on my life. God allowed to make examine myself and that is, are you in ministry to win the approval of man? If your goal is to win the approval of man, your ministry is in vain. God was speaking to me! You're living for Christ and in ministry to serve others and win them to Christ! Your goal is to live a life that is pleasing to God. This was the revelation that gave me the strength and endurance to move forward in the faith, even in the midst of rejection and opposition.

The scripture came to my mind at a time where I became discouraged. I read Mark 16:14-18 NIV, "Later Jesus appeared to the Eleven as they were eating; he rebuked them for their lack of faith and their stubborn refusal to believe those who had seen him after he had risen. He said to them, "Go into all the world and preach the gospel to all creation...." Isn't this the will of God. Our goal as believers is to advance the kingdom of God? If we are believers of Christ, we should examine ourselves as to what are we actively doing to advance the kingdom. Are we showing love and kindness and not bitterness and criticism? Are we witnessing to souls and winning them to Christ? Are we praying for the sick to be healed and are we feeding those who are hungry? Whatever way God lead you in your purpose is how you should go forth in your assignment. Ministry isn't ONLY preaching, teaching and prophesying. Ministry is using our purpose to serve others according to our calling from God. Please remember, It's not about us!

When you can move forward in love and compassion for others, it is the Spirit of God that lives in you because God is love and love is one of the nine fruits of the Spirit you must have in order to do the will of God!

"For I know the plans I have for you," declares the Lord, "plans to prosper you and not to harm you, plans to give you hope and a future." Jeremiah 29:11 NIV

ARISE

In becoming the better version of yourself, you must accept the fact that it is an every day process! You will never arrive to perfection because we are learning! We will never know it all! We never be perfect! It is a daily process and development which is our stepping stone towards achievement and success. I came from the pit of misery and destruction to becoming purposed on a journey to destiny! God knew I had won the victory before I could know it! I had to ARISE and carry my cross for the sake of becoming victorious and no longer a victim of my past!

ARISE, Become The Better Version of YOURSELF!

MY BIO

Angel T. Howard is an ordained Prophetess/Pastor of The Deborah's Anointing International Ministries. She is an author and has always been a writer since the age of ten years old. She is married with two daughters, one adult child in college, and a teenaged child in middle school. She currently resides in Northwest Indiana and holds a Bachelor of Arts in Social Science and Education, and is a Certified Life Coach in the areas of healing, marriage, and finding purpose. Her mission in life is to deliver a message of inspiration and hope that will win souls to Christ for healing, transformation, deliverance, restoration, and the destination to victory!

www.ingramcontent.com/pod-product-compliance
Lightning Source LLC
Chambersburg PA
CBHW060001100426

42740CB00010B/1363